FOCUSED *and* FEARLESS

FOCUSED
and
FEARLESS

A Meditator's Guide to States of Deep Joy, Calm, and Clarity

SHAILA CATHERINE

WISDOM PUBLICATIONS • BOSTON

Wisdom Publications
199 Elm Street
Somerville MA 02144 USA
www.wisdompubs.org

Library of Congress Cataloging-in-Publication Data
Catherine, Shaila.
  Focused and fearless : a meditator's guide to states of deep joy, calm, and clarity /
Shaila Catherine.
     p. cm.
  Includes bibliographical references and index.
  ISBN 0-86171-560-8 (pbk. : alk. paper)
  1. Meditation—Buddhism. I. Title.
  BQ5612.C38 2008
  294.3'4435—dc22

                                              2008002694

eBook ISBN 978-0-86171-981-5
12 11
5 4 3 2

Cover design by Pema Studios. Interior design by Jason Miranda.
Set in Bembo 11/14.8.

Wisdom Publications' books are printed on acid-free paper and meet the
guidelines for permanence and durability of the Production Guidelines for
Book Longevity of the Council on Library Resources.

Printed in the United States of America.

This book was produced with environmental mindfulness. We have elected to
print this title on 30% PCW recycled paper. As a result, we have saved the following resources: 12 trees, 4 million BTUs of energy, 1,125 lbs. of greenhouse gases,
5,418 gallons of water, and 329 lbs. of solid waste. For more information, please visit
our website, www.wisdompubs.org. This paper is also FSC certified. For more information, please visit www.fscus.org.

CONTENTS

ACKNOWLEDGMENTS

THIS BOOK EMERGED primarily from my personal experience during a ten-month meditation retreat in 2004 at the Forest Refuge at the Insight Meditation Society, in Barre, Massachusetts. There is, however, little in this book that can be credited only to me. The lessons, stories, techniques, and teachings contained in this book are one reflection of a lineage of generosity that extends beyond my personal exploration. The contents reflect the influence of many teachers who have shared their wisdom and guided me through difficult lessons as I struggled to develop my mind and understand the nature of things. Most notably, Christopher Titmuss' unwavering encouragement over more than twenty years has challenged me to trust the liberating potential of the Buddha's teachings, even when it feels inefficient, inconvenient, and unpopular to do so. My guru, the late H.W. L. Poonja, revealed a depth of clarity, timeless and pure. Although nearly a decade has passed since his death, he continues to serve as my compass to truth. I have great appreciation for the dedication of the many teachers at the Forest Refuge who guided me during fourteen months of jhana-based practice, especially Myoshin Kelley, Joseph Goldstein, Amita Amy Schmidt, Sarah Doering, Michelle McDonald, Venerable Pa Auk Sayadaw, and Venerable U Jagara. I am grateful to all my teachers, each of whom offered an insight here or there, a challenge to overcome, or a moment of encouragement that kept both my practice and this book developing during the years of its formation.

I am grateful to the community of Insight Meditation South Bay in Mountain View, California, and the many people whose generosity made it possible to spend a year in silence. The support of so many friends and students provided a wellspring of energy that carried me through the more demanding moments of retreat and sustained me through many drafts of this book.

With deep gratitude for their generosity and encouragement, I thank: Betsy Currie, Chade-Meng Tan, LeAnn Bjelle, Glenn Smith, Woods Shoemaker, Adam Winkler, Mikaela and Craig Barnes, Nancy Holt, Rachael Belash, Ron Paisley, Greg MacDonald, Michael Wilding, Shirley Kwok, Steve and Shari Gaber, Jack Erwin, Janet Taylor, Steve and Cheryll Gasner, Edy Young, Drew Oman, Ed Haertel, Doug Slakey, Christine Davis, Jim Podolske, Mary Roy, Maureen O'Brian, Doug Forehand, The Farrah Family, Michael Choy, Gordon Mitchell, Wynette Richards, Joan Mitchell, Linda Rohacek, Richard Sievers, Ellen and David Sugarman, Fred Herman, Lisa Grinnell, Jon Viscoli, Michelle Downs, Meryl Landy, Susan Atwood-Stone, Zina Daniels, Linda Drucker, Sandra Hahn, Brian Bush, Kate Sladen, Elizabeth Romero, MaryJo Whiteman, Mark Graves, Lawrence Tharp, Sue Lucksted, Barbara Byron, Lydia Succi, San Jose Sangha, Arlene Noodleman, Suzanne Kryder, Bobbi and Pat Culbert, Ellen Miller, Cleve and Diana Pardue, Pat White, Laura Crabb, Winifred Hegarty, People of Color Sangha of Albuquerque, Mike Kupfer, Lois Gerchman, Maureen Christine, Jerry Parks, Bill Buchholz, Barbara Vana, Alexcia Trujillo, Smita Joshi, Nathan Williams, Joan Granger, Deborah Hill, George Schroeder, Cassidy Trager, Ed Morgan, and Michelle Goodman.

Transmitting an inner meditative experience into a practical manual required the assistance of many friends and editors. Several friends guided me through the writing process by reading early drafts and sharing skills, suggestions, and questions. This book could not have taken shape without the thoughtful reflections and continuous encouragement of Pat McClelland, Terry Farrah, Lila Kate Wheeler, Glenn Smith, Koelle Bodhi, Dianna Eden, Keren Arbel, Stephen Fulder, Sharon Small, Amita Amy Schmidt, and Leigh Brasington, as well as the contributions of Barry Boyce, whose skillful editing sculpted the final version of this book.

I am especially grateful to Wisdom Publications and my editor, Josh Bartok. Josh's vision and enthusiasm brought this project to life, while his many helpful suggestions and precise corrections clarified subtle points in the text. Books are created through countless unseen contributions— I deeply appreciate the team at Wisdom Publications for their full commitment to this project.

And finally, the truly essential and pervasive support may be the most difficult to distinguish. The love of my family is present as a backdrop to who I am and what I do in the world. My mother, Elizabeth Tromovitch, my sister, Lisa Tromovitch, and my brother, Philip Tromovitch, have given me the greatest of all forms of support—their unfaltering trust, interest, and love. Even when my explorations have drawn me to unfamiliar religions across the globe, or separated me through prolonged periods of silent retreat, I have felt the presence of my family's unlimited love. This is a treasure and blessing that I cannot measure or repay.

INTRODUCTION

From Focused Concentration to Fearless Awakening

RESTING UNDER THE SHADE of a rose apple tree, the young Siddhartha Gotama (whom we would later come to know as the Buddha) spontaneously entered a state of deep concentration, satisfaction, and ease. Much later, after he had studied intensively with two meditation masters and practiced extreme asceticism, he recalled that quiet moment in his youth. Now emaciated by years of rigorous fasting, Siddhartha Gotama was startled by the recollection. After pondering it awhile, he decided to cultivate those naturally pleasant states as the means to awakening. In so doing, he harnessed the potency of the unified mind and transformed a conventional practice of concentration into a catalyst for awakening, for enlightenment. Austere practices of self-mortification understandably lost favor as he taught his disciples to unlock the power of a happy mind.[2]

This meditative technology of intense concentration that leads to sublime states of mental absorption, known as *jhana,* predated the Buddha—but since he was able to use it as a foundation for his enlightenment, it became a critical feature of his teachings. The practice of using jhana as a basis for insight has been preserved to this day. In the discourses of the Pali Canon, the earliest records of the Buddha's teaching, "concentration" appears repeatedly and is taught as a pivotal method for inner transformation. In Pali, *jhana* literally means "to think" or "to meditate."

Consequently, the term is open to a wide variety of uses and interpretations and there has been much debate about its precise meaning. In this book, *jhana* practice refers to a traditional sequence of specific states of absorption where the mind is secluded from sensory impingement and deeply unified with a chosen object. Attention is not distracted by stray thoughts nor affected by the flutter of moods. Even physical sensations and sounds eventually fade as the mind becomes entirely immersed in a single coherent focus.

Jhanas are states of happiness that can radically transform the heart, reshape the mind, imbue consciousness with enduring joy and ease, and provide an inner resource of tranquillity that surpasses any conceivable sensory pleasure. Jhanas are states of deep rest, healing rejuvenation, and profound comfort that create a stable platform for transformative insight. Throughout the development of jhana, we intertwine the calming aspects of concentration with the investigative aspects of insight meditation. The fruit of concentration is freedom of heart and mind.

This book will teach you about and guide you through the traditional sequence of eight levels of meditative absorption that constitute jhana practice—though it will focus in detail on only four. While jhana is a powerful practice not intended for the dilettante, diligent beginners will benefit from the stability and strength afforded by deep concentration and seasoned meditators will find in jhana practice a potent method for intensifying insight.

Although the notion of mastering eight stages of deep concentration may appear daunting at first, the jhana system is easy to follow, sequential, and surprisingly simple. Traditionally this practice was not reserved for special people nor restricted to the monastic order. During the Buddha's day, lay disciples and busy merchants would, from time to time, enjoy the benefits and joys of jhanic abiding.[3] These eight levels of concentration remain readily accessible to contemporary practitioners, so long as they can find sufficient time for retreat, remain ethically clear, and apply balanced effort. Although I've included many teachings useful to beginners, a working knowledge of one's own mind and some facility with mindfulness practices are assumed as prerequisites to the serious undertaking of jhana practice. Nonetheless, I will review mindfulness practice and how it is used to avoid common pitfalls in jhana practice.

This book emerged from my experiences during a ten-month silent retreat focused on the cultivation of jhana as the basis for insight. Although I had more than twenty years of meditation experience, until this retreat I had not systematically used these refined levels of consciousness to develop insight. The methodical techniques of establishing access to jhana, strengthening and sustaining each level of absorption, and then applying the concentrated mind for insight had a powerful effect on my consciousness: it opened me to an experience of unremitting happiness. When I emerged from retreat and shared some of my experiences with friends, I realized that the personal struggles, attainments, and insights gleaned from this retreat described a clear path of concentration and wisdom. With this book, I want to offer serious practitioners this method for attaining profound and unwavering happiness.

Through reading this book, some experienced meditators will discover that they have already experienced some jhanic factors (rapture, happiness, and equanimity, for instance) while engaged in other meditation practices. Indeed, states of extreme happiness characteristic of jhana naturally arise during many intensive meditation experiences. However, cultivating and harnessing them as the basis for insight is a technique unto itself, quite beyond the random "slipping into jhana" that long-term meditators often describe. *Focused and Fearless* can serve as a manual for contemporary practitioners prepared to cultivate jhana as an expression of the stable mind.

When the Buddha was asked, "Why are some people liberated and others not?" he did not say that the most concentrated meditators attain liberation. He replied, "Whosoever clings to the objects perceived by the senses cannot gain liberation. Whosoever stops clinging will be liberated."[4] Liberation through non-clinging is the core of the Buddha's teaching. The human propensity to cling is the problem; meditation is designed to solve it. Working in tandem, the twin practices of concentration and insight create conditions remarkably conducive to awakening.

Some readers may find variances in method and emphasis from teachings received from other teachers. Many approaches have developed over the centuries, each based on an individual teacher's understanding of the ancient texts and how those understandings manifest through his or her own meditation practice. If you would like to authentically experience jhana, you will probably need time in silent retreat under the guidance of teachers. A book can provide a map of the terrain, describe the steps of practice, and indicate signposts along the path, but there is no substitute for diligent practice and the guidance of skilled teachers.

This book is an introductory guide, not a definitive nor exhaustive study. Many exercises and reflections are interspersed throughout. Please try them, even if they slow the pace of your reading. Merely reading exercises will not produce the texture of mind useful to concentration. I encourage you to, at times, set the book down, close your eyes, and collect the mind in silence. If you do, these practices will contribute to a living ease and undistracted presence—even without the attainment of jhanic levels of absorption. But do bear in mind that the cultivation of serenity and wisdom can't be rushed. Please give it the time to work. Don't grow impatient if you don't understand it completely at first. Certain principles are repeated throughout the book and deepen in complexity as the practice progresses.

This book systematically explores the framework of eight classical states of unified consciousness: the four primary jhanas and the four formless realms. It gives instruction on accessing these states, discerning their qualities, and using each as the basis for wisdom. While its thrust is cultivating the deep concentration of jhana, the development of right concentration in the Buddhist tradition must always be intertwined with wisdom. Undertaking jhana practice without the framework of wisdom would be pointless at best, and contains the danger of reinforcing attachment to the pleasures of jhana. Accordingly, I have included wisdom teachings that help to anchor the reader's cultivation of concentration, including non-clinging, the importance of effort, the power of intention, the skillful application of mindfulness, overcoming the negative forces of habit and thought, working with emotions, and learning to let go. I do wish to note, however, that the cultivation of morality, right action within the sphere of the relative world, must also be attended to even though it is not explored in this book.

This book contains five sections. The first, "The Joy of the Focused Mind," positions the practice of jhana as training in relinquishment and an exploration of happiness. The second, "Preparing the Mind for Absorption," addresses themes necessary for preparing the mind to enter jhana. The third, "How to Establish Meditative Absorption," contains instructions for the four primary levels of jhana. The fourth, "Doing the Work of Insight," explores the wisdom that arises when using jhana as the basis for insight. The fifth, "Exploring the Formless Dimensions," examines the four formless realms as an experiential investigation of emptiness. The Epilogue discusses the significant role jhana can play in living a fearless, awakened life.

May readers discover deep peace within their hearts
and bring lasting peace into our world.
May this book contribute
to the liberation of all beings.

PART I

The Joy of the
Focused Mind

CHAPTER 1
Cultivating the Focused Mind

*Just as a rocky mountain is not moved by storms, so sights,
sounds, tastes, smells, contacts and ideas, whether desirable or
undesirable, will never stir one of steady nature, whose mind is
firm and free.*

—The Buddha[1]

CONCENTRATION is a central feature of a contemplative life,
cultivated through formal meditation practice and also
through any of a variety of other daily activities. Concentration brings with it a natural joy that arises as the mind settles and is
absent of distraction. A surgeon may love surgery, not because the oper-
ating room is a pleasant place to be, but because the task demands such
complete attention that the mind is filled with the delight associated
with concentration. Kayakers are often enveloped in rapture even
though their bodies are cramped in little boats and splashed by frigid
water. A concentrated mind is focused, unified, and stable, regardless of
whether the conditions are uncomfortable or luxurious.

In the Pali language of the early Buddhist scriptures, *samadhi* is the
term that has most often been translated into English as "concentration,"
yet samadhi describes something more than the narrow focus implied by
"concentration." It is a calm unification that occurs when the mind is
profoundly undistracted. Samadhi is the beautiful state of an undistracted
mind, described in the Pali texts as "internally steadied, composed, unified, and concentrated."[2] These four qualities indicate that samadhi is not

merely focused on a single object. It is a state of profound serenity that encompasses a balanced, joyful composure, expressing the natural settledness of undistracted awareness.

The Buddhist tradition discusses three levels of samadhi:
- the samadhi of momentary concentration
- the samadhi that grants access to the jhanas
- the samadhi of absorption into the jhanas

Each of these levels is a deeply undistracted state of consciousness, and all three can be the support for liberating wisdom. The momentum of clear and sustained attention brings calm to the mind as it simultaneously restricts energy that might nourish unwholesome or distracting mental states.

Don't worry if, right now, you feel far away from these beautiful calm states. Most people need to bolster their intention and practice diligently to develop the inner conditions for samadhi. All of this can come with time and practice, and this book is the first step to helping you cultivate them.

THE SAMADHI OF MOMENTARY CONCENTRATION

Buddhist disciplines distinguish between the quality of samadhi developed through a continuity of *mindfulness* of changing perceptions and the quality of *samadhi* developed with a fixed focus.

When the breath is used to develop mindfulness, emphasis is placed on clear perception of changing sensations through the full duration of an inhale and exhale. With tremendous precision, the meditator experiences a multitude of fleeting sensations: tingles, vibrations, pressure, heat, for instance. Pressure may increase or decrease. Pulsing may vary in rhythm. The intensity of heat or cold may fluctuate. This meticulous sensitivity to physical variations brings the mind to a state of exquisite clarity that allows you to see the impermanent and empty nature of phenomena and witness the relationship between the mind and body. You can observe how sights and smells can trigger vivid memories, how intentions affect physical movements, and how emotions manifest in the body.

As the momentum of mindfulness increases, concentration correspondingly strengthens. The concentration that develops through *a continuity of mindfulness with changing objects* is called "momentary concentration." The mind momentarily collects, but then it disperses as the flow of sensory experiences ebbs and alters. Thinking can arise, but the thoughts do not diminish the concentrated state. Mindfulness inhibits proliferations of thought because it meets the experience of thinking immediately. The content of thought relates only to the phenomena at hand.

Before samadhi is established, thoughts may multiply through cognitive associations. A personal story is fabricated out of simple sensory triggers. For example, what begins as the simple sight of a stain on my shirt could proliferate into a rapid train of thoughts: plans for how to wash it, reflections on the last meal that might have caused the stain, embarrassed recollections of who I encountered since my last meal, speculations about what those people might think of me, fabrication of excuses for the stain, and on and on.

In contrast to this proliferating tendency, when mindfulness is present, we apprehend the thought quickly. For example, I arrived on my last retreat quite tired and slept through the early morning meditation on the first day. As I sipped some tea after breakfast, my mind was active: sustaining the story of how tired I was, creating the identity of a busy person, justifying my extra hour of sleep because of all the important things I was doing in the previous days. Between sips of tea I became aware that this story was activating restlessness. I reviewed my physical condition and noticed that I was not actually tired. The only thing that seemed to be sustaining tiredness was a perverse identification with the story of exhaustion. As I became aware of the experience of thinking, the story of being tired dissolved. Attention settled easily in the present-moment experience of feeling the cup in my hand, hearing the sounds of activity that surrounded me, and sensing my body and breath.

Ajahn Chah, a master in the Thai Forest Tradition, compared momentary concentration to taking a walk, resting, walking, and resting. The journey is periodically interrupted with the arising of a thought, yet undisturbed, because in a short time the journey is continued. Developed through a continuity of mindfulness, momentary concentration can grow very strong and bring the mind through stages of intense happiness that culminate in wisdom. Although momentary samadhi is not the focus of this book, it is a valid expression of concentration worthy of respect—and extraordinarily useful for insight.

I assume most readers who have done mindfulness practice are familiar with this quality of concentration or can learn about it through the ample literature available on mindfulness with breathing. Therefore, I have narrowed the scope of this book to the sequential development of *samadhi with a fixed object for attention,* as demonstrated in the next two types of samadhi. The purity of mind produced at the threshold to absorption is called *access to jhana* and complete absorption is called *jhana.*

ACCESS TO JHANA

To attain the stage of access to jhana, you don't highlight the changing nature of experience the way you might with mindful breathing. The basic *occurrence* of breath becomes the object for attention rather than the dynamic flow of changing sensations. As concentration deepens, the physicality of changing sensations becomes less dominant. The expression of a steady mind comes to the fore as the predominant mental object. For some practitioners, this manifests as the occurrence of bright light in awareness or a "subtle field of vibrations" in the mind. Each practitioner will discover how this shift in consciousness is perceived, and experiences will vary. As samadhi deepens, the mind gradually withdraws from its orientation to the sensory world.

Sensory orientation is, of course, a deeply ingrained aspect of the healthy functioning of perception. It plays a valuable role in the survival of animals, the development of children, and the structure of social organizations—to name but a few broad areas. However, the critical refinement that sets the stage for the possibility of absorption into jhana and marks these states of concentration as "altered states" occurs as consciousness withdraws its dependence on sensory perception.

With access to jhana, the object for concentration shifts from a perception of the physicality of phenomena to a subtler experience of refined mental factors, or visions of light as the mental reflection of the object. These include (but are not limited to) mental factors of pleasure, focus, mindfulness, happiness, and equanimity. In the access stage, attention dwells consistently in relationship to these positive and pleasant mental qualities. It is a distinctive shift in the direction of seclusion, but still not yet the withdrawal into an altered state of jhana.

Ajahn Chah compared *access to jhana* to wandering about inside your own home. Consciousness is at ease within the confines of a comfortable arena of perceptions. Attention does not move away from the meditation object. Thinking may still arise but it circles closely around the meditative experience. Light and wispy thoughts can arise, often as reflections on the meditation process, yet this mental activity does not disturb a calm tranquillity that pervades the mind. A strong and fundamental purity has been achieved, yet there is still a subtle restlessness that inhibits the depth of stillness required for absorption.

The Buddha said of this stage, "If I think and ponder upon thoughts of letting go, even for a night and day, I see nothing to fear from it. But with excessive thinking and pondering, I might tire my body, and when the body is tired, the mind might become disturbed. It is far from concentration. So I steadied my mind and concentrated it so that it would not be disturbed."[3]

Although there is nothing wrong with thoughts that regulate the meditation experience—such as the desire to calm obsessive thinking and the intention to return to the breath—greater rest and seclusion can be attained by cultivating further stillness. As attention continues to still, an opportunity for absorption (entering the next level of samadhi) may arise.

ABSORPTION INTO JHANA STATES

When the mind abandons its contact with the senses, including discursive thinking, the concentrated absorption of jhana begins. The mind is utterly still and focused on its object. The specific object of focus becomes progressively refined in the development of concentration, from the physical sensations of breathing, to a perception of light. Rapture, pleasure, and equanimity may accompany the bright radiant mind, while attention is continually directed toward the place where the breath is known. As these perceptions grow increasingly subtle, attention

remains connected and the subtle perception of breath is recognized as a
perception of stable brightness in mind.

In jhana, attention is virtually merged into its object, creating an
impression of complete unification. Even if there is sensory impact from
sounds and sensations, the mind remains completely unmoved. Sensory
contact—even strong pain or loud noise—does not disturb the tranquillity
or affect the unification of the mind with its object of concentration. It is
as though you don't hear anything, yet the capacity of hearing is not
impaired. It is as if you don't feel pain, and yet the bodily processes are
functioning. There may or may not be subtle awareness of the impact of a
sound or physical contact, but the mind lets go so automatically that there
can be no sensory residue to disturb the concentration. Because the mind
is so still that even pain will not disrupt the attention, jhana can be sustained for very long periods of time. Although this depth of detachment is
often challenging to attain, once seclusion is established, the sequential
development through the stages of jhana unfolds rather effortlessly.

The standard formula repeatedly presented in the discourses of the
Buddha describes concentration through the development of four primary levels of jhana:

> And what, bhikkhus, is the faculty of concentration? Here,
> bhikkhus, the noble disciple gains concentration, gains one-
> pointedness of mind, having made release the object. Secluded
> from sensual pleasures, secluded from unwholesome states, he enters
> and dwells in the first jhana, which is accompanied by thought and
> examination, with rapture and happiness born of seclusion. With
> the subsiding of thought and examination, he enters and dwells in
> the second jhana, which has internal confidence and unification of
> mind, is without thought and examination, and has rapture and
> happiness born of concentration. With the fading away as well of
> rapture, he dwells equanimous and, mindful and clearly compre-
> hending, he experiences happiness with the body; he enters and
> dwells in the third jhana of which the noble ones declare: "he is
> equanimous, mindful, one who dwells happily." With the abandon-
> ing of pleasure and pain, and with the previous passing away of joy
> and displeasure, he enters and dwells in the fourth jhana, which is
> neither painful nor pleasant and includes the purification of mind-
> fulness by equanimity. This is called the faculty of concentration.[4]

Developing this faculty requires appreciation both of the power of seclusion and forms of happiness that go beyond sensory gratification. The next two chapters explore these elements that are so vital to bringing about jhana.

☞ THE FOUNDATIONAL PRACTICE ☜

THIS INITIAL MEDITATION forms the basis of jhana practice. Though deceptively simple, it leads to profound focus and transformative insight when practiced daily. The many exercises and reflections interspersed throughout this book build upon the primary technique of developing concentration through careful attention to the breath.

CONCENTRATION MEDITATION For concentration meditation, we establish a very simple task: we choose one object and maintain concentration on that. The method I teach uses the breath as the initial focus for attention. We give ourselves the task of observing the sensations of the breath as it enters and exits at the nostrils. Narrowing the focus to a single object discards many of the stray thoughts that occupy and divert precious mental energy. The simple practice of repeatedly bringing attention to the breath and letting it rest there forms the basis of this meditation. Here are some basic instructions:

Sit in a comfortable posture. Feel how the body is sitting. Feel the contact with the chair. Gently bring attention to the breath. First feel the whole breath, and how the chest and abdomen expand and contract. Then, settle the attention on the sensation of the breath at the very tip of the nostrils; observe that initial point of contact with the breath. Observe the sensations of breathing without altering or manipulating the breath. Let the breath come naturally. Attend to the breath as it is now, not as you think a breath should appear. Observe the whole breath throughout the duration of inhale, exhale, and pause; inhale, exhale, and pause.

If the attention drifts off into thoughts, bring it gently back to the breath. The mind will probably stray many times. When the mind is lost in thought and mindfulness is weak or absent, the conditions are not present to choose alertness. When you wake up to the bare fact that thinking has subsumed the attention, you can redirect your attention to breathing. Without judging your capacity to meditate, simply return to the perception of breathing. Attention is not developed by riveting the attention to the breath with super glue or hammering it into the nostrils with nails. Attention becomes unwavering by the consistent willingness to gently begin again.

With this exercise you are cultivating your capacity to let go of distractions and strengthening your ability to direct attention. It diminishes habits of distraction and cultivates a peaceful and calm awareness. Please set some time aside each day to do this fundamental meditation exercise. I recommend twenty to sixty minutes a day as the general guideline for a committed daily practice; however, it is fine to adjust the time as your lifestyle and interest allow. A daily practice of any length can bring great fruits in concentration and wisdom.

☞ ADDITIONAL TOOLS

MINDFUL MOVEMENT Gentle stretching, mindful walking, or mindful movement can enhance the calmness and composure of mind. Physical expressions of composure through posture and movement support inner unification. Although gross movements can certainly be performed mindlessly—as many people walk daily from their cars to their offices without conscious awareness of their surroundings, footsteps, or breath—the discipline of mindful movement cultivates concentrated attention by coordinating gestures of the body with the rhythm of the inhale and exhale; the flow of feeling, energy, and balance; and sometimes visualizations. Different people tend to prefer different styles of mindful movement, so rather than recommend a single approach I suggest incorporating some movement imbued with awareness into your daily practice. It could be a structured discipline like yoga, tai chi, qi gong, line dance, or swimming. It could also be something less structured, such as going for a walk or walking the dog with the intention to be fully aware. The key is to feel yourself moving in space. Bring calm attention to the sensations of the dynamic body.

COUNT YOUR STEPS If you want more structure for cultivating concentration while you take a walk, you can count your steps. Count from 1–10, then 1–9, 1–8, and so forth, until you get to 1–1. Then, repeat the process in ascending order: 1–1, 1–2, 1–3, 1–4 . . . 1–10. There is no value in attaining a big number. No one really cares how many steps it takes to walk around your block. But the counting gives the mind something to do, keeping it out of trouble, supporting the spirit of concentration. You can try counting for some time, and then let the numbers go and rest with direct awareness of walking. Counting focuses attention, but if we obsessively or continuously count, the added numerical concepts can eventually distract us from the vividness of present-moment awareness.

CHAPTER 2
Joy of Seclusion

Which is worth more, a crowd of thousands,
or your own genuine solitude?
Freedom, or power over an entire nation?
A little while alone in your room
will prove more valuable than anything else
that could ever be given you.

—Rumi[1]

T HE BUDDHA DESCRIBED the transition from ordinary consciousness to the altered state of jhana thus: "Secluded from
sensory pleasures, secluded from unwholesome states, one
enters and abides in the first jhana."[2] This chapter explores the search for
seclusion through training the mind. It also considers the deeper implication of solitude as an awakening beyond separation.

First let it be said that "seclusion" does not imply repression or
denial; it is not a state of alienation, loneliness, or division. The seclusion
that supports a meditation practice is rooted in wisdom and clarity.
Knowing what leads to suffering, you wisely choose a path that leads to
happiness. The Buddha addressed this point quite simply:

If, by giving up a lesser happiness,
One could experience greater happiness,
A wise person would renounce the lesser
To behold the greater.[3]

Sparked by this basic instinct toward happiness, we follow the trajectory of training that will eventually carry us beyond conceivable delights.

The Buddhist teachings describe three kinds of seclusion: (1) physical aloneness that is experienced as we remove ourselves from complex social dynamics; (2) mental seclusion that describes the aloofness of the mind while it is absorbed in jhana—this marks a separation from unwholesome states and sensory pleasures; and (3) liberation as detachment from the root causes of suffering. This implies a suspension of conceptual proliferations.[4]

THE SECLUSION OF BEING ALONE

Physical solitude creates a temporary separation from the distractions and activities that fill daily life, but true external simplification involves more than renunciation of material possessions. It is a process that divests the heart of the activities and roles upon which personality relies. The Buddha suggested, "A bhikkhu resorts to a secluded resting place: the forest, the root of a tree, a mountain, a ravine, a hillside cave, a charnel ground, a jungle thicket, an open space, a heap of straw."[5] We could, of course, expand that list to include the modern option of a formal retreat center.

At the rudimentary level, this detachment may be likened to a spiritual vacation. A retreat may be for any length of time, from a single day of silence to many years. It can be a relief to take time away from the exaggerated responsibilities of your routine. Most people need some degree of periodic solitude to learn to calm the anxious heart and quiet the distracted mind. Alternating time for inner retreat with time fully engaged with career, family, and social concerns makes for a balanced approach to the lay lifestyle. Ultimately, silence supports depth in meditation, but it is through our social interactions that our understanding matures and is tested. The Buddha's life is an exemplary model for balancing seclusion with the compassionate engagement with society. There were periods in his ministry when he remained aloof from his disciples, and many times when he taught, led, and served the community.

I have a deep love for silence. It has been an indispensable asset on my own path of inner discovery. At the age of forty-three, I have spent approximately seven years in silence. Not everyone will need to or have the opportunity to undertake extended retreats, and concentration can still be developed in active social settings—but spiritual satisfaction is something you must discover alone. You might stay in a monastery, reserve a room at a retreat center, go camping in the mountains, sit in a city park, or abide comfortably in a quiet room in your own home. The place does not matter, although retreat centers offer the advantage of skilled teachers and safe conditions for the settling of the mind.

Unable to imagine the exquisite joy that arises from a quiet mind, many people presume a silent retreat would be boring, but when you enter retreat you leave behind your array of projects, distractions, and entertainments. You can allow the mind to unwind in a secluded shelter without the need to defend your safety or maintain your social roles. When you can arrange for a spiritual retreat, it is important to make the most of it by putting your worldly affairs in order before entering the silence. Don't bring entertainments with you. Give your mind a real vacation from your daily life routines. Let silence reveal a depth of knowledge that is usually unseen in the rapid swirl of daily personal achievements.

Concentration states depend upon the "protected" conditions of a retreat. They are, like all things, impermanent—and they dissipate after the retreat. Even so, the insights that arise due to the purity of concentration remain accessible long after the states of concentration have ended. Concentration does not need to be permanent to be important.[6] In the transition back to your ordinary routine, worldly activities may seem to be moving ridiculously fast. This period of adjustment poses no serious threat. It may be just a few hours, or a few days, weeks, or longer, depending upon the length of the retreat and the depths of concentration, but as you ease into your routine responsibilities, the wisdom gleaned through your meditation practice will emerge and inform your life.

> ### ⌒ FOR REFLECTION
>
> How do you fill the space in your life? Do you preserve space for solitude, or is it squeezed out by compulsive busyness, noise from the radio, or trivial errands? Is it easy or difficult to be alone with yourself? Do you go from one relationship to the next, or is there space between relationships when you are content alone? How densely have you organized your life? If you were to describe how you spend your days, would your life sound like a schedule or a life you are happy to live?

Inspired by some early experiences in my meditation practice, I actively sought situations of solitude. At a small forest monastery in Chonburi Province, Thailand, I spent one retreat on a platform made of wooden planks. It had no walls, but was partially covered by a grass roof. My intention was, simply, to meditate there, alone. I did not leave the platform except briefly for the single daily meal, toilet, and a bath at a nearby stream. I wanted to allow the meditation practice to flow unrestricted by schedules and social conventions. I quickly discovered that I was never actually alone. I shared that simple platform with two snakes, the wind, birds, bugs, and the universe. The moon visited at night, the rain freely blew through, and the air was filled with flying and floating creatures. I lived among a natural community of friends.

Young and not yet understanding the deeper meanings of solitude, I sought greater seclusion in a cave in Krabi District, Thailand. The only entrance was through a tunnel that bent in such a way that no light penetrated. But even underground, in the total darkness of that cavern, life abounded. Bats cluttered the ceiling and a large white snake periodically appeared to feed on the bats. Sometimes local villagers entered with flashlights scavenging for bat droppings that are used as garden fertilizer. Even underground, I was not alone.

We may search for a quiet place to meditate, but true external solitude is not necessary, and may not even exist. I have come to understand solitude as an experience of relationship, specifically our relationship to reality. Lovers of solitude value this relationship and give it attention. We devote time for meditation, time to listen to silence, time to breathe in the vastness of space that surrounds us, time to make friends with ourselves.

In a dialogue on solitude with a monk named Migajala, the Buddha elaborated on the attributes of two types of meditators, one described as "a lone dweller," the other as "one dwelling with a partner." The Buddha explains:

> There are, Migajala, forms cognizable by the eye that are desirable, lovely, agreeable, pleasing, sensually enticing, tantalizing. If a bhikkhu seeks delight in them, welcomes them, and remains holding to them, delight arises. When there is delight, there is infatuation. When there is infatuation, there is bondage. Bound by the fetter of delight, Migajala, a bhikkhu is called one dwelling with a partner. . . .
>
> Migajala, even though a bhikkhu who dwells thus resorts to forests and groves, to remote lodgings where there are few sounds and little noise, desolate, hidden from people, appropriate for seclusion, he is still called one dwelling with a partner. For what reason? Because craving is his partner, and he has not abandoned it; therefore he is called one dwelling with a partner.[7]

Experiences can be pleasing and agreeable. If you seek gratification through that contact, infatuation will entrap consciousness and craving will be your companion. From a meditative perspective, solitude is not concerned with how many people populate your residence. Solitude is a contemplation of the question: What companions are we housing within our minds? Solitude does not demand we make other people go away; rather, in solitude we consider what states we are entertaining within our own minds. Is craving the company we wish to keep? Physical solitude minimizes the complexities of social life. It is, however, only a first step.

THE SOLITUDE OF A QUIET MIND

You take your mind with you whether you are at the beach, on a hike in the forest, in a formal meditation retreat, or spending a quiet day in the garden. You may be sitting in a quiet place, but if your mind is agitated with judging thoughts, future plans, restlessness, or fantasy, you are not yet secluded for meditation. When I lived in India, serving my teacher, H. W. L. Poonja, one student requested a private meeting with Poonjaji. He said, "I want to see you alone before I leave." Poonjaji replied, "You are invited to see me alone. You come alone to me. Don't bring anyone with you, not your clothes, not your body, not your mind. Then you can see me alone."[8] He was not suggesting the student meet him without a shirt and pants but asking for a deeper level of relinquishment—a stripping away of the personality masks, social ranks, and self-image that habitually accompany us.

Do you ever stand that exposed, emptied of the facades of identity, without your roles, without identification with social status, utterly empty of concepts, not preoccupied with who you are and how you are perceived?

Inner solitude invites us to empty our minds of thoughts, reactions, and obstructive mental states like lust, aversion, restlessness, and doubt. Although the basic level of instruction for jhana practice is to simply set distractions and hindrances aside, mindfulness and understanding are needed to set them aside skillfully. Frantically batting thoughts and difficult mental states away as unwelcome intrusions while trying to rush into jhana won't work. You need to examine thoughts until their nature is unmistakably obvious. Then you will be able to sweep them aside easily and without denial.

It is imperative for the sincere meditator to unwaveringly witness the functions of desire, aversion, restlessness, and doubt, witness these forces arising—but without acting them out, without buying into them. See them arise as empty thoughts, and see them pass just as quickly. If they are not seen clearly, these mental states can obstruct progress in concentration. Doubt can assail the mind with indecision, worry, or chronic judgment. Unabated, the momentum of uncertainty can paralyze spiritual progress. Yet doubt is nothing more than a thought. Through examining the experience of doubt, you will come to understand doubt, rather than be consumed by it. Doubt is a category of thought that you can definitively set aside. The very instant you realize you are thinking you have an opportunity to affect the patterns of mind. Thoughts of self can clutter attention with a plethora of diversified tales—preventing composure, stillness, and unification. Concentration abandons this diffusing activity. When you clearly perceive a thought, natural disinterest replaces identification with the stories. As the mind calms, mental seclusion is established.

The strategy for insight meditation is to meet difficult mind-states head-on and illuminate them with wisdom. In this way vipassana practices are described as "practicing near suffering." By escorting the attention to meet the basic and often painful facts, insight develops. On the other hand, when strengthening samadhi, disengage from obstructive energies quickly. Set the hindrances aside. Let them go. Clear a space in the mind. Infuse it with happiness. Don't give much attention to the hindrances, but instead preserve your energy for purifying the mind within the realm of happy wholesome states. In this way jhana practice is said to be "near to happiness." With the repeated dismissal of distractions, the mind settles and the hindrances lose their charge until they eventually stop arising.

☞ SETTING THOUGHTS ASIDE

It can be useful to develop a variety of methods for setting thoughts aside, like a meditator's tool kit.

One method is to "sweep thoughts into trash bins." One by one observe each thought, and then imagine you can toss it into a bin, clearing the space of mind from the clutter of mental proliferations. Take a moment to look at the thought, know it, but then diligently toss it aside.

Or, imagine thoughts flying at you like baseballs. You catch each one and roll it back. Don't pocket it. Just look at it, know what it is, consider it for a moment, and toss it away. And if it comes back, do it again.

The secluded mind is separated from unwholesome states. This sets the stage for absorption. Hindrances are not permanently uprooted, but they are very remote. At this point you must be firm in your resolve. Intrusions on the seclusion could shatter the tenuous foundation of concentration. The gross struggles with obstructions that habitually siphon off our energy have been overcome. Now energy is recaptured and accumulated for samadhi. These are the conditions that are prerequisites for jhana.

ULTIMATE SOLITUDE

The culmination of seclusion goes far beyond a quiet state of mind. The Buddha described true seclusion as an experience that is free from attachment. In a discussion with a monk named Elder, he said, "And how, Elder, is dwelling alone fulfilled in detail? Here, Elder, what lies in the past has been abandoned, what lies in the future has been relinquished, and desire and lust for present forms of individual existence has been thoroughly removed. It is in such a way, Elder, that dwelling alone is fulfilled in detail."[9] Thus, inner seclusion is a way of being that is freed from attachment to past, future, and even present perceptions. Consciousness ceases to take its stand on forms, feelings, perceptions, or thoughts. Nothing is taken up as a basis upon which to construct personal identity. This realization of the unfabricated nature of things brings the uncluttered mind to perfection. We don't just clear away physical and mental rubbish, and then rest in that neat and tidy mental space. The very constituents of personality are exposed as utterly empty. There is nothing there to hold, and no one to try. Nothing exists that would structure a relationship between assumed constructs of I and you, this and that, there and here, past and future.

Awakening is a realization that is utterly unshakable; what's more, it occurs to no one, requires no confirmation, and attains nothing. Such knowledge will transform your fundamental orientation in life. With no place to stop, ease is limitless; happiness is unbounded, and freedom realized. In a famous verse, the Buddha says,

Where water, earth, fire and wind have no footing,
there the stars do not shine,
the sun is not visible,
the moon does not appear,
darkness is not found.

And when a sage, a worthy one, through wisdom
has known this for himself,
then from form and name,
from pleasure and pain,
he is freed.[10]

Ultimately, seclusion is the separation from suffering—not sensations, feelings, or perceptions. Physical and mental seclusion creates conditions conducive to deep investigation. The seclusion of jhana is likened to learning to ride a bicycle with training wheels. The concentration states help you to stay balanced while you practice. Through the practice you let go in so many ways, until finally you ride without the crutch of those conditioned states. The Buddha described realization beyond the support of jhana:

> There is that sphere of being where there is no earth, no water, no fire nor wind; no experience of infinity of space, of infinity of consciousness, of nothingness or even of neither-perception-nor-non-perception; there is there neither this world nor another world, neither moon nor sun; this sphere of being I call neither a coming nor a going nor a staying still, neither a dying nor a reappearance; it has no basis, no evolution and no support. It is the end of suffering.[11]

COUNTING THE BREATH

As you direct your attention to the experience of breath at the nostrils, add a count in the pause between breaths. Breath in, breath
out, count 1; breath in, breath out, count 2; breath in, breath out,
count 3. Count the breaths from one to ten, then from ten to one,
then from one to ten. Limiting the number to ten reduces the tendency to try to accomplish something. Several rounds can help
focus the attention on the simple activity of breathing. This exercise emphasizes the directing function of attention. The danger
with counting exercises is that excessive attention can be given to
the conceptual number producing a superficial trance while automatically counting. You can work to counteract this danger by sustaining interest in the experience of each individual breath.

CHAPTER 3
Happiness

Whatever happiness is found in sensual pleasures,
And whatever there is of heavenly bliss—
These are not worth one sixteenth-part
Of the happiness that comes with craving's end.

—The Buddha[1]

E VERYONE WANTS TO BE HAPPY and not suffer. We strive for
pleasing and successful experiences. We avoid what is uncomfortable or unpleasant. Wanting to be happy in and of itself is
not a problem. Problems arise when we limit happiness to the narrow
scope of sensuality and personal comfort. The spiritual life introduces the
possibility of deep joy independent of sensory pleasure.

At the heart of Buddhist teachings is the recognition of the four
noble truths: to understand the fact of suffering; to abandon the cause of
suffering; to realize the end of suffering; to cultivate the way leading to
the end of suffering.

These teachings can make Buddhism appear to be a philosophy
that emphasizes suffering. However, the Buddha realized these truths
after he saturated his consciousness in the sublime happiness of jhana.
Happiness is the essential context for a liberating insight into the basic
facts of discontent.

This chapter provides an overview of jhana from the perspective of pleasure. Pleasure includes the common happiness of pleasant mental and physical experiences and also the sublime happiness associated with the subtle state of equanimity. Later chapters will give step-by-step instructions on how to attain each level of absorption with the unique qualities of pleasure inherent in each jhana.

Images and stories of the Buddha portray him as a happy man who lived the simple life of a renunciate, delighted in the calm clarity of meditation practice, and led a thriving community of seekers toward awakening. He appears to have lived content and carefree, responding to his disciples with compassion that was sometimes tender and at other times sharp. The Buddha had a remarkable wit and on occasion taught profound subjects through humorous anecdotes and puns. Speaking in the common dialect, the Buddha stayed close to the hearts and humor of the people. The ancient discourses are riddled with jokes (often explained in the translator's notes, since word play is one of the primary modes in which the Buddha's humor is preserved).

As I teach from the discourses of the Buddha today, my students often burst out laughing at the odd twists, brazen instructions, and amusing similes that permeate these ancient teachings. Interspersed with profound teachings on the nature of suffering, the Buddha made jokes about such things as the name of the questioner. He displayed surprising humor regarding human foibles. He teased the disciple Malunkyaputta, who asked endless skeptical questions. He consoled the despairing Venerable Sona with similes of music.[2] He comforted the dullard Cula Panthaka when he stood weeping outside the monastery.[3] He tricked Nanda, who was struggling with lust, promising five hundred pink-footed nymphs.[4] He gladdened the hearts of merchants, soldiers, potters, farmers, kings, queens, and prostitutes alike. The Buddha urged, instructed, cajoled, and consoled his followers to awaken to the liberating truth of things. He was not, in any way at all, dour.

The community of disciples who practiced with the Buddha were also happy and cheerful. The association of Buddhism with suffering can make you think the disciples must have been a grim order of alienated renunciates, disaffected and discontent, who selfishly pursued extreme withdrawal from society for personal satisfaction. This was not at all the case. The ancient records of the Buddha's ministry describe a community that was amiable, dedicated, humorous, and happy. On one occasion, King Pasenadi of Kosala visited the Buddha. Seeing the joy and delight that pervaded the community he praised the monastic sangha. The king observed, "Here I see bhikkhus smiling and cheerful, sincerely joyful, plainly delighting, their faculties fresh, living at ease, unruffled, subsisting on what others give, abiding with mind [as aloof] as a wild deer's."[5] The king attributed the cheerfulness of the monastics not only to a congenial social order but also to the depths of inner happiness available to those skilled in the attainments of jhana.

When the Buddha recounted his own practice, he described joy independent of physical comfort and unshaken by the hardships of famine, illness, and verbal abuse—and beyond what can be experienced through the senses.[6] "There are two kinds of happiness; the kind to be pursued and the kind to be avoided," the Buddha said. "When I observed that in the pursuit of such happiness, unwholesome factors increased and wholesome factors decreased, then that happiness was to be avoided. When I observed that in the pursuit of such happiness unwholesome factors decreased and wholesome ones increased, then that happiness was to be sought after."[7] The Buddha asks us: What pursuits lead to wholesome forces developing? And what pursuits lead to unwholesome forces thriving? The Buddha was a proponent of an efficient, long-term, sustainable approach to happiness, never settling for resigned acceptance of limited conventional comforts.

HIERARCHY OF HAPPINESS

The Buddha described a threefold hierarchy of happiness, classically designated as *carnal happiness, spiritual happiness,* and *happiness that is more spiritual than spiritual happiness.* Carnal happiness is based upon the sensual pleasures derived from sights, sounds, odors, tastes, touches, and even thoughts that are "desirable, lovely, agreeable, pleasing, sensually enticing, tantalizing."[8] Many of us live our lives knowing no other kind of happiness, but there is an even greater delight than what the senses can offer. This higher pleasure is reflected in states of rapture, joy, and equanimity, developed through concentration and clarified in jhana. In the language of the discourses:

> There are these five cords of sensual pleasure. What five? Forms cognizable by the eye that are desirable, lovely, agreeable, pleasing, sensually enticing, tantalizing. Sounds cognizable by the ear . . . odors cognizable by the nose . . . tastes cognizable by the tongue . . . tactile objects cognizable by the body that are desirable, lovely, agreeable, pleasing, sensually enticing, tantalizing. These are the five cords of sensual pleasure. The pleasure and joy that arise in dependence on these five cords of sensual pleasure; this is called sensual pleasure.
>
> Though some may say, "This is the supreme pleasure and joy that beings experience," I would not concede this to them. Why is that? Because there is another kind of happiness more excellent and sublime than that happiness. And what is that other kind of happiness? Here, secluded from sensual pleasures, secluded from unwholesome states, one enters and dwells in the first jhana.[9]

Jhana offers an alternative for those willing to turn away from the familiar obsession with sensory pleasure. Each level of jhana is characterized by sequentially more refined qualities of pleasure. A direct experience of the higher happiness in jhanic states creates a corresponding dispassion toward coarser pleasures. Instead of resisting attraction to pleasure, the Buddha skillfully invoked the mind's natural interest in happiness to realize a more stable happiness than what sensual delights can offer. When something better is discovered, coarser pleasures lose appeal. My teacher, H.W. L. Poonja, often said that once you know the taste of bees' fine honey, you will not crave coarse brown sugar.

The Buddha did not stop his exploration of happiness with the "spiritual happiness" of concentration states. His discovery of happiness encompassed the joy that is intrinsic to awakening. This unexcelled happiness manifests from the liberated mind freed from attachment, attended by insight, and not restricted to the temporary boundaries of concentrated states. The Buddha described this unwavering happiness as being "more spiritual than the spiritual," more sublime than the temporary pleasures of either sensual pursuits or concentrated meditative attainments.

SENSUAL PLEASURE

The Buddha said that "Pleasure is a bond, a joy that's brief, of little taste, leading to drawn out pain. The wise know that the hook is baited."[10] Sensual pleasures are inherently brief, but they are not bad or immoral. Desire for sensual pleasure is simply not an effective strategy to find lasting happiness. Wherever there is attachment to sensual pleasures, there follows fear of unavoidable change. The mindful realize this truth.

It is important to explore your relationship to pleasurable activities. I often hear people say that they "love" doing something. Hiking, for example, may be a generally pleasant activity, but like any activity, it is not a reliable source of happiness. Is a walk on a forest path entirely pleasant?

⌒ MINDFUL PRESENCE TO TASTE

Try to be totally and precisely mindful of the experience of eating a brownie, cookie, or something you really like. Resist the temptation to just wolf it down or, on the other hand, to savor it with indulgence.

Instead see what you might notice by eating it with complete awareness.

Take note of the changing qualities of pleasure, when it intensifies or diminishes. Observe the distinctions between a physical sensation of pleasant feeling, and a thought of craving or a commentary on the delights.

In the rush of daily life, we often miss the details of pleasure. Entranced by the conceptual notion of a "good" taste we may not notice contrasts in color of the food against the backdrop of the ceramic plate, a slightly salty flavor stimulating the tongue, the changing textures of crispy, crunchy, smooth, or gooey feelings as the morsel turns over in our mouths.

To develop appreciation of pleasure with daily sensory experiences, extract the conceptual assumptions from the physical knowledge of pleasure.

Notice the interactions of mind and body in this intimate experience of a favorite taste. See what there is to learn.

Will it remain pleasant if you continued to walk for nine hours, for fourteen hours, in the summer and in the winter, in the day and in the night?
Some aspects are pleasant and some unpleasant.

Sexuality and love may be exquisitely pleasurable, but the intensity
of sexual contact can shift rapidly between pleasure and pain. Sexual
pleasure is not permanent. Every sensory experience is limited, condi-
tional, and unreliable as a basis for happiness. To unhook the attachment
to these fragile pleasures, bring mindfulness to your experience of pleasant events throughout your day. What occurs that sparks pleasure? How
do you respond to it? Open yourself to pleasure, but resist adding the
attachment that wants it to last.

THE HAPPINESS OF A CONCENTRATED MIND

We must stop searching for gratification through sense spheres if we wish
to attain the first jhana. Most people have been conditioned since birth
to look toward successful work, home life, and relationships as the strategy for attaining well-being and lasting happiness. Most people, too, have
discovered that it has never actually worked to do that! Whatever success
we have attained can quickly be lost. An achievement such as winning in
an election, a tournament, or a competition brings only temporary success. At another time a different competitor will take the prize. The possessions we value can be lost. A cherished home can be destroyed by fire.
Our lifestyle could be disrupted by war, famine, or violence. A tidy
retirement fund can be eroded by medical costs. Anyone can die at any
time. Seeing the vulnerability in this familiar cycle of craving, accumulation, change, and loss, a wise person looks elsewhere for happiness. It
does *not* matter at this point if you believe that there is a happiness higher
than material success. It is enough to know what has not worked in the
past. Take the risk of trying another way. Detach from what you already
know will not bring you lasting happiness; this release sets the stage for
deep concentration.

The Buddha instructed his disciples to not merely recognize a
present-moment feeling, but to *discern the genesis* of the feeling.[11] For the
deepening of concentration, it is useful to distinguish sensually based
feelings from feelings that arise through spiritual practice. These would

include the delight of non-remorse associated with virtue, the rapture that arises with concentration, the happiness that comes with wholesome states such as love and compassion, the contentment that comes with simplicity and renunciation, the equanimity of tranquil states, and the bliss of release. These feelings are not conditioned by lust, hate, or delusion; they are a vital support for the cultivation of concentration and insight. Invoking these states propels the spiritual journey beyond the conventional confines of sensual experiences.

Awareness practices usually develop mindfulness through present-moment sensory experiences. The cultivation of jhana takes a different approach. Mindfulness is required, but the locus of attention soon shifts from sensory phenomena to a refined mental object. The first stage of concentrating the mind involves turning attention away from the shallow stimulation of sense pleasures that agitate and diffuse consciousness. This is the critical shift of orientation that makes access to the "pleasant abidings" of jhana possible.

The Buddha described five qualitatively distinct feelings of happiness found within the progression of jhanic absorptions: happiness born of seclusion, happiness born of concentration, happiness associated with mindfulness and equanimity, the feeling of equanimity that is neither pleasant nor unpleasant, and the "peaceful abidings" characteristic of the formless spheres.

As absorption deepens, the mind is saturated with increasingly sublime delights. These satiate the mind as it lets go of gradually more subtle fixations. Detaching from the habitual allure of the domain of sensory pleasures prepares attention to find a deeper resource for happiness. Each jhana state has certain characteristic features that distinguish the particular absorption, but the nuances of each are subjectively experienced by the individual practitioner. The intimate pleasures of jhana present a risk of attachment that could stall a meditator's progress. Becoming overly impressed with a relatively minor degree of jhanic rapture is the beginner's pitfall. When the mind is freed from the restrictions of physical pleasures and jhana attained, the potential for joy is virtually infinite.

HAPPINESS IN THE FOUR JHANAS

Absorption in the first jhana frees the mind from unwholesome states and the impingement of sensuality. Just as there comes a time when continuing to chew a bite of brownie no longer is pleasant, there comes a point when you are no longer delighted to dwell in the bliss of detachment. You are ready to "swallow" the brownie and move on. It is no longer intriguing. Conviction will grow that conditioned states are not reliable sources for happiness. Empowered by this understanding, the mind naturally withdraws from the pleasure distinctive of the first jhana, curious to discover an abiding that is more subtle.

As consciousness unifies in the second jhana, it is filled with rapture, pleasure, and delight. The rapt interest of the second jhana is described as "happiness that is born of concentration." Here, the mind and body are drenched, filled, and infused with these ecstatic heights of jhanic rapture. Yet, although initially exciting, the intensity of rapture eventually almost "grates" on the nerves. The mind eventually will prefer a quieter, less agitated state of pleasure. As dispassion toward rapture grows, the pleasure characteristic of the second jhana naturally fades. There is no need to rush through or reject the rapture. Experiencing the delight with clarity is sufficient for this level of pleasure to come to fulfillment and then subside. One can stay with the delight for as long as the mind is soaking it up. Then, mindful of the fading of that delight, one enters and abides in the third jhana.

The third jhana is characterized by happiness, yet divested of delight. It possesses a sublime quality of happiness that is associated with mindfulness and equanimity. It is a calm and deep sense of contentment and peace likened to the half-smile that artists render on Buddha images. A half-smile implies full acceptance and deep happiness, regardless of conditions. This third absorption provides a smooth resting place for the heart. One feels joy in a mindful connection to things, a contact that does not seek pleasure through the experience. In the state of jhana sensory experiences are not the focus; the mental factor of mindfulness is highlighted. This brings a quality of joy to the third jhana: happiness due to mindfulness and equanimity.

Third jhana can feel so sweet that you might wonder if you would ever honestly grow disenchanted by it. During one long retreat I was instructed to remain with the third jhana until the sign of the fourth jhana naturally arose—to endure as much contentment and joy as the mind could tolerate until it naturally and genuinely threw off engagement with pleasure. I had no idea how long that would take!

The texture of consciousness was smooth, with contentment saturating not only the meditations, but also the meals, walking, sleeping, showering, working, and so forth. One week passed, then two. I glided along on a creamy cloud of quiet joy, wondering if I could ever tire of this fantastic state. Sustained through the momentum of concentration and the protected conditions of retreat, absorption required virtually no effort to maintain. It was utter bliss. To my surprise, by the end of the third week there arose a clear sense that "This is enough."

Even this most sublime and peaceful joy was ultimately unsatisfactory. Genuine dispassion arose naturally, without the harsh imposition of renunciation tactics. Gentle saturation and natural relinquishment brought forth deep faith in the liberating force of concentration. In the wake of this realization the mind willingly released its engagement with the joy characteristic of the third jhana. No longer enchanted, I found contentment fades to reveal the more peaceful neutral feeling of the fourth jhana. This is an important transition. This recognition of the limitations of pleasure allows the mind to shed engagement with the whole spectrum of pleasure and pain.

The fourth jhana is characterized by a deep stillness, complete focus, and equipoise. The shift can occur only when we are willing to let go of joy. This release is not disappointing. In the absence of obvious pleasure, there is nothing unpleasant. The mind settles; it stops swinging between worldly dualities: happiness to sadness, excitement to dullness. Still and quiet, consciousness abides undisturbed, beyond the range of pleasure and pain. The fourth jhana has an exquisitely pervasive neutral feeling, but without a trace of blandness, described as the feeling of equanimity. Though it is an accentuated state of evenness, it is without the slightest implication of mediocrity.

Resting with equanimity, we have shed yet another layer of agitation. This is a deeply stable state, praised by the Buddha as a powerful platform for insight, spiritual powers, or absorption in the "peaceful abidings" of the formless perceptions.[12] With deep equanimity there is no agitation pulling consciousness toward one thing or away from another, no struggle, no resistance. The mind rests in a complete state of ease, cooled out, unperturbed, equanimous. The quality of equanimity is so profound and important that I will discuss it in more detail in the next chapter.

THE HAPPINESS OF A LIBERATED MIND

The Buddha took a broad approach to pleasure. His discussion of happiness began with the common pursuits of sensual experiences. It developed through meditative concentration that includes jhanas imbued with rapture, happiness, and equanimity, and extended to the peaceful abidings of the formless perceptions. He also described a pleasure beyond the realm of conditioned experience: the happiness of a liberated mind. The Buddha declares that when he speaks of pleasure he "describes pleasure not only with reference to pleasant feeling; rather, friends, the Tathagata describes as pleasure any kind of pleasure whenever and in whatever way it is found."[13] At each level of this development of happiness we abandon the gross for the subtle. This process of cultivating the finer happiness and letting go of the coarser pleasures gradually purifies the potentially seductive relationship to pleasure until finally we experience the release of true detachment. This final release is what the Buddha referred to as bliss that is "more spiritual than the spiritual."

The happiness of freedom is not conditioned by pleasant or unpleasant feelings. It does not require comforts, ease, wealth, health, solitude, or society. The happiness of a liberated mind is not limited to the protected conditions of meditative absorptions. The peace of liberation goes beyond the temporal states of rapture, joy, and even equanimity. Enlightenment brings a complete release from all constrictions. It is the happiness that describes the end of suffering, a happiness that is "more spiritual than the spiritual."

THE HAPPINESS OF NONATTACHMENT

What is true happiness?

To begin to explore this, notice the mind that grasps at perceptions, and notice when there is no grasping in the mind. When you feel the mind without grasping, even for a moment, let yourself fully experience that quality of ease, from head to toe. There is happiness in the expression of non-attachment. Can you find it? Rest into that state of ease beyond attraction and repulsion. Try it in fairly neutral encounters, with physical pleasure, or in the face of pain.

The joy of pure detachment is discovered whenever you are not struggling against the fact of things.

With the daily meditation and the counting exercise introduced in Chapter 1, you have been focusing attention at the point of contact where the breath meets the nostrils. With some practice, you may notice that your attention gradually becomes steady and is not so easily scattered by stray thoughts or the barrage of passing sights, sounds, and sensations. The mind is beginning to compose itself in present-moment awareness. As you begin to feel this gathering of mental energies, notice any lightness or happiness that might arise. Notice the ease and even relief that comes from ceasing to roam through the fields of sensory stimuli. As this ease intensifies, it will eventually manifest as the quality described as "delight and happiness born of seclusion."

This describes the pleasure that characterizes the first level of jhana. Stay aware of this quality of ease. Let your entire body and mind be saturated with the feeling of happiness born of this seclusion. This happiness is entirely wholesome. It is a healing and joyful energy, intrinsic to the concentrated mind. This happiness is not based in craving; it does not depend on nor condition states of greed, hatred, or delusion. There is nothing to fear from this feeling. Throughout this practice, I encourage you to experience non-sensual happiness fully and completely. Let the mind be drenched in it. Allow the experience of spiritual happiness to deepen. Open to wisely experiencing the boundless depths of spiritual happiness.

There are no limits to what a concentrated and free mind might discover!

CHAPTER 4
Equanimity

*The way I see it, if you want the rainbow,
you gotta put up with the rain.*

—Dolly Parton

Such it is.

—The Buddha[1]

NEITHER THE COARSE FEELING of unpleasantness nor the agitated feeling of pleasure, equanimity is, the Buddha said, one of the highest kinds of happiness, beyond compare with mere pleasant feelings. Superior to delight and joy, true equanimity remains undisturbed as events change from hot to cold, from bitter to sweet, from easy to difficult. This neutral feeling is so subtle that it can be difficult to discern.

Equanimity is steady through vicissitudes, equally close to the things you may like and the things you do not like. Observe when the tendency to move away from what you do not like ends, and the tendency to hold on to what you like is equally absent. Personal preference no longer dictates the direction of attention. Equanimity contains the complete willingness to behold the pleasant and the painful events of life equally. It points to a deep balance in which you are not pushed and pulled between the coercive energies of desire and aversion. Equanimity has the capacity to embrace extremes without getting thrown off balance. Equanimity takes interest in whatever is occurring simply because it is occurring.

Equanimity does not include the aversive states of indifference, boredom, coldness, or hesitation. It is an expression of calm, radiant balance that takes whatever comes in stride.

The taste of a favorite meal, perhaps eggplant parmesan, may be exquisitely clear: the sweetness of cooked tomatoes, the aroma of basil, the soft texture of the eggplant that melts on the tongue, the saltiness of the parmesan cheese. Each taste may be discerned with acute precision and clarity. They are also enjoyed as a unique blend and appreciated for their combined qualities. When equanimity is dominant, the experience of craving another morsel is absent. That eggplant parmesan will instead be fully experienced with equanimity rather than delight. For many people such balance around taste would be a unique moment.

Some of my beginning students have told me, "But I don't want that kind of happiness. I enjoy the *gusto* of delight. I relish a passionate involvement with my life. I love the excitement of experience." I understand. As a concept, equanimity may appear unappealing, but students nonetheless discover, quite to their surprise, that the exquisite peace of balanced states has a taste of happiness beyond pleasure and beyond pain. Every experience of liking something has as its counterpart disliking something else. The fickleness of personal preference agitates consciousness. The deeply balanced state of equanimity makes a sustained investigation of things possible. Out of this combination of concentrated stability, penetrative investigation, and mindful awareness, consciousness may awaken the unshakable nature of happiness.

Spiritual practitioners thrive in unpredictable conditions, testing and refining the inner qualities of heart and mind. Every situation becomes an opportunity to abandon judgment and opinions and to simply give complete attention to what is. Situations of inconvenience are terrific areas to discover, test, or develop your equanimity. How gracefully can you compromise in a negotiation? Does your mind remain balanced when you have to drive around the block three times to find a parking space? Are you at ease waiting for a flight that is six hours delayed? These inconveniences are opportunities to develop equanimity. Rather than shift the blame onto an institution, system, or person, one can develop the capacity to opt to rest within the experience of inconvenience.

Equanimity matures when you deal with what is difficult without being thrown off balance by it. It is in the difficult or even tragic moments, when we receive a diagnosis of cancer, or learn of the death of a friend, or are suddenly disabled in an automobile accident, that our mettle is tested. Understanding that things occur due to causes and conditions, we don't struggle with the fact that the event occurred; we let the body be a body. It is the nature of physical form to decay and die. No wish will change this natural law. The concentrated mind then rests composed, even as the body is affected by accident, illness, and death.

In 1996, in the midst of several years of living and practicing meditation in Asia, I returned to California to visit my family. It was scheduled as a three-week holiday. During this visit, when some friends and I were traveling to a trailhead to take a day hike, we were involved in a head-on collision. My life instantly changed. Although I was able to walk away from the accident, my injuries caused intense pain that dominated my experience for years. Returning to Asia was simply impossible. During the years I was occupied by medical treatments and physical therapies, I met many fellow accident victims. We were all struggling to regain some degree of function, to have a life that we valued and enjoyed.

In my case, I used meditation skills to protect the mind. Any time my mind drifted into thoughts of things I could no longer do, how my life had been ruined, or the beginnings of a mental story that bemoaned my situation, I quickly brought my attention back to mindful clarity. This repeatedly distinguished between the physical and the mental qualities of suffering. It was a practice that required diligence. Observing the interactions of thought, emotion, and sensation had to be continuous throughout the day and night. It became a practice that guided my mind toward the deep peace of equanimity even in the face of physical pain and an uncertain future. I did not have to struggle against the pain or grapple toward pleasure. In the absence of desire and aversion, there is the quiet happiness of equanimity. This kind of happiness is steady and strong; it pervades the mind even when the body is racked by searing physical pain.

I have on occasion suggested that some students actually enter challenging situations in order to refine equanimity. I recommend avoiding car accidents, but favor foreign travel as one excellent way to develop equanimity off the meditation cushion. I lived in India during my late twenties and early thirties. The initial experience was a confusion of incomprehensible events. I did not even recognize the street sounds. The cuisine was unfamiliar and more spicy than my digestive system was accustomed to. Many customs appeared strange. Having only known a suburban-California lifestyle, I found India unpredictable, uncontrollable, and confusing.

We may not realize to what extent we impose our expectations on things until those expectations are left unmet. I had always expected post offices to have stamps, banks to have cash, drug stores to sell aspirin, and international airports to have money-changing services, until I traveled. On a trip to China, I arrived midmorning at an international airport. The airport money changers were all closed until late afternoon. Without local currency I just had to sit in the airport for six hours until the exchange counters reopened. If we live protected by our routines, we grow to expect our days to go the way we plan them, and for the most part in California it works. Traveling encourages us to rest a bit more and enjoy being where we are, with all its beauty and frustration. I may have on my "to do list" to buy stamps today, but that does not guarantee that the post office will have stamps for sale that day. Traveling asks us to demand less and accept things as they are, to remain balanced and equanimous whether or not things go according to plan.

When I practiced in Thailand, I joined with a large group of monks, nuns, and laypeople who were walking in the jungle in a remote region for several weeks. It was a practice called tudong that develops equanimity through renouncing luxury and working intentionally with austere conditions. For us, these conditions included a virtual absence of possessions and comforts, sleeping on the ground covered only by a mosquito net or a black plastic trash bag on cold nights, bathing by the banks of the rivers, accepting the very simple food we could carry (rice and chili paste) or gather in the forest (bamboo shoots and bitter leaves). Some days water was scarce. We walked all day, sometimes long into the night, usually barefoot.

This was no high-tech backpacking trip. It was a practice of renunciation, acceptance, and equanimity that brought tremendous happiness. I was quite surprised to find myself sitting down to rest, exhausted, aching, and hungry yet very definitely happy. Equanimity has a quality of deep peaceful bliss. When we are not insulated by highly structured routines or pampered by luxurious comforts, equipoise develops by resting in the presence of the things we cannot control, predict, or even comprehend.

In India, my teacher was not interested in experiences confined to a formal meditation session. Insight must be lived. When Poonjaji saw me enter very quiet, rapturous states while sitting still, he would send me to the bazaar, to the kitchen, or to run an errand. He insisted that no distinction be made between the tranquillity of the sitting meditation and the busy haggling of the Indian bazaar. A peace that was worth attaining must remain utterly undisturbed and undistracted in the chaotic moments as well as the still moments, equally present to an experience of comfort or pain, equally balanced when things work out conveniently or inconveniently. Equanimous, we cease imposing our personal preferences and demands on life.

Two of my grandparents lost their short-term memory as they aged. Visiting them was challenging. Conversations were repeated over and over and over again. Sentences repeated, questions re-asked, worries restated. This became an important place for my practice. It is too easy to reject, avoid, or resent the frustrating dimension of interactions like these. I noticed that with my grandparents the content of the conversation topics was not important. The words were simply a means of connection, reassurance, expression of loneliness or fear, love, appreciation—all very basic interactions. If I focused on the content in communicating an idea, exploring a philosophy, or sharing a story, there was no reason to talk with them at all. But if I focused on the connection and the love, then the lack of variation in the words and subject matter didn't matter. I could happily answer the same question over and over again. We could discover the same flower nine times in four minutes. When we accept the difficult things in our lives, they become supports for developing equanimity, happiness, and peace.

A student recently told me about attending a church service that included a point when parishioners greet each other with a handshake or hug as a sign of peace. The young woman sitting to her left leaned over and full of joy told her, "I'm pregnant." The man sitting to her right greeted her next with the statement, "Did you know my wife died?" Equanimity asks us to remain balanced and present with both the pain and the joy—no matter how extreme each may be.

Intense or profound moments can draw out a pure quality of presence without conscious effort. I sat with my grandmother in the hospital, her hand in mine, as she died. It felt connected, peaceful, and somehow harmonious. There was deep acceptance and an awesome wonder of the incomprehensibility of life and death. The profundity of her peace superseded all struggle and brought forth a state of serenity and wonder in my heart. What would it be like to bring the same quality of stable presence, deep release, attention, and wonder to mundane daily interactions with our family members?

Equanimity is not limited to the painful areas of life. Equanimity also protects us from being swept away by praise, flattery, and success. Careless excitement in response to praise can cloud good judgment. A friend recently showed me a new dress that she could barely afford. She purchased it when the salesperson said that it made her look ten years younger. On the other side of the spectrum, self-hatred or anger can fester when we are blamed, criticized, or find our faults exposed. We live in a world where we may be barraged by both praise and blame. As a teacher who gives public lectures, I have many opportunities to experience these vicissitudes. Students often approach me after my lectures. Some people are deeply moved and offer me high praise. Other people who sat in the same room and heard the same talk may react with anger, boredom, or annoyance.

How equanimous are you when people express their views of liking or not liking what you do? Do you take it personally or understand they are simply expressing their own bias? Does praise or blame disturb your balance?

During the time of the Buddha there was a lay disciple who repeatedly approached the monks asking for teachings. The first talk he heard was comprehensive and detailed. This layman walked away complaining that the monk was long winded. The next time he came to the monastery, he approached a silent monk; this time he left complaining because there were no teachings. The third time this layman requested teachings, Ananda, who was aware of the previous two visits, offered a talk of medium length, neither too long nor too short. But this man again complained that the talk was mediocre, neither detailed nor succinct. When all this was reported to the Buddha, the Buddha simply observed: there is always blame in this world.[2] Praise and blame, gain and loss, pleasure and pain, are inevitable facets of human existence. Meditation practice invites us to find a range of happiness that includes the full spectrum, so that we remain joyful, balanced, and happy in the face of change.

⌒ CLARIFYING EQUANIMITY

Daily activities outside the formal meditative experience are a useful training ground to explore this refined quality of the happiness of neutrality. Mindfulness of simple daily events such as buttering toast, eating bland food, washing dishes, commuting with traffic, drinking water, or folding clean clothes can clarify the characteristic of equanimity.

Notice the feelings and behaviors associated with equanimity during your engagements at home and work.

Notice when the mind is free from the tension of judging and craving, when you meet the present moment intimately and fully without being pulled by desire or aversion.

You don't need to wait until the fourth jhana to cultivate this critically balanced factor!

PART II
Preparing the Mind for Absorption

CHAPTER 5
The Wisdom of Letting Go

See how letting go of the world is peacefulness.
There is nothing that you need to hold on to and nothing that
*   you need push away.*

—The Buddha[1]

Letting go is supreme happiness.

—The Buddha[2]

THE WISE UNDERSTAND THE IMPORTANCE of letting go—even letting go of the things we strive for and attain. Developing wisdom demands that we courageously abandon anything harmful and diligently cultivate wholesome states. Development and relinquishment together carry one systematically through the jhanas, strengthening the wholesome forces and distilling the mind to its essence. At each level of absorption new perceptions are discovered as others are abandoned. We use the deep happiness of jhana to encourage our practice of letting go. As we release control over body and mind to absorb into the peace of jhana, we let go into the cradle of jhanic bliss.

Meditative training is more about letting go than it is about attaining levels of absorption. Spiritual life invites you to relinquish all that binds you, whether that is your cherished fantasies, destructive attitudes, assumptions, views, or treasured roles, beliefs, and ideals. Relinquishment is not a weak conceptual thought; it registers very deeply in the purity of a concentrated mind. In fact, the guiding principle of jhana practice is relinquishment, and release is both the method and aim of concentration. "If you don't want to suffer, don't cling" could summarize the main thrust of all the Buddha's instructions. But if you can't follow that simple instruction completely and need (as so of many us do) more complex approaches to help you along or keep you busy until you finally tire of clinging, an extensive array of meditation tools have been devised by generations of Buddhist practitioners. And yet, if at any point you are unsure what to do in this practice, just let go.

As one teacher advised, "You can't go wrong with not clinging."[3]

☞ FOR REFLECTION

Look into the stories, fantasies, fabrications, desires, aversions, reactions, and doubts that periodically occupy your thoughts. Notice what your mind conjures up in the first moments after waking up in the morning—that period between waking and breakfast is a fascinating window into your habitual thought patterns. Where does your mind go when you sit down for a few moments to rest without the distractions of radio or TV?

Take ten minutes now and lie down on your bed watching the mind without falling asleep.

What patterns of thought dominate? Where does your mind wander when it is not directed by the structure of a task? Can you identify your habitual thinking pattern? Is it blame? memory? fantasies of success? complaining? worry? insecurities about finances, relationships, opinions, self-image? are you planning your next activity?

The Buddha boldly declared, "Nothing is worth adhering to."[4] In a vital discourse, the Buddha instructs Sakka, the ruler of the gods, on this topic. The dialogue begins with Sakka asking: "How is one liberated by the destruction of craving?" In reply, the Buddha said that by learning that "nothing is worth adhering to" one gains an understanding that is applicable to all things. From the perspective of this wise understanding, you can experience whatever feelings may arise—pleasant, painful, or neutral—with wisdom, recognize the impermanence of feeling, and not cling. Not clinging, the wise person is not agitated and abides in peace.

Satisfied, Sakka asked no further questions and returned to his home, resuming his heavenly businesses and becoming preoccupied with the various affairs of the daily life of the gods. He was an important god of his time, with many godly responsibilities and duties to perform, many entertainments to pursue, places to go and people to see. Sakka's meditation practice became quite lax. He made excuses for neglecting it, complaining, "We are so busy; we have so much to do."[5] Something always seemed to be more important or more compelling.

Perhaps your situation is not so different. You may read a spiritual book, hear a lecture, or attend a meditation retreat. You appreciate these teachings, value them, perhaps feel inspired, but then go home and become preoccupied with the various affairs of your life. Now, having read that nothing is worth adhering to, allow this teaching to affect the quality of your life. The understanding that nothing is worth adhering to inspires the relinquishment that makes absorption possible. By clearing the craving from your mind, you prepare it to delve into the depths of concentration.

Meditation is designed to solve a specific problem: attachment. Awakening is not the experience of spiritual ecstasy accompanied by rainbows and fireworks. Awakening is the experience of a profound relinquishment of clinging, abandoning the cause of suffering. By understanding that the problem lies in the clinging, we learn to let go.

Many practices cultivate the skill of letting go through renunciation, contemplating death, and perceiving impermanence. Letting go does not require strenuous effort. It is not necessarily one more task to perform. It is, simply, what occurs when you are not clinging: a direct expression of wisdom arising in a moment of experience. Simple wisdom tells us, "When you are being dragged, let go of the leash." When you feel the pain of grasping and understand the holding on as the cause of your suffering, the solution becomes obvious.

The Buddha illustrated his teaching on relinquishment with the simile of a quail tethered by a thin rotting vine. It is a trifling bond, but for the frail bird it is a strong fetter. For an elephant, however, a rotting vine is no tether at all.[6] The thing that binds may be feeble or strong; the measure is not in the fetter itself, but rather in the ability to abandon or in the tendency to be bound. Thus, to escape the fetter of clinging, we develop the facility to abandon and cultivate a vivid knowledge of the unfettered mind.

FOUR WAYS OF ABANDONING TROUBLESOME THOUGHTS

You may sit down to meditate with the best of intentions but find yourself inundated with uncontrollable memories, intense desires, complex plans, or insidious doubts, fears, or hopes. You may *aspire* to let go, but find it difficult to do.

The things that obsess one person may not attract another person. Power is not inherent in the thing to which one feels bound. Through meditation we discern our relationship to our thoughts: what are our patterns and what is sustaining the attachment? In the "Discourse on the Simile of the Quail," the Buddha observed four ways of working with the thoughts of attachment that may beset the earnest meditator.

The first approach is to indulge distracting thoughts. A person taking this approach is considered *fettered, bound, not free*. The second approach is to reject, deny, avoid, or react against repetitive thoughts. Although this practice removes the thoughts, aversion becomes a binding force. The third approach is to quickly abandon and remove memories and thoughts during meditation. Mindful, the meditator is free of indulgence and aversion. Interestingly, the Buddha also described the practitioner of this approach as *fettered, bound, not free*. The mindful person recognizes when the mind gets obsessed by thoughts and skillfully returns to an awareness of the present moment by letting go of the habitual thought patterns. This person practices admirably, but still is not fully free. Wisdom has not yet uprooted the cause of obsessive thoughts. Thus, this practitioner knows how to let go of distractions that arise, but has not penetrated the process deeply enough to prevent further distractions from occurring. Caught in an alternating sequence of distraction, mindfulness, and letting go, the practice continues.

The Buddha describes the fourth way, saying, "Some person, having understood that attachment is the root of suffering, divests himself of attachment, and is liberated with the destruction of attachment. Such a person I call *unfettered, not fettered.*"[7] Wisdom has penetrated to the root of the problem for this meditator and extracted the fundamental cause of obsessive thinking. In this system of four approaches, the first two ways, indulgence and rejection, describe the two extremes of reactivity. The third way is practice: developing mindfulness and cultivating the ability to let go. The fourth approach achieves another level altogether: liberating wisdom. With this understanding well established, the Buddha continues the discourse with instructions on establishing the sequence of jhana.

The wisdom that understands attachment as the root of suffering reveals the possibility of a transformation that doesn't require us to abandon one obsessive thought pattern after another. This transformative wisdom clears away the distractions that inhibit concentration, and directly liberates the mind from all forms of clinging. It manifests in the moment of contact with any sensory experience, in the moment of feeling a feeling or thinking a thought. The experience of wisdom is not just letting one particular problem pass; the Buddha taught that *nothing whatsoever* should be clung to. When you know this so clearly that clinging loses its power, you possess the wisdom that liberates.

ABANDON ONLY WHAT IS NOT YOURS

Some people fear that letting go could diminish the quality of their lives, health, abilities, achievements, or personal property. To this, the Buddha said, "Whatever is not yours, abandon it; when you have abandoned it, that will lead to your welfare and happiness for a long time."[8] This invites a profound reflection on what one can authentically claim as one's own. As we discern the impermanent, conditioned character of all material and mental processes, we eliminate perceptions, sensory experience, and material things as fields for possession. On the surface it seems like we are asked to give up everything, but simultaneously comes the realization that there is actually nothing possessed and consequently nothing that can actually be given up. The great abandonment is to let go of the concept of ownership.

Letting go in meditation is the relinquishment that involves no loss. Recognizing impermanence leads to the realization of the pure and ungraspable nature of things. Knowing this basic fact of things, one has nothing to fear. And the extraordinary delight that arises with realization surpasses all temporary pleasures, softening any residual fear that may want to grasp again what can never actually be possessed.

☞ FOR REFLECTION

Have you had any recent experiences of clearly letting go? They happen all the time, although we rarely investigate the experience. You make a plan in the morning, but a flat tire demands that you let go of your agenda for the day. You might like milk in your tea, but when you don't find any in the refrigerator you release the desire rather than suffer irritation. A friend might be emotionally distraught, and you realize there is nothing you can do to make her happy; although you care about her and listen, you don't hastily jump in to "fix" her feelings. You might want to be recognized and appreciated by a colleague, and only discover relief when you release the desire for that acknowledgment.

Notice moments of letting go throughout your day.

What feelings occurred with the experience of that release?

What burdens your life that you would be happier living without?

UNDERSTANDING FEELING

For a person with an untrained mind, attention can become entangled by grasping as it moves toward pleasant encounters and avoids unpleasant feelings. Notice how you respond when you don't get what you want. Also, observe how you respond when you succeed and do get exactly what you want.

The Buddha's following poetic instruction on feelings refers to the basic quality of a feeling being pleasant, unpleasant, or neither-pleasant-nor-unpleasant.

Just as many diverse winds
Blow back and forth across the sky
Easterly winds and westerly winds,
Northerly winds and southerly winds,
Dusty winds and dustless winds,
Sometimes cool, sometimes hot,
Those that are strong and others mild—
Winds of many kinds that blow;
So in this very body here
Various kinds of feelings arise,
Pleasant ones and painful ones,
And those neither painful nor pleasant.
But when a bhikkhu who is ardent
Does not neglect clear comprehension,
Then that wise man fully understands
Feelings in their entirety.[9]

This basic response to any sense stimuli is the affective experience
of sensory contact. Throughout the development of concentration, one
must be mindful of these qualities—pleasant, unpleasant, and neither-
pleasant-nor-unpleasant—because when one does not see the *feeling-
tone,* habits of desire and aversion are reinforced.

Feel the undercurrent of the affective tone distinct from any conceptual assumptions about what you like or dislike. Discover what is
actually pleasant, and what is unpleasant, or neutral, just now. It may not
be obvious. A favorite meal might be pleasant generally, but also might
include bits of unpleasant chewing, disturbing textures and sounds, and
sudden changes in flavor. A pain in the body might include aspects that
are pleasant, such as warmth, tingling, and softness. Let your attention
drop below the level of *concept* and personal history to directly experience the quality of feeling.

For the spiritual aspirant committed to uprooting lust, aversion, and
delusion, mindfulness of feeling-tone is an indispensable skill. Unless we
clearly recognize how feeling affects perception, the three poisons will
be reinforced. For example, an unmindful connection with a pleasurable

experience can activate the underlying tendency to lust, generating a stronger conditioning toward desire. An unmindful experience of something painful can ignite the underlying tendency to aversion, further conditioning resistance, hatred, or fear. And an unmindful encounter with a neutral experience may trigger the underlying tendency to delusion. Subtle neutrality often goes unnoticed. In the absence of clear attention, preconceived ideas easily distort perception, perpetuating ignorance.[10] Feeling is a crucial link to observe, a strategic point for release. Consistent awareness of the present-moment feeling, wedged just between simple contact with a sensory stimulus and the grasping reaction, can not only cool the agitated mind but also uproot the source from which suffering springs.

I just stepped outside on this early spring day and stood for a few moments basking in the late morning sun. Although the sun warmed my face and my right side, a crisp coolness in the air chilled my left hand, which was shaded. My habit of mind is that warmth is pleasant and cold is unpleasant. Rather than instinctively shoving my hand into my pocket at this moment, I looked into the feeling. Cold is not a static feeling. It is composed of many changing sensations. The icy coldness was at first characterized by an unpleasantly sharp sting. It was followed by moments of pleasant tingles and warm pulses that intensified into unpleasant throbbing. Soon these sensations softened into a basically pleasant vibration. Within the area where I had felt the initial coldness, many changing sensations quickly arose and passed—some pleasant, some unpleasant, and some indistinguishable.

Try this yourself. Rather than act according to the assumption that something is entirely pleasant or unpleasant, attune your attention to the flow of feeling. Let the attention rest in the current of feeling as the framework for mindfulness; experience the dynamic flow of feelings. What is directly felt as pleasant, unpleasant, and neutral can be surprising.

To illustrate this point, let me use the example of chocolate cake. I like chocolate cake—and one time I had a piece of homemade chocolate cake for dessert and a scoop of rice left on my plate from the meal. It was plain white rice, nothing special. As I ate these two, bite by bite, my attention focused in on the *quality* of feeling. I let the process slow down, exploring in meticulous detail the actual experience of a bite of rice and then a bite of chocolate cake. What were the tastes, how did they evolve through the process of eating? I settled into the experience of texture and temperature as the two foods moved from the plate to be consumed through contact with my tongue and teeth. I noticed what occurred when my eye landed on the cake or the rice, observing the initial desire, preference, interest, and craving. Without rushing, I took the time to explore my consumption of these morsels. I learned something that amazed me.

During that entire examination, I could find nothing about the cake that had a more pleasant feeling than the rice. It was the opposite actually; the chocolate had a roughness and bitterness that periodically flared into an abruptly unpleasant sensation. When the craving subsided and attention rested on the stream of changing feeling, the actual experience of cake did not confirm my habitual view of cake. I can no longer assume that I like cake better than rice.

Liking and not-liking are triggered by an unmindful relationship to feelings. By maintaining focused awareness on the stream of changing feelings, one can break the link to craving long enough to suspend habitual reactions. Cake becomes just cake, and rice becomes just rice.

EXPLORING FEELING-TONES

Although many insight meditation students can be mindful of what is arising, they nevertheless find themselves reacting to particular pains and discomforts. Students may diligently notice the details of the burning, stabbing, searing, pricking sensations that compose pain, but are frustrated because their minds resist the basic fact of pain. In a situation such as this, it may not help to force yourself to meticulously notice more nuances in painful sensations. Instead, shift your attention to the unpleasant feeling-tone accompanying the pain. It doesn't matter if it is a bitter taste, caustic music, indigestion, or searing shoulder pain; all are accompanied by an unpleasant feeling tone. If you shift your attention to become mindful of the subtle feeling-tone, the specific perceptions and personal narratives that trigger unpleasant feeling become relatively inconsequential. Know it as unpleasant; accept it as it is.

☞ THE SUBTLE IN THE MUNDANE

This exercise explores how the three kinds of feeling may trigger reactions of craving, aversion, and dullness, or be a tool for cultivating equanimity. Choose three food items: one that you generally like, one that you distinctly dislike, and one that you feel fairly neutral about.

Place enough of each on your plate to permit several bites of each item.

Slowly and mindfully eat each item, bite by bite, noticing the qualities of pleasantness, unpleasantness, and neutrality in the experience.

Carefully notice the impulses, textures, temperatures, stimulation, affects, and opinions related to each perception.

Observe not only the stimulation through taste, notice the experience of seeing, smelling, tasting, touching, thoughts, comparisons, views, emotions, and so forth.

Is there a desire to increase contact with the things you like, or to avoid contact with the food you dislike?

As you move back and forth between slow mindful bites of each item, allow a harmonious investigation and balanced equanimity to pervade the experience of the bare fact of each perception.

Take at least twenty minutes to mindfully explore this exercise. Slowing down will permit you to notice subtle aspects of an otherwise mundane experience of eating.

When hearing an unwanted sound during meditation, some people may get irritated and angry, search for ear plugs, and yell, "Stop that racket!"—thinking the sound is disturbing their meditation. The sound might be all right as just a sound, but they experience agitation because they remain unmindful of the connection between sound and the unpleasant feeling-tone, or unaware that they are reacting to assumptions about what sounds are acceptable during meditation. This often occurs at retreat centers located near freeways. Yet in remote forests the wind blowing through trees can make an even louder sound than traffic but will generate few complaints. The actual volume and quality of the sound may not be so different—and from this we can learn it is our assumptions, and not the fact of the sounds themselves, that trigger the reaction.

Imagine yourself eating a piece of berry pie. Even before finishing the serving, you begin to think about a second helping. It may not be more pie you want; in fact, a second piece might bring unpleasant feelings of bloatedness. The desire may not be to have more pie, but rather, to sustain the pleasant feeling-tone. Craving for pleasure stimulates greed for more pleasant sensations. Unaware of the dynamic of feeling, we reinforce the assumption that more pleasure will come through more experiences—if one piece of pie was good, more is better. This habitual drive for *more* strengthens the pattern of greed.

You can save yourself a lot of anguish by investigating your response to the fundamental qualities of pleasure and pain. If you are unmindful of a pleasant feeling, the underlying tendency to greed gets activated. If you are unmindful of an unpleasant feeling, the underlying tendency to aversion gets activated. If you are unmindful of a neutral feeling, the underlying tendency to delusion gets activated.[11] People commonly try to increase the pleasant, react against the unpleasant, and are dulled, confused, or inattentive to the neutral feelings. A skillful meditator will develop the flexibility to direct awareness to these subtler layers of experience and investigate the interaction of pleasure and greed, pain and aversion, neutrality and delusion.

THE FREEDOM OF RELEASE

Wherever clinging is perceived, that is the place to release. As your equanimity grows, it becomes easier to let go. Wisdom infiltrates your days, sometimes consciously, and often subtly. Wisdom may manifest as the ability to keep your mouth shut when you feel the impulse to come back with that witty retort that would only increase the conflict.

Wisdom gives one greater courage to face the grief of a loss, to understand loss not simply as personal tragedy, but also as a manifestation of the broader dynamic of life's suffering. It leads one to discover a deeper appreciation of life, inspires us to live aligned with our highest aspirations. Most people notice improvement in the quality of their lives through the cultivation of this training; this brings confidence that the practice is working. Students who have practiced awhile say, "I may not be enlightened yet, but I am at least a bit more patient," or "I don't feel very different, but my family says I am easier to live with." The benefits of developing patience, kindness, equanimity, calmness, compassion, and the ability to bear the pain in life cannot be underestimated.

CHAPTER 6
Dynamics of Emotion

Reality is not the result of a process; it is an explosion. It is definitely beyond the mind, but all you can do is to know your mind well. Not that the mind will help you, but by knowing your mind you may avoid your mind disabling you. You have to be very alert, or else your mind will play false with you. It is like watching a thief—not that you expect anything from a thief, but you do not want to be robbed. In the same way you give a lot of attention to the mind without expecting anything from it.

—Sri Nisargadatta Maharaj[1]

THE POPULAR CARICATURE of the meditator is someone in full lotus posture—totally cool, even-tempered, utterly unemotional, sitting perfectly still and peaceful like a statue. But in actual experience, meditation is neither static nor stoic. As sentient beings, we feel the full range of emotions and feelings. Some will be difficult, others delightful. Calmness and peacefulness are so subtle you may not even notice them. Rage, grief, sorrow, and terror are so intense that you can sometimes notice little else. A mindful engagement with sensory and emotional life intimately informs meditation. Steadfast mindfulness is an essential precondition for creating a strong foundation for jhana, but mindfulness does not require the withdrawal characteristic of jhana. It develops in the midst of sensory contact.

MINDFULNESS IS YOUR GUARDIAN

The Buddha urged, "For one's own sake, diligent mindfulness should be made the mind's guard."[2] Mindfulness protects concentration from the impulsive intrusion of lust, hate, confusion, and infatuation. Mindfulness balances the mind, bringing harmony between the extremes of restlessness and sleepiness, agitation and dullness, wanting and not-wanting, doubt and faith. If your mind is left unguarded and a pleasant thought occurs to you and you are unaware that it has arisen, the mind might begin to go wild: images proliferate; fantasies of pleasure emerge; rippling responses run through the body; tension from grasping forms; concepts of "me and mine" are reinforced. In an unguarded, unrestrained mind, attention is lost in fantasy. Although the initial contact may be pleasant, the associative sequence can create a wake of mental agitation; suffering results. The problem is *not* that a pleasant thought arises; the problem is that the mind is unprotected. When mindfulness is absent or muddled, clinging finds an opportunity, and identification with the experience ensues.

You don't need to shut your eyes and ears or practice in a sensory deprivation chamber. Mindfulness is alert, screening for obstructions and reactions. It does not prevent perception; it only restrains the tendency to grasp at the contact. Experience shines freshly as unique moments that come and go in a relaxed and clear mind. The habit of attachment is inhibited.

The Buddha taught:

> On seeing a visible form with the eye, or hearing a sound with the
> ear, or smelling an odor with the nose, or tasting a flavor with the
> tongue, or touching a tactile object with the body, or cognizing a
> mental object with the mind, a monk does not seize upon the
> object's general appearance or its details. Since, if he left his sense
> faculties unguarded, evil and unwholesome states of covetousness
> and grief might invade him, he applies himself to the restraint of the
> sense faculties, he guards them and achieves control over them.[3]

Mindful awareness is the guard we post at the door of each sense. For example, if you experience an unpleasant tactile sensation, such as cold on the arm, you might begin to complain about the weather. Although there has never been a time when the weather changed in response to human complaints, we still make them. Stories circulate in the mind about not having enough warm clothes; judgments reinforce the view that this climate is unfit for human habitation; criticisms are aimed at companions who we feel are being cheapskates by keeping the heat too low. Hatred grows and the heart closes. Feeling alienated and separated, we become irritable, callous, easily annoyed.

In this kind of scenario, self-condemning thoughts proliferate: "I'm not good enough. I'm not worthy to get enlightened. How can I become enlightened if I don't even wear the right clothes for the season?" Such an unguarded mind suffers. The suffering is not caused by the sensation of cold on the arm. Lack of mindfulness is the problem. Mindful attention to the initial contact will prevent suffering from entering. The sooner mindfulness meets the mental embellishments that arise, the easier it will be to interrupt the cycle of suffering. A moment of discontent becomes nothing more troublesome than a fleeting perception of discontent. A lyrical teaching of the Buddha states:

> *Having seen a form with mindfulness muddled,*
> *Attending to the pleasing sign,*
> *One experiences it with infatuated mind*
> *And remains tightly holding to it.*
> *Many feelings flourish within,*
> *Originating from the visible form,*
> *Covetousness and annoyance as well*
> *By which one's mind becomes disturbed.*
> *For one who accumulates suffering thus*
> *Nibbana is said to be far away.*
> *When, firmly mindful, one sees a form,*
> *One is not inflamed by lust for forms;*
> *One experiences it with dispassionate mind*
> *And does not remain holding it tightly.*
> *One fares mindfully in such a way*
> *That even as one sees the form,*

And while one undergoes a feeling,
[Suffering] is exhausted, not built up.
For one dismantling suffering thus,
Nibbana is said to be close by.[4]

WHEN WE HURT

Living with a human body with physical needs for food, sleep, and
warmth, vulnerable to illness and injury, you will experience pain. If you
can distinguish between physical suffering and mental suffering, pain
will not impede concentration. I have practiced with traditional Asian
masters who encourage using pain as a strong object for concentration.
Because attention is easily drawn to intense pain, focus remains undistracted. In this book, however, I recommend using the breath as a more
neutral object of concentration, since for jhana, neutral or pleasant states
are preferred.

Yet, given the nature of the body, pain will inevitably arise. We can't
avoid it. If mindfulness is weak when we feel pain, an undercurrent of
aversion could fester, creating a mental dimension of suffering intertwined with the physical pain. The traditional Buddhist teachings illustrate this through the story of a man who is stabbed by a dart and
immediately stabbed by a second dart.[5] The Buddha explains that the
first dart is like the pain that comes with life—bodily feelings. These
might arise from illness, accident, a mosquito bite, hunger, thirst, cold.
The second dart—mental feelings—we inflict on ourselves with reactions of desire, aversion, craving, and ignorance.

The Buddha concludes the teaching with the instruction:

> If he feels a pleasant feeling, he feels it detached. If he feels a
> painful feeling, he feels it detached. If he feels a neither-painful-
> nor-pleasant feeling, he feels it detached. This, bhikkhus, is called
> a noble disciple who is detached from birth, aging and death; who
> is detached from sorrow, lamentation, pain, displeasure and
> despair; who is detached from suffering, I say.[6]

No one can completely control physical life. We may exercise, eat well, and live healthy lives, but our bodies are subject to illness, injury, and decay. We cannot end feeling, but we can train our minds to experience feelings with a balanced awareness free from aversion. We respect our physical vulnerability by not forcing ourselves beyond reasonable limitations, and by not fearing aging, judging wrinkles as bad, or believing that our joints should not ache as we age.

As you practice bringing mindfulness to pain, and become aware of the sensations themselves—distinct from thoughts and interpretations about them—you narrow the range of possible obstruction. Although physical pain may fatigue the body, it need not spark the parallel mental suffering of frustration, agitation, or annoyance. Practice experiencing pain as only a single dart; free yourself from the extra suffering of stabbing yourself with the second dart of aversion. You might still have pain, but you will be peaceful and happy nonetheless.

At one retreat a student appeared particularly restless. He struggled to maintain the silence: he wrote notes to the coordinators, conversed during work periods, requested personal items he'd forgotten, and perused books to identify plants, animal tracks, and local bird species. On the second day of the retreat, he urgently requested buckets and rags to wash his car. By the third day, he was collaborating with the cook to produce a recipe book. When I met with him, it was apparent something was agitating him deeply; these distractions were manifestations of an inner state. Clearly it wasn't the car that needed attention.

In our conversation he nonchalantly mentioned the recent death of his wife and told me he was supporting a daughter with cancer. In the telling he felt his pain; intense grief bubbled to the surface. With a courageous heart and a box of tissues nearby, he gently opened to his anguish. A deep calmness settled over his experience. He experienced it as painful, yes, but he also saw it as the truth of his life. When he felt the authenticity of his feelings, he knew that his heart was big enough to experience the intensity of both grief and love.

Restlessness, a common obstacle to concentration, is often a cover for painful states that hide below the surface of busy, agitated energies. Pain may be calling for your attention. Is there loneliness, fear, grief, or sadness you are staying too active to feel? Gently ask yourself if you can open to this pain. You don't need to rip your heart open all at once, but see if you can touch some of your pain—it may give you strength.

The seclusion of jhana is supported by the clear connection of mindfulness, not by dullness or aversion. This essential point is frequently misunderstood if one tries to rush the attempt to gain meditative attainments. Avoid the temptation to imitate seclusion by blunting your senses or diffusing your perceptions to create the illusion of seclusion. There is nothing whatsoever dull about jhana. The serene mind is not sleepy, diffused, or inert; it is without the slightest trace of uncertainty. Each jhana state incorporates mindfulness and a bright attention. You need to trust mindfulness as your mind's guard. Vividly encounter any experience of body, mind, or the world as it unfolds, before, during, and after absorption into jhana with mindfulness as protection.

☞ MEETING PERCEPTIONS

Notice how your attention meets perceptions.

Do you feel that the attention is lurching toward perceptions to embellish experience? Rest back. Allow experience to arise and pass.

Observe phenomena from the stability of your seated posture.

Each time the attention pounces on a thought, a sight, a sound, rest back again.

Imagine a comfortable armchair positioned in a room with large picture windows opening out to a vast view. Imagine yourself sitting in the chair observing the expansive view. You don't need to chase thoughts or follow after feelings to be aware of them.

Simply observe how each thought arises and passes like a bird flying across the sky.

Remain comfortable and steady in your grand and royal seat!

ENLIGHTENING PLEASURE

At times, positive emotions will arise. You may see an injured bird as you walk through the forest and recognize genuine compassion as your natural response. You may step out of your home into the cool morning air and realize you are infused with a spontaneous appreciation of life. In watching a spider build a web, you may discover the commitment necessary to repair a troubled relationship. While struggling with illness, you might be filled with unlimited love. While sitting in meditation, you may discover a great peace pervading your heart.

In the meditative process you will encounter a variety of qualities related to happiness and peace. Pleasure arises quite spontaneously as the mind settles. Allow yourself to fully experience the wholesome and healing states that arise with concentration, whether its expression is intense or subtle. Open to them, allow their healing character to infuse you with energy. You do not need to push away jhanic pleasures by thinking you should work harder to overcome your personal problems. Allow the pleasant feelings to vibrate in every cell of your being. Sometimes we must endure rapture so intense that it feels as though our bones could break from the ecstasy or burst from the flood of joyful bliss. Give these feelings of happiness and pleasure your attention; allow the body to be healed in their gentle embrace; let them calm, still, and balance the attention. Happiness and peace develop effortlessly and, like all phenomena, naturally fade and pass away. The pleasure known through jhana is described as a subtle accompaniment to the state; it is much fuller and calmer than the ecstatic intensity felt in the early stages before absorption.

In the introduction, I referred to some of the events leading up to the Buddha's enlightenment. Already quite experienced in the systematic attainment of jhana, he remembered a moment in his youth when the pleasures of jhana spontaneously arose as he rested in the shade of a rose apple tree. This recollection led to a pivotal shift in his relationship to pleasure. Recalling this spontaneous experience of happiness, the emaciated recluse wondered, "Could that be the path to enlightenment?" And he came to think that it might be so. Then the thought arose, "Why am I afraid of that pleasure that has nothing to do with sensual pleasures and unwholesome states?"[7] His examination of pleasurable feeling continued. He noticed there was nothing to fear from pleasure that arose in a steady mind, and he ceased the severe austerities of fasting. His concentration deepened, and his mind grew ripe for awakening. As he sat under the Bodhi tree with the resolve to awaken, he traversed the jhanas and, using jhana as the basis for insight, realized enlightenment.[8]

Tremendous strength resides in feelings of peace and happiness. The Buddha instructed his disciples to liberally allow the jhanic factors of delight, interest, happiness, joy, and equanimity to so pervade, suffuse, irradiate, and saturate their bodies and minds that no part is left untouched.[9] We can actively harness the potency of these feelings to fortify our concentration.

The Buddha illustrated the process of completely immersing oneself in the field of wholesome pleasure with four similes, each linked to the experience of a level of jhana: (1) soap powder sprinkled and thoroughly blended with water as it is kneaded into a ball; (2) a lake fed by a cool spring that permeates unimpeded every area of that lake; (3) a lotus that lives entirely immersed in a cool lake, drinking of the water, never rising out of the water, completely enveloped in the coolness of the water; and (4) a man completely covered by a clean white shawl so that no part of his head or body is exposed.

These images equate total immersion with a saturation of mind and body with the wholesome aspects of heart. When the state recedes, however, you don't need to conjure up ways to make it stay, because it was known, honored, valued, and fully met as it appeared. It is equally recognized when it fades, changes, or dissipates. As the Buddha noted, feelings arise, but they do not "invade the mind and remain."[10]

CONFRONTING DIFFICULT EMOTIONS

During the absorption of jhana, wholesome states dominate the mind. But prior to absorption and after emerging from jhana, the mind may in fact feel all sorts of things. Mental states are not trading cards you can exchange, swapping unpleasant ones for preferred feelings. You don't need to be trampled by difficult feelings or repress them, but you do need to know them in the clear light of mindfulness.

Trust the capacity of the heart to be spacious enough to feel not only the things you like but also mental states that are difficult. The challenge of difficult emotions is the impulse to avoid confronting them. Denial is ultimately unconvincing, however. Often when we try to remove ourselves from the feeling, just slightly, we discover that we are dwelling on the story of the emotion. The story creates a slight separation from the direct feeling of the painful state. For example, you might remember something hurtful that a friend said and rehearse various defensive responses during your meditation session. Thinking removes your attention from what anger, disappointment, and betrayal actually feel like in this moment right now. If you experience a repeating memory, it's your opportunity to explore the feelings that underlie the story.

In a situation of highly charged emotions, you'll find it helpful to gather the support of stillness. Bring awareness to the posture. If you are sitting, take a deep breath and stay sitting. If you are standing, take a deep breath and keep standing. Feel your feet on the floor. Sense the stability of your body. Scan your body and know the sensations you are feeling. Physical sensations serve as a tangible guide to the felt sense of the mental state. Are you experiencing contraction? Are specific areas of tension, quivering, shaking, pulling, or throbbing dominant? Locate the feeling in the body and let the attention rest in the embodied experience of the emotion. Emotions are never static. Notice how they flow and change: intensifying, dissipating, or fluctuating within a cluster of related sensations. Every time the mind reengages the storyline, disentangle yourself from the conceptual level and return to the felt sense of the feeling.

I recall a painful conversation during which I was informed that I had been rejected for a position that I had earnestly sought. This was the culmination of a long process of qualifying for the position, and an equally long exploration of my desire to attain it. After the decision was finally announced and all hope was exhausted, waves of sadness and loneliness flowed through me. Needing some space to attend to these feelings, I went for a walk. Each time I noticed that my mind was retelling the story I intentionally dropped the story and settled into the bare feeling, opening to the sadness and disappointment. Although my feelings repeated through much of the walk, they were neither constant

☞ WORKING WITH DIFFICULT THOUGHTS

For this exercise, intentionally bring to mind a thought that will trigger some emotion. It may be a memory that sparks annoyance, anger, or sadness. It might be an expectation that causes envy, fear, or shame.

As you give rise to the difficult thoughts, be conscious that they form stories in your mind, but feel the impact of these emotionally charged thoughts in the body.

Is there tightness in your chest, shoulders, and face? Are there sensations in the belly or limbs?

Notice how those physical sensations manifest and evolve.

Notice how the emotional quality shifts, perhaps from anger to fear, pity, sadness, shame, worry, love, melancholy, or desire.

Emotions are dynamic processes that are in a state of flux. If you don't refuel them through obsessive thinking, they will change and fade.

We learn to be present to the full range of emotions by feeling their changing energetic expressions in the mind and body.

For example, anger might bring heated, agitated explosive feelings radiating from the chest; sadness might carry a sinking vulnerable quality in the belly; fear might create an unstable quivering sensation in the knees or throat. Attending to the physical manifestations of emotions keeps attention focused on the process long enough for you to learn directly about how these difficult states impact your mind.

When the mind is obsessed by a difficult emotion, it may construct repetitive stories about who did what and why. Caught in the storyline, you might dwell on painful narratives and not discover how to free the mind from the painful thoughts. Let go of the story and investigate the emotion directly. When you allow feelings to evolve through their natural changes, the emotional landscape clears, like clouds passing on a stormy or windy day.

nor overwhelming. I saw a bulldozer pushing a pile of dirt around and for a few moments stood fascinated. A friend walked past me on the path and I felt tender appreciation fill my heart. When a rabbit hopped by, I felt joyful delight. When my attention moved freely between these various responses, disappointment did not burden my mind. After several waves of feeling, it passed, leaving a residue of lightness, acceptance, and confidence in its wake.

Noticing change and observing the spaces between feelings can bring a balanced perspective to emotion. Emotions are an expression of empty phenomena that arise in response to stimulus, are experienced, and cease.

The Buddha described a human being as a guesthouse; many kinds of feelings come, stay for a while, and then travel on.[11] Try greeting all emotions as visitors or guests. Allow them to visit, accept that they arise due to conditions, but don't adopt them as permanent residents.

CHAPTER 7
Effort, Ease, and Intention

Leave everything as it is in fundamental simplicity,
and clarity will arise by itself.
Only by doing nothing will you do all there is to be done.

—Dilgo Khyentse Rinpoche[1]

IN THE HONESTY OF SILENCE you will encounter your own mind without pretense. You may sit still and yet discover that your mind is anything but still. At times it may feel as though you have sat down with a monster. A great challenge lies before you. How can you embrace this companion who is sometimes monstrous, insulting, and raucous? How can you develop a deep friendship with your own mind, so deep that your mind becomes your trusted ally?

No matter how restless and uncooperative your mind might appear, concentration improves with practice—yet stillness cannot be imposed by strenuously wrestling down distractions. Concentration grows through the willingness to encounter, understand, and eventually remove all that agitates the mind. Like the folk saying goes, "Dirty water has more fish." The messy aspects of the mind create a dynamic force that supports spiritual development as we meet challenges with clarity and skill.

Effort is an integral aspect of the Buddha's teaching. Just moments before his death, the Buddha urged his disciples, "Strive on untiringly!"[2] This injunction crystallized a teaching of diligent effort that pervaded the Buddha's forty-five-year ministry. Skillful application of effort is fundamental to the art of meditation: you must apply yourself completely, yet without the caustic energies of force. You need both the utmost fortitude and the gentlest touch—applying just the right amount of energy to be fully present to the facts of things.

As you begin the concentration practice, you may notice tension caused by overexertion. It is common to blame the effort for the unpleasant feeling of tension, and then rebel against discipline. If you incline toward the other extreme, of not making effort, you may never gather the strength to progress. Self-doubt, withdrawal, laziness, resistance, uncertainty, or holding the view that non-effort is superior can weaken resolve and stall the development of concentration.

Please don't throw the baby out with the bath water.

The problem is not effort per se, but how to adjust it; usually only a slight modification is required. Explore effort and ease dynamically. Continue to notice how you are applying attention to meet the present object of meditation.

HOW LITTLE IS ENOUGH?

The art of meditation explores how attention meets its meditation subject. Meditative attention shines like a light beam, illuminating the subject, but not interfering with its natural process of change. What is the quality of effort that meets its object without excessive aggression? Overly intense observation might bash right through your focus. Stiff control might cause you to lose alignment with the graceful unfolding of things. Excessively zealous energy may backfire into an inner rebellion of self-judgment, tension, and doubt.

Try doing less rather than more. Half the effort might be sufficient to bring composure and balance to attention. You may not even be aware you are doing too much until you stop. Tension in the face and eyes may indicate excessive striving. Strive for the attitude of zeal that does not impose itself onto its object but softly rests into the meditation subject. Then explore it. Meditators describe this connection as "dropping back to observe," "dropping into experience," "settling into the experience," or "merging with the perception."

Efforts that don't support the task at hand can creep unnoticed into meditation. Reduce any unnecessary muscular effort in your jaw, eyes, facial muscles, chest, or hands. When I lead retreats, I sit in the front of the room facing my students. We usually meditate with eyes closed, but I peek. Sometimes I see indications of excessive striving—faces puckered, mouths scrunched, foreheads wrinkled, postures rigid, chins jutting forward as if to reach for the breath. Such exaggerated physical effort interferes with the clarity of concentrated attention.

Relax! Breathe! Enjoy! Don't force the practice. Gather the dispersed energies of mind in a loving and consistent way. Loving diligence is stronger than the tense shell of striving. A composed, coordinated, gentle attention is usually enough to meet the rapidly changing perceptions that unfold.

GUARD YOUR MIND AS A COWHERD GUARDS THE COWS

In the early stages of concentration, most people need strong resolve to abandon distractions and unwholesome tendencies of mind. To illustrate the need for timely energetic attention, the Buddha used a simile of a

---

⌒ ADJUSTING YOUR ENGAGEMENT

During your meditation session, notice the quantity and quality of energy you apply to observation. Is there interest or dullness, precision or diffusion, intensity or passivity?

Notice the conditions in which greater energy is available, such as when interest is piqued. And notice when there is less energy, such as when attention is dulled by fantasy.

Sense your ability to adjust the quality and quantity of energy and effort during a meditation session.

How much effort is required initially to direct the attention to the breath?

Try it again, and see if the same quality and quantity of effort are needed.

Try again when there is noise in the room, or pain in the body, or you feel a little sleepy.

Notice the varied modulations of effort needed to precisely meet each of these changing conditions.

☞ **FOR REFLECTION**

Consider the following questions during work, recreation, or
home activities.

Under what circumstances do you find more vigorous energetic effort is required?

When is equanimous relaxation more appropriate?

Notice tasks at home or work during which alert attention and
relaxation are both present and in balance.

---

cowherd working in the autumn when the crops thicken. The cowherd
knows that he could be punished, fined, or blamed if he allows his cows
to stray into the crops. So during this season the cowherd guards his
cows by constantly poking them, to check them and curb them. The
Buddha said, "So too I saw in unwholesome states danger, degradation,
and defilement."[3] Mindful of how unwholesome thoughts lead to afflic-
tion, a wise meditator actively removes harmful thoughts and hindrances. Obstacles must be met with resolute dedication.

Effort becomes gentler as concentration deepens. As the mind
moves from coarser toward more refined states of consciousness, harmful agitating thoughts cease to arise; thoughts of kindness, compassion,
letting go, and peace dominate. The Buddha, continuing with the simile
of the cowherd, teaches that activity of mind is more spacious when the
contents are wholesome: "Just as in the last month of the hot season,
when all the crops have been harvested by the villagers, a cowherd
would guard his cows simply by staying at the root of a tree since he
needs only to be mindful that the cows are there, so too, there was need
for me only to be mindful that those states were there."

TUNING A MUSICAL INSTRUMENT

During the Buddha's days, there were many eager young monastics,
deeply intent on awakening. Having left their homes to undertake the
holy life of a recluse, some were excessively energetic in their meditative
pursuits. Young Sona, desperate to become enlightened, was one such

monk. He was not yet mature in his practice; the impact of his overexertion caused genuine inspiration to sour into discouragement:

> As Venerable Sona was meditating in seclusion, after doing walking meditation until the skin of his soles was split and bleeding, this train of thought arose in his awareness: "I am one of the most energetic disciples of the Blessed One, yet my mind has not attained liberation from the taints by non-clinging."[4]

Dear Sona was deep in doubt, discouraged and ready to quit. Fortunately, the Blessed One appeared before him and gave these instructions on effort:

> "Now Sona, before, when you were a house dweller, were you skilled at playing the lute?"
> "Yes, Lord."
> "And when the strings of your lute were too taut, was your lute in tune and easy to play?"
> "No, Lord."
> "And when the strings of your lute were too loose, was your lute in tune and easy to play?"
> "No Lord."
> "But when the strings of your lute were neither too taut nor too loose, but adjusted to an even pitch, was your lute then well tuned and easy to play?"
> "Yes, Lord."
> "Similarly, Sona, if energy is applied too forcefully it will lead to restlessness, and if energy is too lax it will lead to lassitude. Therefore, Sona, keep your energy in balance, . . . and there seize your object."

There is no single correct *setting* for our effort that will apply to all situations. Tuning the instrument of effort occurs continuously, with each inhale and exhale, in each moment of connecting and sustaining the attention. We adjust our energies moment by moment, as automatically as we adjust how much exertion is needed to lift an empty tea cup and how we automatically shift that degree of effort to lift a full pot of soup. As we encounter the phenomenal world we adjust the vigor with which we interact with things. Through meditation we learn to refine this capacity so we apply our minds wholeheartedly to perception. Just as a child intuitively determines the variations in strength needed to push a toy car or shove the living room sofa, so too we learn how vigorously to relate to a lustful fantasy and how to soften our vigor when encountering a subtle perception of joy.

The Buddha taught a multifaceted approach to effort. He did not merely demand that students just keep trying harder. Skillful effort requires the wisdom to bring forth the quality and quantity of energy that keeps the attention balanced, stable, and aware.

INTENTION: THE POWER OF THOUGHT

A disciple once asked the Buddha how he realized the end of suffering: "How did you cross the flood?" The Buddha replied, "By not halting, and by not straining, I crossed the flood."[5] The power of intention guides the unfolding of the meditative path, enabling smooth progress without strain. Our intentions establish the direction for what we will cultivate. Once an intention is set, the mind and body instantly orient toward that perception. Before you are consciously aware of a physical movement or personal decision, intention has mobilized and established the inclination. This interaction of mind and body occurs in all activities—the familiar impulse to reach for the doorknob on a closed gate, the movement of a hand brushing hair off the face, the decision to drink when we are thirsty.

Actions don't happen only in the body; they result from an intricate interrelationship of body and mind. Momentary impulses, springing from your contact with the myriad perceptions you encounter, shape the countless choices you make everyday.[6] Being mindful of intentions presents an opportunity to explore how this mind-body process works, how a thought leads into an action.

Intention is the basis of all deliberate action. Intentions are subtle forms of thought that link a mental impulse to physical action. As the Buddha said, "Intention, I tell you, is action.[7] Intending, one creates action by way of body, speech, and mind."[8] Some intentions will lead to happiness; others will generate suffering. The dynamic interaction of thought and action perpetuates the binding force of karma and reveals the potential for liberation. Intention is a potent force, powerful enough to either reinforce or interrupt conditioned patterns.

Although largely unnoticed, intentions permeate virtually all actions and choices. An intention impels the movement from the sitting posture to standing; or will move you from the living room to the office. Intentions generated by the mind manifest in speech. Intention will also move you from one level of jhana to the next jhana. And intention will be the impetus for emerging from the absorption state at the proper time.

☞ NOTICING INTENTION

As you prepare to end your next meditation session, notice what moves you from sitting to standing. How is that shift organized? What initiates the change in postures? Observe the arising of intention as a moment of being "about to" do something.

Practice playing with intention during meditation when you're experiencing subtle pain, perhaps an itch. The impulse arises to scratch. Don't move. Keenly observe that mental impulse to move. Observe the intention to scratch arise and keep watching until you observe the intention to scratch pass. You may notice that the tingling itchy sensation is distinct from the mental impulse to scratch.

What happens if you inhibit the intention to move and just stay still, awake and aware to the whole realm of mind-body phenomena?

Explore the links between body and mind, between sensation and intention, between stimulus and response.

Notice what forces come together to mobilize a mindful movement. How does a decision occur?

Intentions often lie hidden, obscured by the complex and rapidly changing activities we busy ourselves with. The Buddhist practice shows the way to achieve liberation from all greed, all hate, and all delusion and confusion, which involves more than simply becoming a good person. Most people attracted to meditation already live with a decent standard of morality and ethics. Awakening, however, has the potential to completely uproot even our slightest negative tendencies. No one likes to think of herself as cruel or filled with ill will, but little nasty thoughts may have infected the mind and become intertwined with complaints, gossip, criticisms, or a chronically judgmental attitude. Whether the judgments are directed at ourselves or others makes little difference; both poison the heart with ill will. The aim of this practice is to refine intention so that only the purest impulses—those that support awakening—interest the mind.

I have learned to see my pattern of justification as a signal to stop and reflect. When I notice a residue of justification in my mind—a train of thought, usually repetitive, that explains why I did something, that holds on to past actions defending my strategies—I stop what I am doing to consider: What were my intentions that brought forth the action I am obsessing about? Since my mind became so unsettled and agitated, since restless justification manifested, perhaps my action was rooted in an impure intention. By reflecting, we create the opportunity to choose which intentions to support and which to withdraw our energy from.

Inevitably, we all make mistakes. Focusing on purity of intention more than on perfection of action allows us to accept our imperfections and personal limitations. When we trust our intentions, we learn without dwelling on mistakes and condemning ourselves. We cannot control the results of our actions, but we can have tremendous influence over the intentions from which our actions spring.

☙ FOR REFLECTION

Out of the many intentions you may notice, which ones do you select to act on?

What are the ones you regret having acted on? Remember some times that you chose restraint, and were glad.

☙ COMPOSING YOUR INTENTIONS

It can be helpful to write out your intentions for practice.

What is your highest purpose? Focus on your deepest aspirations for yourself and all beings. This can serve to inspire you when progress appears slow. Knowing your intentions can keep you going even when you are tired, bored, or busy. Try to use language that resonates for you personally; write it to inspire yourself; and then use it to remind yourself of your deepest aspirations.

I wrote out my intention at the start of one personal retreat. When the meditation became difficult, when my body throbbed with aches and pains, when I wanted to take a nap, lose myself in fantasy, or distract myself with books, I would recite it, encouraging myself to realign with my deeper values. Since I am greatly inspired by the early discourses of the Buddha, I included some lines that refer to his teachings. I share it as an example, but please compose one that is meaningful to you.

> *Today I have a fortunate opportunity,*
>   *not easily come by,*
>   *supported by the sacrifice, trust, and generosity*
>   *of many benefactors.*
> *Let me not waste this precious chance to free the mind*
>   *from habitual obstructions,*
>   *to unclog the conditioned tendencies of judging, selfing,*
>   *craving, and distraction.*
> *May my practice this day be energetic and bright,*
>   *earnest,*
>   *steadfast in the face of any difficulty.*
> *Concentrated, focused, unwavering.*
> *Happily, I apply myself with vigor,*
>   *Until this mind is utterly freed*
>   *Beyond the range of grasping,*
>   *Having willingly done,*
>   *What needs to be done.*

INTENTION AND THE STILLNESS OF ABSORPTION

As concentration deepens, the activities of mind are sequentially stilled; unwholesome thoughts are set aside until the thoughts that arise are of an entirely wholesome flavor and sparked only by immediate experience. When you review such a mind, you'll find nothing to fear. As the Buddha discovered, "If I think and ponder upon this thought even for a night, even for a day, even for a night and day, I see nothing to fear from it."[9] It is essential to examine this purified mind, to know that you can trust yourself. Recognizing the beauty of a purified mind brings the confidence to deeply relax. There is no longer any need to struggle against disruptive tendencies. Enjoy the mind that has no ill will, cruelty, or greed present. It is safe to relax.

When the Buddha found his mind entirely free of unwholesome states, he recognized that the very presence of thinking disturbs tranquillity. He noticed, "with excessive thinking and pondering I might tire my body, and when the body is tired, the mind becomes disturbed, and when the mind is disturbed, it is far from concentration. So I steadied my mind internally, quieted it, brought it to singleness, and concentrated it. Why is that? So that my mind should not be disturbed." After energetically removing everything unwholesome, after reflection that confirms only wholesome thoughts are present, you may wish to consider the

---

☞ FOR REFLECTION

What is the purpose of your efforts?
What is beyond the touch of even your best effort?
What is accomplished through effort and what is effortless?

---

possibility of going beyond good and bad thoughts. This is a pertinent step for progressing in concentration practice: here one enters the domain of jhana.

BREAKING OUT FROM THE SHELL

The Buddha likened developing a mature practice to incubating eggs:

> Suppose there were a hen with eight, ten, or twelve eggs, which
> she had covered, incubated, and nurtured properly. Even though
> she did not wish; "Oh, that my chicks might pierce their shells
> with the points of their claws and beaks and hatch out safely!" yet
> the chicks are capable of piercing their shells with the points of
> their claws and beaks and hatching out safely. So too, a bhikkhu
> who thus develops various wholesome faculties supportive of
> wisdom and concentration is capable of breaking out, capable of
> enlightenment, capable of attaining the supreme security from
> bondage.[10]

You can cultivate many things through dedicated interest: patience, generosity, joy, understanding. You can develop conditions that are conducive to concentration and supportive of wisdom. You can "sit on your eggs" by diligently nurturing the meditative explorations. Giving yourself to the spiritual life is like sitting on the nest. But the actual rate of maturation is not under your control. It would be senseless to wish, "May I attain the fourth jhana today," and expect that wish to be fulfilled without any practice. You can diligently nurture your practice, but maturation occurs due to the ripening of conditions, not from how fervent your wishes are.

No one will make you meditate, no one requires you to cultivate deep spiritual happiness, no one can insist that you become aware. Meditation practice is not a prescription, obligation, or punishment. In the absence of authoritarian requirements, we must each discover for ourselves the tender discipline that sustains us. Spiritual discipline is a precious resource for maintaining a practice, even when it feels dry, tedious, and difficult. We need effort to progress on this path. Only after all need for effort ceases are we entitled to make the ancient declaration of enlightenment: "What had to be done has been done."[11]

CHAPTER 8
Calming the Restless Mind

Whatever one frequently thinks and ponders upon,
that will become the inclination of his mind.

— The Buddha[1]

TO ATTAIN THE JHANAS, we need both concentration and wisdom. The basic instruction for concentration training is marvelously simple: let all distractions go and steadily focus on your meditation subject. Yet wisdom training requires us to be sensitive to what is being let go. Both concentration and wisdom practices require a composed and clear mind that is neither stuck nor distracted. Since distraction can take many forms, it is helpful to have a toolkit of practices that allow us to work with various modes of distraction. This chapter offers the reader several helpful approaches for investigating and dealing with distraction that emphasize both *letting go* and *clear understanding,* a combination vital for developing wise concentration.

Once a student decides in principle to let go of distracting thoughts, a common question arises: "How?" In the early days of my meditation practice I employed a rather unsophisticated technique that I now call the Caveman Approach. In *The Flintstones* cartoon, Barney Rubble's son Bamm-Bamm wielded a favorite club and pursued a single theme in all his actions. Whatever he encountered, he clobbered with his club. When an unwary thought arose during meditation, my mind would bash it immediately with a walloping *Bamm-Bamm!* This is a very coarse technique, and not one I recommend.

Instead, when practicing letting go, notice how your mind tends to respond to unwanted thoughts. Does it respond by clobbering them with judgment? If a painful feeling arises, do you wham that away too? Certainly thoughts and feelings that lead to harm must be wisely abandoned, but the single-minded aggression of Bamm–Bamm tends to increase self-judgment, fear, and aversion, exhausting the zealous meditator rather than providing the understanding that can support deep release.

And yet we need determination to avoid entertaining unwholesome thoughts. The Buddha teaches:

> A monk does not tolerate an arisen thought of sensual desire; he abandons it, dispels it, obliterates it, annihilates it. He does not tolerate an arisen thought of ill will, and an arisen thought of violence, and arisen evil unwholesome states; he abandons them, dispels them, obliterates them, annihilates them. This, Ananda, is called the perception of abandoning.[2]

In addition to this determined approach, we also need a more developed and precise tool, the "sword of wisdom," which represents the power of sharp decisiveness. You must identify where the problem lies and cut directly through that attachment. There is no use bashing sensations, thoughts, or perceptions. Effective removal is more surgical: cutting the link of craving. This can take the form of a stern but clear "No, thank you!" That cuts the energy off at the root—not because you're angry or denying, but because you don't choose to go where they will lead. You don't need to maintain habits that lead you into agitated distraction or mental obsessions. Tell unruly, undisciplined thoughts to go away and mean it. As your concentration strengthens, you will find this approach increasingly effective.

Students, distraught at the persistence of their thoughts, ask, "How can I quiet my mind? How can I get rid of thoughts? How can I stop my mind from wandering?" If we are to free the mind from the influence of restless thinking, we must understand the forces that push and pull at the mind, jerking it along the trail of associative thought.

☞ WORKING WITH RESTLESS THINKING

In the first ten minutes of one of your meditation sessions, notice your thinking rather than the sensations of breath. Without judging yourself for the presence of thought during meditation, count each thought.

Observe closely, so you can count each discrete thought. Each thought has a beginning, middle, and end.

When each thought ends, let the mind relax quietly until the next thought arises and is counted.

Count even subtle thoughts about the meditation and judgments of how the process is developing, in addition to the coarser thoughts about past events and future plans.

It isn't necessarily better to get a higher or a lower "score"— but to perform this exercise, you need to distinguish between the occurrence of thought and the content of thought. De-emphasize the content of the story and focus simply on the energetic occurrence of thinking.

The primary challenge in developing awareness of our thoughts is not recognizing that they are thoughts. You do not need to get rid of thoughts, just cease to believe them. If you are not seduced by the story that they represent, the thoughts will not disturb your mind. Tenzin Palmo, a nun in the Tibetan tradition wrote:

> There is the thought, and then there is the knowing of the thought. And the difference between being aware of the thought and just thinking is immense. Normally we are so identified with our thoughts and emotions, that we are them. We are the happiness, we are the anger, we are the fear. We have to learn to step back and know our thoughts and emotions are just thoughts and emotions. They're just mental states. They're not solid, they're transparent.[3]

A well-settled mind is not devoid of thought, but at the same time it is not seduced by the stories. You needn't buy into the storyline just because you thought it. Instead of believing your thoughts, inquire: Can I actually know this? Is this sure? Work directly with the energy of thinking, unseduced by the content of the thought. When you connect with a thought as just a thought, there is no distraction. It is just what it is, nothing more and nothing less.

☞ CATCHING THOUGHTS

This exercise encourages the observation of the arising and passing of thoughts.

Try to catch each thought at its inception—as soon as a thought arises, try to catch it. Ask yourself, "What is a thought? What can I catch?" Give your full attention to the observation of mental objects, not breath. How fast can you observe the arising of thoughts? See the moment thought begins and disappears. Between each thought, rest back into the quiet mind, until the next thought appears out of nothing.

Rest between thoughts, alert for the next thought to catch.

AS THOUGHTS PROLIFERATE

Many meditators find that certain thoughts proliferate—thoughts about the past and future often preoccupy our minds during meditation. You might feel disappointed about an event that you witnessed, but the event is long past. It has already changed and gone. Or, you might feel insecure about an activity you have to perform in the near future and hope for reassurance and support. The event, however, has not even occurred. The grasping—and consequently the place for letting go—is in the presently arising desire for recognition. Here is where the illusion of self is fabricated; here is where it can be abandoned. By momentarily ceasing to construct self-concepts through daily experiences, you simplify and clarify your relationship with all things.

As you practice mindfulness and concentration, you learn to rest in the first moment of contact at any sense door, before it evolves into a chain of discursive thinking.

One student described a series of thoughts to me: She had lost her hair clip that day; she knew she had to go buy a new one. She felt annoyed that she had to go shopping; the thought arose that she was stupid to lose it; how could she lose it? Now she has to spend more money; her job is not paying well; she never has enough money; she will never have enough; deep feelings of worthlessness and failure dominated her mind; she decided she had better get a new job, but wondered what else she could do. Over lunch, she read through the want ads in the newspaper. She felt trapped, angry, afraid, and depressed. Finally, she remembered she could observe her own mind. All this anguish was nothing more than a proliferation of thought sparked by an absent hair clip. If she had brought mindfulness to the first thought "I lost my hair clip," noticing that was a thought rather than identifying wholly with the elaborate story, the suffering would have ended there, eliminating the whole chain of distorting associations.

This may seem like a trivial example, but our days can be filled with such low-grade distress. Misperception blows event after event out of proportion. Although unrestrained associative thinking is a deeply ingrained habit, you do not need to entertain it. You can train yourself to mindfully rest in the direct recognition of any sensory experience, without the entanglements of the scattered and restless mind. Look into your own vivid experience of seeing, hearing, smelling, tasting, touching, and thinking.

Personal history makes each of us vulnerable to our own set of chronic thoughts. Be heartened: these patterns are arising in order to be released. When a familiar scenario recurs, one you have set aside dozens of times before, you may need to investigate it more precisely and understand it more thoroughly before you can abandon it completely. The next time you find repeating thoughts dominating your meditation, try using the exercise below.

☞ TALKING BACK TO YOUR MIND

If while you are cultivating concentration, you discover that your mind is preoccupied with thoughts of people, relations, work, reputation, activities, roles, past events, future plans—talk back to it! Send those thoughts away. Talk back in a tone of voice that is clear but not abusive. Tell the thought, gently but firmly:

That is not my concern.
There is nothing to be done right now.
This is not the time for this subject.
That is uncertain, unknown, not sure.
That may not be true; I just can't know if it is really true.
That is long past; it is over and done with, too late now.

Arguably, some topics merit reflection and responsible attention. However, most thoughts merely reflect habitual tendencies and can be seen clearly, then abandoned, without pulling attention away from the meditation object of the breath. If certain thoughts persist, you may need to temporarily set aside the practice of concentration to mindfully explore the process of thinking, glean insight through investigation, and then return to concentrate on breathing. At times it may be wise to activate the meditation with mindful reflection, however any reflection on thought implies a corresponding absence of attention to the breath, thereby weakening concentration.

UNDISTRACTED COMPASSION

The problem of distraction doesn't exist *"out there,"* in the objects. You don't need to remove objects, prevent perceptions, or control your external environment to abide without distraction. It's in the thick of life's activities where you will learn to discern the difference between a distraction and a genuine, free, wise, and compassionate response to life.

Several years ago I was in Nepal with a group of friends receiving a series of teachings from a Tibetan Lama. This teacher lived in a monastery at the top of a hill. Each day we would ascend the hill by a

☞ LAUGHING AT THOUGHTS

Be clearly aware that a thought is occurring. Notice the theme of the story. Disentangle the energy of thinking from the content or storyline the thought is narrating.

For example, you may find yourself repeatedly planning what you will say in next week's staff meeting. Give the story a title or name such as "presenting me," "endless agendas," "my witty retort." Give the repeating thoughts funny names: "The story of my life," "The tragedy at dinner." These repetitive stories are like songs we sing over and over again.

Humorous names can depersonalize the thought patterns, minimizing their power over the mind and a playful or humorous name makes it easier to deflate any charged energy in the thoughts and recognize them simply as thoughts.

---

trail that passed a few little village shops near the base, then wove back and forth in switchbacks until it reached the monastery perched at its summit. One day we were hurrying up the trail. I turned to notice that two friends had fallen behind. They had stopped at the outskirts of the tiny village and were standing near a sobbing young girl. She had been sent to the shop to purchase two eggs but had accidentally broken one and was afraid to go home for fear her mother would beat her. My friends had stopped and talked with her, and had sent a boy with two rupees to buy another egg.

By the time my friends and I finally ascended the hill that day, the room was full and the doors were closed. We sat outside, perched against the building near an open window, catching only a smattering of words. Yes, we missed the formal teachings that morning—after all, we had traveled halfway around the planet to receive these teachings from a renowned senior lama—but I didn't consider this a distraction from our spiritual quest. It was the practice—a compassionate response to immediate needs.

WHEN CONSCIOUSNESS IS NOT DISTRACTED OR DIFFUSED

As we have noted, the most common way to overcome distraction is by concentrating on an object such as the breath. This is one way of dissolving the scattered tendencies; at the same time, it may introduce a kind of subtle fixation. The Buddha taught:

> A practitioner should so investigate that, as she investigates, her consciousness is not distracted and diffused externally, and internally is not fixed, and by not grasping anything she should remain undisturbed. If her consciousness is not distracted and diffused externally, and internally is not fixed, and by not grasping anything she remains undisturbed, then there is no . . . suffering in the future.[4]

The feeling of consciousness being *scattered externally* commonly occurs to people before they have developed a meditation practice, yet they may not notice that it is possible for a multitude of discordant experiences to occur without scattering the mind. Imagine walking through a crowded train station during your daily commute, but not veering off your path. Discordant images—people, noises, smells, and announcements—just occur; they do not disturb your route. In other situations, a variety of experiences could distract your attention. Perhaps music is playing, the telephone is ringing, a child is calling for attention, and your hands are wet from washing a salad; you feel pulled in many directions at once. What, then, turns an experience into a distraction rather than just another complex moment of sensory encounters in the fabric of daily life?

The Buddha explained that consciousness becomes scattered when it "is tied and shackled by gratification."[5] This occurs when the mind revels in the gratification of sensory contact—attention follows after sights, sounds, tastes, sensations, and thoughts. Sensory experience does not in and of itself distract us; the mind is not inevitably fettered by contact. The problem resides in the movement of desire. We are bound by seeking gratification through sensory perceptions and then using those perceptions to construct a personal identity. Therefore, the Buddha cautioned that the meditator should not be "stuck internally," or "internally fixed."

The ardent meditator, endeavoring to establish the jhanas, might be disappointed to learn that one can be stuck internally through attachment to the rapture and happiness available in jhana. Is jhana practice inherently flawed by its dependence upon sustained attention? Is sustained attention synonymous with fixation? These are criticisms jhana practitioners must consider.

Whether the bondage is to internal states or to external objects, the principles regarding the cause of suffering are the same. The rapture, joy, and bliss of jhana are not in and of themselves problematic, nor is the pleasure that naturally arises in a concentrated mind—unless there is clinging. If consciousness follows after the signs of rapture, joy, contentment, equanimity, or any subtle meditative attainment, then it could be establishing a relationship to inner experience that is "fettered by the fetter of gratification."[6]

After dwelling in each jhana, it will be important to reflect upon your relationship to the dominant jhanic factors, to rest into the absorption with detachment—unified without any reaching out to gain, indulge, or experience anything from it. You will need to explore your relationship to pleasure by examining the subtle and intense delights of concentration. As the concentration practice develops, you must maintain a parallel contemplation on fixation and inquire, "What is the stillness of a unified mind, and what is the static fixation of clinging?" You must know when the mind is stuck, and when it is simply at rest. When fixation breaks, you will see the dynamic nature of things in high relief.

As your observation skills develop, you might discover attention remains vibrant during the space between breaths and a clear awareness pervades the space between thoughts. Those spaces are opportunities for deep rest as things fluidly arise and pass in awareness. Sounds, sensations, or thoughts appear and disappear, as temporary as a bird flying through the sky-like space of mind; they leave no trace, no markers, no wake. From this well-settled sense of spaciousness, you can notice when the mind seems to contract around a perception. Often something we either desire or are averse to triggers our more noticeable reactions. If you can discern this contraction, instantly let it go and rest back into spacious awareness. You will experience the ephemeral nature of experience as it flows and changes, and feel the mind narrow and expand, undistracted in the moments of contraction and release.

You cannot control the experiences of living. There will always be unpleasant sensations, challenging thoughts, and abrasive sounds. Difficult events happen: illness, death, betrayal, cruelty. These are part of our world. You cannot avoid them, but you can cultivate such a vast quality of awareness that your mind remains undistracted. If you mix a teaspoon of salt in a glass, its impact is strong. If you mix a teaspoon of salt in a lake, the impact is much more tempered.[7] Meditation will not eliminate abrasive conditions from your life, but it can temper their impact and enhance your ability to remain balanced in the face of life's challenges.

UNDISTURBED TRANQUILLITY

Jhana practice introduces the mind to the stability of mental unification; it drenches the heart with tranquillity. Free of desire or aversion, thoughts remain quite simple. A concentrated mind is essentially undisturbed. A mind influenced by jhana is so coherent, almost crystalline, that it reenters the world of sensory contact without binding itself to the various perceptions that habitually preoccupy unconcentrated attention.

After emerging from a deep absorption, the mind is pliable, concentrated, and ready to investigate. You can use this steadiness to explore the nuances of the objects that you perceive, or turn your attention from external sensory objects and become aware of knowing itself. Exploring the process of perception is a subtle inquiry. We do not reject things; we simply are no longer fascinated with them. We look into the process of perceiving rather than the content of our perceptions.

One of the great contributions of the modern art movement was the production of nonrepresentational art. Art works were created from an interest in the varied uses of materials—canvas, paint, wood, metal, paper, and so forth—rather than from a wish to represent a person, still-life, or landscape. A line was just a line; it did not represent the contour of a realistic or imaginary object. These innovations challenged the viewer to see without indulging in stories, to view the canvas as canvas, the paint as paint, a curve as a curve. Art broke through the conventional expectations that limited it to the representation of historic events and personalities or the recording of social, natural, or fictitious scenes. Similarly, meditation challenges us to experience a thought as a thought, a feeling as a feeling, a sight as a sight, without embellishing each encounter with a personal story of representational significance.

☞ JUST NOTICING

Set this book aside for 5–10 minutes to just sit quietly.

Notice what you are experiencing.

What do you feel in the body? What mental states and emotions flavor your experience now? What thoughts circulate in the mind?

With mindful awareness, explore each experience of body and mind, free of the elaborate stories they trigger.

Notice the thinking as just thinking—an energetic impulse in the mind.

Notice the feelings as just feelings, without explaining or justifying them.

Bring awareness to each precise momentary experience.

Turn your interest to the phenomenal process of the interaction of mind and body, rather than seeing experience as individual story—of my day, my life, my friends, my family, my desires.

Let the mind rest, spacious and at ease, as mind and body processes are effortlessly known, arising and passing, disturbing no one, affecting no one, belonging to no one.

You may wish to let this exercise transition into one of mental relaxation.

Just relax the mind.

Just relax.

Repeatedly relax.

Just relax allowing a naturally alert awareness to experience the nature of things.

If you keep examining—not until you find something, but until you realize seeing without grasping, inquiring without fixating, exploring without expecting, knowing without controlling, living without suffering—you will discover a purity of happiness that is unbounded. It is a happiness beyond anything contrived by concentration: the deep joy of release.

PART III
How to Establish Meditative Absorption

CHAPTER 9

Happiness
and the Five Factors of Absorption

There is, in taking things, a thirst, a clinging, a grasping. You must lose it. You must lose it altogether, above, below, around and within. It makes no difference what it is you are grasping at: when a man grasps, Mara [the Deceiver] stands beside him.

—The Buddha[1]

THE FORCES THAT CONFOUND our concentration are personified in the Buddhist teachings by a character named Mara. He represents the inner forces of temptation that hinder progress. This mythical symbolic figure arrives on the scene in various forms and represents a wide range of obstructive mental states that prevent concentration.[2] As we have noted, the mind must be free of such hindrances for stable absorption to occur. If we are able to counteract the forces of Mara and apply antidotes to the various obstacles to a stable mind, we can begin the entry into jhana. This chapter and the next present instructions for dealing effectively with obstacles and creating the conditions necessary for entering jhana. In preparation for absorption, they take up in a more pointed, instructional way topics introduced in earlier chapters.

Classically, Mara manifested as fear, desire, or doubt just before a recluse approached jhana or liberating insight. Symbolically, Mara appears at critical junctures in our lives, when we stand at the brink of a choice. He might aggressively confront the unwary meditator with a stream of vengeful thoughts. He might be disguised as something pleasant, thereby seducing us with comfort, honor, and privilege. Mara may arise in a multitude of disguises: as friends cajoling us toward trivial activities; as temptations toward drink or distraction; as the rationalizations within our own mind that whisper, "You have too much to do today to waste time just meditating; accomplish something useful!"; as the inertia that reaches for the TV remote-control rather than the meditation cushion; as the self-critical voice that condemns us before we try; or as the overconfident disposition that exaggerates our abilities and cannot accept defeat. When encountering any of these inner forces, you are metaphorically confronting Mara. Facing Mara, you are facing your shadow. Will we make the great stride toward liberating understanding or fall back again into the grip of habit? Vanquishing Mara you overcome the "inner demons" that threaten to limit your spiritual potential. Mara represents the challenges that test our mettle and spiritual maturity.

The depictions of Mara in the Buddhist scriptures offer a liturgy of heroic stories that tell of the courage of meditators coming face to face with their darkest fears, including monks who surmounted lust when Mara appeared disguised as the alluring seductress and nuns who staved off their deepest fears when Mara accosted them in the forest.[3] Even the Buddha received a number of visits from this character. In each encounter there is a single antidote to all of Mara's antics: mindfulness. Mindfulness is the secret weapon for which Mara's army has no defense. Exposed to mindful scrutiny, obstructive forces always and inevitably weaken.

Mara provides a metaphorical image that can help depersonalize our relationship to hindrances. You might laugh when doubt arises, viewing the doubt as Mara playing a trick on you. You might poke fun at a tendency to find fault with your friends, seeing Mara appearing as the judge. You may cajole the greedy mind that buys needlessly, storing up possessions like a chipmunk stuffing its cheeks with peanuts, for this is Mara's mischief. And the time will come that, with faith clarified and confidence verified, you will return the challenge to Mara, as Venerable Samiddhi did: "My mindfulness and wisdom are mature, and my mind well concentrated. Conjure up whatever forms you wish, but you will never make me tremble."[4] When we can stand firm in the face of Mara, we rest unruffled by whatever life may bring us.

WHERE MARA IS BLINDFOLDED

Jhana is an attainment that is said to have "blindfolded Mara" because it creates a field of unification in which hindrances of desire, aversion, and obsessive thoughts cannot arise. For the duration of the absorption, your energies are liberated from the struggle with hindrances and available to cultivate entirely wholesome qualities. Jhana is an approach to training the mind in the absence of Mara, rather than in confrontation with Mara. In jhana the strength comes not through rubbing up against obstacles, but through familiarity with a way of being that is unhindered by them. By turning away from the corruptions, the mind thrives in a range of purity temporarily unimpeded by malicious forces.

Prior to entering jhana we learn about difficult mental states and work with them mindfully until we can set them aside without struggle or identification. Within jhana, internal energies coalesce, and strengthen. When you emerge, this well-concentrated mind is again ready to meet all variety of sensory contacts. Should you discover that you emerge near an ambush from Mara (perhaps an attack of impatience, anger, or wanton greed) you need not bother to berate yourself for the occurrence of painful states—it is just Mara visiting again! We continue to work through the hindrances by facing them squarely when they arise after emerging from jhana. They may erupt with volcanic force or sneak up so gradually you hardly detect them. Although the refined mind might be humiliated by these unwholesome tendencies, little by little, the integration of samadhi and vipassana will wear away the forces of obstruction.

Confidence floods the heart when you look into your own mind and can honestly declare, "No hindrance is present."

THE FIVE JHANIC FACTORS

Access to jhana occurs when hindering unwholesome factors are in abeyance and when five corresponding wholesome mental factors grow strong.

⌒ WORKING WITH OBSTRUCTIVE ENERGIES

1. During your meditation, notice when hindrances or temptations arise. Recognize those forces and name them. Feel how
each arises in body and in mind. Precisely acknowledge each of
these states by saying to them: "I see you Mara," or "I see you
anger," or "I see you doubt."

Observe their arising, how they change, and how they
disappear.

Notice the stream of associated thoughts or emotions triggered by hindrances.

Notice how their arrival affects the degree of concentration,
carefully observing any breach in mental cohesion.

Consider Mara a mischievous neighbor who visits for tea.
There is no cause for argument, yet his antics become tiresome,
so you keep a keen watch over him when he is near, and escort
him to the door when the opportunity arises.

2. You are not plagued by hindrances every moment of every day.
Notice any moments that seem empty of hindrances. When
judgment, anger, lust, fear, laziness, restlessness, confusion, and
doubt are not arising, what is the quality of mind? Allow the
absence of hindrances to gladden the mind.

3. After recognizing the presence and absence of the obstructive
forces during silent meditation, bring the exploration into your
daily life.

Notice in activities and interactions when the mind is
affected or obsessed by unwholesome forces, and when it is free
from obstructions.

These five jhanic factors and the hindrances they overcome are:
(1) *the ability to direct the attention to a chosen object* overcomes dullness;
(2) *the capacity to sustain the attention on the object* overcomes doubt;

(3) *feelings of delight, rapture, and interest that arise through the concentration accrued by sustained attention* overcome aversion; (4) *pervasive feelings of happiness, peace, contentment, and joy* overcome restlessness; and (5) *the stability of single-pointed focus* overcomes lust and greed.

Each jhanic factor is an antidote to a particular hindrance. They are paired as opposites; the development of one automatically weakens the other, offering an alternative model for eroding obstructive forces. Much of a meditator's early samadhi training will be devoted to developing these jhanic factors. Once they are established, the progression through the jhanas follows systematically. When these jhanic factors are fully developed, the mind cannot be overwhelmed by hindrances.

The Buddha recommended that practitioners periodically review their minds to notice if anything needs to be abandoned or developed. If when you look into your mind, you discover a mind free of hindrances, the instruction is to "abide happy and glad, training day and night in wholesome states."[5] Even after the hindrances have been set aside, the jhanic factors must be fortified or absorption will remain elusive. Don't hurry to get into jhana; take your time and cultivate the basic factors. They are a powerful resource with or without the specific states of absorption.

The first meditation instruction given in Chapter 1 was to be aware of the sense of breath at the nostrils. As you develop this basic exercise, be patient but diligent; each time the mind wanders, simply bring it back to the breath. Being aware of the breath and returning the attention when it wanders off constitute an exercise that cultivates the abilities to direct and sustain attention, the first two factors essential for samadhi. With some practice the mind will succeed in connecting with and sustaining attention on the focus of breath intermittently. As the momentum of sustained focus grows, attention is gradually infused with pleasure—the mind settles down. When the mind stays at one point without straying wildly, a feedback loop is created that further enhances stability and happiness. When delight, joy, or equanimity are primary, the mind is less inclined to wander into thoughts of past or future. Consequently, when the first four factors gain strength, the experience of one-pointed focus grows, further unifying the mind with its object.

VITAKKA: DIRECTED ATTENTION

The first jhanic factor, *vitakka,* refers to the capacity to direct attention at a particular perception; it is the aiming or connecting function of attention. Think of this process as shining a light on an object in a dark room, striking a baseball with a bat, aiming a pistol at a target, or poking a needle through a buttonhole when sewing. It is the clear directing of attention to its chosen object. The *Visuddhimagga,* an ancient commentary written by Buddhaghosa in the fifth century, uses the analogy of a gatekeeper who inspects people as they enter and exit the gate.[6] The gatekeeper is not concerned with the business the merchants transact in the marketplace or which village they travel to when they depart. The gatekeeper simply checks each person as they pass through the gate. Just so, we direct our attention to the area between the nostrils and upper lip and examine what we find there. We don't need to follow the breath inside the body or contemplate external phenomena. We keep our focus precise.

The directed application of energy associated with vitakka has an invigorating quality that refreshes and revitalizes the mind. As the attention collects at a chosen point—perceiving the breath—distractions diminish. It is not sufficient to want to feel the breath; nor will one connection be enough. You must repeatedly apply attention to the meditation object. You might aim and connect several times on the inhale and several times on the exhale. My first teacher likened this to training a puppy to sit. You have to repeat the lesson many times. Bring the pup back to its place and tell it again to "sit!" When it wanders, bring it back and again say, with patience and kindness, "sit!" After a while, puppies learn. So will your mind.

The function of vitakka is likened to ringing a bell with a striker. To produce a sound the striker must actually meet the bell: there must be a connection. Waving the striker around in the air would be unproductive. Only when there is clear aim, a directed swing, and the striker meets the bell, is sound produced. Similarly, it is not enough to have an idea about breathing; your attention must distinctly reach the breath. Many methods can strengthen this aiming capacity. Counting breaths is one popular tool. Counting maintains a clear focus. If the mind wanders off into thoughts of past or future, you come right back with the next number and continue your task. Repeatedly directing your attention to the presence of breath at the nostrils develops vitakka.

☞ MORE WITH COUNTING BREATHS

Work again with the counting exercise introduced in Chapter 2. Count the breaths from one to ten. Then from ten to one. Then from one to ten. As you count, emphasize the direct experience of the breath rather than the conceptual numbers. Give 95% of your attention to the actual feeling of the contact with breath, and the remaining 5% to maintaining the numerical sequence.

With each breath, count 1, 1, 1, 1, 1, then 2, 2, 2, 2, 2, 2, and then 3, 3, 3, 3, 3, 3, 3, 3, and so on. Repeat the numbers throughout the duration of each inhale and exhale, actively lifting attention up to the breath with each repeated number. Repeatedly applying attention allows no opportunity for distracting thoughts to arise.

This traditional counting technique was inspired by the method ancient caterers used for measuring rice. A cook would repeat aloud the number of measures as he simultaneously pulled out bits of grass, straw, dirt, or pebbles from the rice batch. He would measure out one cup, saying "1, 1, 1, 1" as he sorted the debris from the grain. He would add a second cup counting "2, 2, 2, 2, 2" continuing to pull out bits of dirt. By repeating the numbers throughout the task of cleaning, the cook would keep track of the correct measurement and not become distracted by the related activity of cleaning the rice.

Vitakka is a subtle activity of thought that counteracts drowsiness and dullness. The hindering force traditionally called "sloth and torpor" is marked by a dull withdrawal, inertia, heaviness, lassitude, boredom, slumping, nodding, and, in its extreme form, sleepiness. Vitakka vividly connects to its object, allowing no opportunity for the torpor that dullness and boredom feeds upon.

☞ DIRECTING ATTENTION

Here are three ways outside of formal meditation you can playfully explore the remarkable capacity of attention to focus on and discern specific aspects of experience.

1. Listen to a recording of a symphony. Focus on individual instruments. Apply the attention to just the clarinet, then shift to the bass, then notice only the melody of the flute.

2. Sit on a park bench for fifteen minutes or so. Chose four or five things to notice—perhaps the pressure where your thighs touch the bench, traffic sounds, the smell of cut grass, the warmth of the sun, or your posture. Systematically shift the attention through those items, spending about twenty seconds attentive to the first sensory experience, then twenty seconds or so focused on the second sensory experience, and so on through your selected sequence. Rotate through a sequence of sense contacts several times at a comfortable pace noticing the capacity you have to aim attention.

3. Sit in your home near an open window. Notice sounds that are close such as a heater, people in the building, plumbing, a gurgling stomach, the sound of saliva being swallowed. Then shift your attention to hearing far-off sounds: airplanes, distant traffic, unrecognizable street sounds. Move the attention back and forth between the near and far sounds. Notice the capacity to maintain a continuity of hearing while directing the range of that function.

VICARA: SUSTAINED ATTENTION

The second jhanic factor, *vicara,* the mate to vitakka, is the capacity of mind to sustain the attention on the object to which it has been directed. Vicara is the quality of attention that stays with and penetrates the object of perception. When vicara is strong, you can remain aware of the full length of the breath from the beginning, middle, and through to the end of each one. Vicara sinks into its object and gets to know it with penetrative clarity. Because vicara is an explorative aspect of thought, the term has been translated variously into English as "examination," "sustained thought," "pondering," "contemplation," and "investigation." In the context of jhana practice, the specific function of vicara is to sustain the attention on the chosen object. Sustained connection stabilizes and smoothes consciousness.

Vicara has been likened to the resounding of a bell. Vitakka directs the attention to the object (or strikes the bell) then vicara sustains the attention (like the lingering resounding of a bell). Repeatedly directing attention to the breath brings a sustained knowledge of the breath. Vicara holds the attention on a mental object, permitting concentration to deepen.

☞ MOVING HANDS WITH SUSTAINED ATTENTION

Choose a place to meditate that is relatively quiet.

Place your hand and forearm comfortably in front of you in a way that permits you to easily bend your elbow raising your lower arm slightly in front of the body. This movement will cause the hand to gently pass through the air.

Slowly move your lower arm and hand up and down while focusing your attention on the sensations in the palm of the hand. Keep the attention focused in the hand, sustaining awareness on these changing sensations.

Bring a penetrative quality to the attention so that your focus remains steady on the hand, even as the sensations change.

Encourage the attention to sink into the sensations and remain stable there.

Gradually make the movements slower and smaller until the hand comes to rest on your lap.

Maintain the steady focus of attention with the sensations of the hand as the movement and sensations grow increasingly subtle.

Then shift the attention to the sensations of the point of contact of the breath. Employ a quality of penetrative sustained attention that stays with the sensations as though attention locks on to its subject.

Both vitakka and vicara are aspects of conceptual thought. They represent a skillful use of thought during meditation that focuses otherwise dispersed inclinations of the thinking mind.

Vicara's function is to dispel the hindrance of doubt. By sustaining awareness long enough for deep contemplation, vicara eliminates the opportunity for confusion and uncertainty to overtake awareness. The mind does not "back away" from presence, or wander off its subject, or separate from the investigation of things before the perception is thoroughly known. Sustained attention makes it possible to develop genuine confidence in your penetrative knowledge of a meditation subject.

PITI: RAPTUROUS INTEREST

When vitakka and vicara are steady, a feeling of lightness and pleasure naturally occur. The mind becomes bright and alert. The body may feel invigorated. The posture may be uplifted. This quality of pleasure, *piti,* is infused with vibrant interest. *Piti* is usually translated with terms such as "rapture," "delight," "pleasure," "zest," "happiness," or "bliss." Sometimes this pulsating pleasure will be almost excruciatingly intense; at other times soft and quiet. Piti grows by being noticed. It is not necessary to frantically rev up the bliss. You don't make delight arise through effort. Sensitivity to the pleasant quality is quite enough to support its development.

Piti manifests in many forms, and not necessarily as the tantalizing electrified spectacle implied in such dramatic words as "rapturous bliss." Often it is experienced as simply an uplifting inner smile. It might begin as a subtle sense of lightness and ease. There may be goose-bumps, shivers, tingles, and vibrations. There may be surging and uplifting feelings. There can even be spontaneous trembling or jerking of the limbs. You will learn to identify the characteristics of piti in its intense, pervasive, and subtle manifestations.

You may need to ride some energetic waves of this bliss as you explore rapture without becoming agitated by the intensity of energy. When piti develops into a quality that is full, subtle, and steady— traditionally described as "all-pervading rapture"—it has strengthened into a force stable enough to be considered a jhanic factor.

☞ DISCERNING THE PLEASANTNESS OF THE PLEASANT

Find an experience that is pleasant: looking at a sunrise, feeling the smooth fur of a cat, holding a warm cup of tea, or any other such simple thing.

Practice moving the attention between the object and the pleasant feeling it elicits. Shift your attention between the object of pleasure (the visual image, feeling of warmth or softness) and the pleasurable feeling it evokes. Practice allowing the attention to settle within the experience of pleasantness without adding attachment.

If the desire for more arises, notice that attachment. Ask yourself—what is this feeling of attachment? Does attachment increase the pleasure, or decrease it? Many people will recognize attachment by a characteristic feeling of contraction or separation. How do you notice attachment to pleasure as distinct from a simple experience of pleasure?

Refocus attention and continue to move awareness between the pleasant perception and the perception of pleasantness. Allow the pleasure to fill your awareness. Don't hold yourself back from the pleasant feeling. Allow the lightness of simple pleasant contact and feeling to suffuse the mind and body.

This aspect of happiness infused with interest lubricates the sustaining function of attention. Influenced by piti, the mind grows increasingly cohesive. Rapturous interest provides moisturizing energy that glides attention smoothly into its chosen object of perception. As the rapt quality of interest draws mental and physical energy together, piti becomes the catalyst and ally for the stabilizing of attention. While consciousness is saturated in delight and a feeling of fullness permeates the mind, the meditator is infused with energy that inspires one's quest.

Piti is the antidote to the hindrance of aversion—and most people enjoy piti at first. It is dramatically pleasant: a sharp contrast to the painful state of aversion. The struggle to direct and sustain the attention eases.

Something finally seems to be happening in the meditation when this delightfully inspiring energy appears. The alluring pleasure of piti attracts the mind, facilitating greater stability of attention and deeper unification with the meditation subject.

SUKHA: DEEP EASE OR PERVASIVE CONTENTMENT

Sukha is a quality of happiness that is much quieter and smoother than piti. *Sukha* is usually translated as "peace," "joy," "contentment," "pleasure," "ease," or "happiness." Sukha has a sweet and smooth quality in contrast to the activated quality of piti. Sukha is neither the jazz and thrill of delight nor the still calm of equanimity. When sukha is strong, the mind is exceptionally bright and undisturbed. It is the mental equivalent of submerging in a comforting warm bath: all-embracing contentment. Through intimate experience of sukha, you will discover a deeply settled state of joy that is neither tranquilized by equanimity nor agitated by interest.

With the peace and contentment of sukha washing through the mind, the heart rests with confidence. When sukha is predominant, the meditator is undisturbed and feels no desire to get up at the end of the meditation: meditation sessions can last very long without distraction.

☞ EXPLORING PLEASANT DAILY EVENTS

For one week write a list of pleasant events that occur each day.

Make a note of the quality of the feeling: how the body feels, how the mind feels. Notice happiness wherever it arises. Be in touch with a felt sense of joy and contentment regarding the normal pleasant things that happen in a day—a hot shower, sunlight sparkling on a pond, the soft touch of fleece, a compliment from a friend, a good night's sleep.

If a pleasant experience sparks excitement, let the thrill settle. Then, focus on a quieter sense of happiness. Sukha is not revved up with interest and excitement; it is revealed by deeply settling into contentment. Rest into pleasant daily experiences and notice for yourself what aspects of pleasure agitate attention with the desire for more, or relax the mind in deep contentment.

The vastness of ease, a characteristic of sukha, overcomes the hindrance of restlessness. When sukha is strong, everything feels OK as it is. There is no restless lurching toward habitual planning or repetitive thinking. Deeply settled, content, pervaded by sukha, the mind rests joyfully in present-moment experience.

EKAGGATA: ONE-POINTEDNESS OF ATTENTION

The fifth jhanic factor, *ekaggata,* describes the capacity of mind to remain focused and one-pointed with a chosen object. Ekaggata's characteristic quality is to lock on to the chosen object with an intimacy that rivets the attention, stills the mind, and settles into unwavering focus. The connection is so steady there is no impetus to wander. This singularity of attention does not diverge; it is not lured from its meditation subject by the seductive force of desire, lust, or craving. It is not thrown off its focus by the rattling energies of restlessness. Although it is described in terms similar to the sustaining factor of vicara, ekaggata has a steadier texture; it does not possess the explorative quality inherent in vicara. Whereas vicara is compared to a bee entering a single flower and buzzing around in the pollen, ekaggata is compared to a nail or post that is anchored to one spot. Ekaggata brings certainty, deep stability, and clarity: its one pointed focus completely unifies attention with the object until consciousness feels virtually undifferentiated from its object.

The characteristic stability of ekaggata transforms the hindrance of desire. Desirous energy tends to want more: it lurches to reach for the next good thing or clutch at present experience hoping it will last longer. Based in craving, desire is never satisfied, and the mind affected by desire cannot rest. No matter how much a person possesses, as long as greed arises the mind is discontent. The Buddha remarked that even if the Himalayas were turned into gold, it would not satisfy one man's greed.[7] After one pleasure is attained, the next is sought, perpetuating the fantasy of future fulfillment. In contrast, the focused intensity of one-pointedness needs nothing more. With ekaggata there is no sense of deficiency, nothing lacking. The mind is completely unified and "one with the experience."

SETTING THE STAGE FOR ABSORPTION

These five elements of concentration—connecting, sustaining, rapture, joy, one-pointedness—take center stage during jhanic experience. Each level of absorption has its characteristic blend of these factors. Skill in entering and maneuvering through the levels of absorption depends upon cultivating these five factors.

These are not the only mental functions present in jhana. In a detailed description, the Venerable Sariputta lists each factor that can be observed during jhana.[8] The primary jhanic factors—connecting, sustaining, rapture, joy, one-pointedness—are perceived. Contact, feeling, perception, volition, mind, zeal, decision, energy, mindfulness, equanimity, and attention are also present in jhana. Notice that even within the state of absorption, mindfulness and attention remain present. These mental functions make it possible to clarify exactly what is and is not there.

In jhana, consciousness is alert. Jhanic states are intensely clear. Absorption states do not resemble sleepy relaxation or dull spacey tranquillity. Nor is absorption defined by the mere presence of rapture and happiness. It's important to note that the occurrence of jhanic factors is not synonymous with a jhanic state. Practitioners, with a strong desire to succeed, might mistake the simple arising of jhanic factors for absorption states. Sublime pleasures often seduce eager meditators; the development of the jhanic factors become distracting obstructions if it sparks excitement, pride, or attachment.

On the other hand, subtle meditative pleasures may go unrecognized; this lightness of piti is easily dismissed by experienced meditators as just how meditation usually feels. It may take some time to discern the subtle significance of this familiar quality of piti in the shift from the more distracted mental states of worldly perceptions toward the protected seclusion of an inner abiding.

As you experience and explore the absorption states, you will come to recognize the difference through keen observation of the changing clusters of factors and their effect on consciousness. Gradually, through honest introspection—repeatedly examining, exploring, and dwelling with these experiences—you will understand how these factors can intensify perception or produce absorbed states of non-ordinary consciousness.

In this approach to jhana, highly developed discernment of the jhanic factors achieved through practice is critical. As a meditator becomes more skillful in passing through each stage, she will come to know through direct experience what is present and what is absent in consciousness. An adept practitioner recognizes the multitude of mental functions that operate within absorption, observes the absence of certain mental functions, and understands what cannot coexist with absorption.

CHAPTER 10

Access to Absorption: At the Threshold of Peace

Whoever, whether standing or walking, sitting or lying down, calms his mind and strives for that inner stillness in which there is no thought, he has the prerequisite to realize supreme illumination.

—The Buddha[1]

THE FIRST FORMAL INSTRUCTION I received for jhana practice surprised me. My teacher told me to meditate in any way that supported the development of three qualities: mental brightness, spaciousness, and relaxation. I had expected the early instructions to emphasize vigorous focus on a narrow object. It soon became clear, however, that demanding effort can create tension; in the wake of tension, aversion and hindrances thrive. Conversely, a mind that is relaxed, bright, and spacious contributes to mental and physical ease and encourages a natural release into present-moment experience.

For concentration to deepen the mind needs to relax. It cannot stay on the defensive. A mind that is glad is easily concentrated. In spiritual life gladness is not the giddy excitement expressed by titillation or thrill. The deeper forms of gladness arise when you trust your virtue. Happiness arises when you can trust the purity of your own heart's intentions. In short, it is a happiness of non-remorse. It is through sincere reflection and our inner ethical commitments that we purify our intentions and grow to trust ourselves. If our ethical foundation is uncertain, tranquillity will remain shaky, the mind will be unable to confidently settle into this living process of purification.

We can improve the texture of the mind by influencing the kind of thoughts we tend to think. When you observe thoughts that diminish the qualities you appreciate, abandon those thoughts and give a thought or two to something virtuous, respectable, joyful—perhaps a thought of kindness.

☞ THOUGHTS OF KINDNESS

When I practiced in a Thai forest monastery, I (along with all residents) was asked to generate thoughts of friendship and kindness for several minutes before leaving the mosquito nets we slept under at night. We would bring a person to mind and mentally recite a simple phrase of good will—"May you be well, happy, and at ease"—or an equivalent wish. With repeated practice, this simple reflection on kind wishes has the potential to soothe an ill temper, calm an anxious mind, and bring joy to the heart. Try this throughout your day.

BASIC INSTRUCTIONS FOR STABILIZING THE MIND

This book focuses on the technique of using the breath as your initial object for meditation. The Buddhist tradition suggests a number of objects for jhana meditation, including colors, light, the basic elements (earth, fire, water, and wind), foul aspects of bodily experience, or beautiful inner qualities such as loving-kindness, compassion, joy, and equanimity. Each object has the potential to raise the mind to correspondingly distinct levels of absorption. Traditionally, an experienced teacher tailors the meditation subject according to the student's disposition, meditative ability, interest, and intention.

The breath serves as a powerful, and popular, meditation subject. It can bring the mind to the highest formless states. It is the preferred meditation subject for the majority of practitioners. Although certain indi-

viduals might find jhana easier to attain with a different meditation subject, the skills developed working with the breath can be applied to any
meditative endeavor.

In the commentarial tradition, the designation of a state called *access
concentration* arose as a convenient term to describe the conditions that
immediately precede jhana. Although there is no direct reference in the
discourses of the Buddha to access concentration as a distinct state, the
conditions that lead to jhana are clearly described—and when these
conditions arise, access to jhana is possible.

The following instructions for attaining access to jhana refine the
basic meditation instructions given in Chapter 1.

Once you are sitting in a comfortable and alert posture, with a
mind inclined toward qualities of ease, brightness, and spaciousness,
apply an actively penetrative attention to experience the initial sensations of the breath touching the nostrils or upper lip. Choose a small
point at the nostrils or upper lip area—wherever you feel the sensations
of the breath most distinctly. The actual location will vary from person
to person, depending on the angle of the nose, structure of the jaw,
shape of the lips, and facial features; there is no best or correct place.
Feel where the breath naturally touches you. Whenever the attention
drifts off that point of sensation, guide it back, simply and diligently.
Each time the awareness wanders off with thoughts of past or future,
simply drop this preoccupation with thoughts by reaffirming the
directed focus of your activity. Ignore everything else: environmental
sounds, pain, thoughts, or plans. If emotions, great insights, a review of
yesterday's shopping list, a plan for redecorating your kitchen, a replay
of a movie you recently watched, or any profound or mundane thought
should arise, invest no interest in these events and guide the attention
perseveringly back to the breath.

Although this instruction is simple to understand, within just a few
minutes of practice you will surely notice that the mind tends to wander
away from that point of contact where the breath is felt. It may wander
through past thoughts, future plans, or a commentary on the present
experience of sitting with a book in your lap feeling the breath at your

nose. Whatever thoughts arise, interesting or boring, supportive or destructive of your self-esteem, let them all go equally and unequivocally. The discipline here is to discard all entanglement without judging yourself and return happily to the meditation subject, with a mind that is spacious, bright, and relaxed.

Let sounds, sensations, and thoughts go their own way; there is no need to follow them. You may initially notice a multitude of perceptions: sounds might impinge, pain might be felt, thoughts might meander through consciousness. These are all normal sensory experiences. You don't need to push them away, but you don't need to maintain interest in them either. Keep sequestering the mind close to the breath, abandoning the urge to move toward the various sensory experiences that will inevitably arise. This streamlined practice, sustained over time, creates a powerful momentum of concentration by connecting and sustaining the attention on a chosen object.

Initially the breath may appear with distinct physical properties: vibration, temperature, tension, pressure, roughness, for instance. To develop concentration, keep steadily aware of the continuity of connecting and sustaining (vitakka and vicara) without great emphasis on the physicality of changing sensations. As the attention remains connected for longer periods of time without distraction, there will be a corresponding withdrawal of perception from other bodily senses. Awareness of distinct sensations related to the sitting posture will diminish. Awareness of room temperature will fade. Sounds might occur as remote innocuous notes without pulling the attention toward them. Aches, pain, tensions, or twinges in the body will hardly be noticed. Parallel to this growing separation from physical sensory experiences, pleasant mental qualities of bliss, lightness, delight, rapture, pleasure, and happiness will grow, supporting the sustained connection. You will gradually experience clear awareness—samadhi is not a dull or drifting state—yet the objects you perceive will not be bound to the gross field of sensory perception.

As we've noted, meditation requires diligent effort and clear intention. You cannot demand that distractions vanish, but you can cultivate a deep willingness to repeatedly and happily let go. If you try to adhere to the breath and wrestle violently with anything that threatens that hold, you will quickly become tense and probably decide to quit before you have barely begun. But if you allow yourself to *enjoy* letting go of distractions, to feel happy to reconnect, and unburdened by pressure to accomplish a certain number of consecutive breaths, happiness will arise through the simple joy of relinquishment.

When attention is continuously applied, intrusive thoughts subside. If a thought should arise, there will be no fuel for proliferation. It is just a tiny transparent thought that wisps through the mind without causing disturbance, like a momentary bubble on a stream or an ephemeral cloud in the sky. The few thoughts that do arise are entirely wholesome and often concern the meditation practice. Alertness thrives; the mind brightens. When access to jhana is available, there are no hindrances in the mind: no craving, no judging, no doubt, no agitation, no greed. The pulsing activities of vitakka and vicara continue. Relaxed, bright, and spacious, with a momentum of concentration supporting the process, the mind coheres around its object.

THE COUNTERPART SIGN

At some point the physicality of the breath will diminish and the mind will collect through the mere functions of connecting and sustaining attention on the subtle knowing of breath. Focus the attention below the nostrils, either at the subtle feeling near the upper lip, or in the space just off the body near that point. Stay focused on the whole breath—from the very start of the inhalation through to the end of the exhalation—without attention wavering. Be attentive to a continuous perception of breath as the object, rather than particular sensations associated with the breath.

The deepening of samadhi involves this distinctive shift from the physicality of breath sensations as the object of concentration to what is called the *counterpart sign* or *nimitta*. The nimitta often appears as a vibrating pearly bright light resonating with the in- and out-breath, or a soft luminous perception likened to cotton wool. Please don't jump to the conclusion that the first appearance of light in the mind is the nimitta. The mind progressively brightens long before the breath nimitta appears. Many meditators stall their progress by following after "false nimittas"—changing colors, changing images, flashes, motley fields of light, or visual impressions of light that remove the focus of attention from the breath-point to another location (most commonly above the eyes, or in the head).

The breath nimitta usually appears as a stable, smooth, white radiance associated with the focus on the breath. It is a mental reflection of the breath and includes no physical aspect; the light and breath may appear to have merged into a single mental experience of breath. The counterpart sign arises as a result of the concentration and serves as the first landmark of a state conducive to absorption. By learning to notice when this sign arises, you will be able to retrace your steps in the future and attain jhana when desired. Discerning the nimitta is the first step in stabilizing this refined object for concentration. From this point forward, there is no attention to coarse physicality. The term *nimitta,* or counterpart sign, will refer to the object of breath when the breath is known as a stable, luminous, mental focus without sensation.

A skilled meditator should have the capacity to direct the attention at any time either back to the physicality of the sensation of breath or to the mental experience of the counterpart sign. If the meditator decides to remain attentive to physical sensations, rapture will still arise, but it will be known as physical delight. If you accept the subtler luminous mental sign as the object for concentration, this shift to the subtler mental perception will lead to absorption. To attain access to jhana, you would choose the perception of pleasant, radiant light as the new nimitta and allow the attention to remain steadily focused on the luminous perception that is known by directing attention to the upper lip area. But to confirm that you do have the option, it is helpful to sometimes choose the physicality. There is a choice: stay with physical sensations or shift to the counterpart sign.

The momentum of samadhi naturally inclines toward the subtler experience of mental brightness, but skillfulness always includes options. Concentration can be very strong. The mind should never be propelled through this system nor "sucked into a vortex" of concentration. A wise practitioner will moderate the pace, fully developing the meditative skills, before moving to the next stage. By valuing both the release into a profound depth of experience and the insight that arises with dynamic proximity to the senses, you can explore the intertwined trainings of concentration and insight—simultaneously exploring how attention connects with both physical and mental objects of perception.

ACCESS TO JHANA

How strong does concentration need to be to be sure access is attained? Access to jhana has been achieved when there is a sustained experience of a unified mind free of all hindrances and imbued with strong factors of vitakka, vicara, piti, and sukha. Attention, undistracted by thoughts or sensory perceptions, remains intensely focused on the mental nimitta. The mind is utterly bright, the heart relaxed.

Fundamentally, *access* describes an absence of hindrances conjoined with the presence of strongly developed jhanic factors. These conditions are recognized prerequisites to jhana, as the Buddha describes:

> And when he knows that these five hindrances have left him, gladness arises in him, from gladness comes delight, from delight in his mind his body is tranquilized, with a tranquil body he feels joy, and with joy his mind is concentrated. Being thus detached from sense-desires, detached from unwholesome states he enters and remains in the first jhana. . . .[2]

With the absence of hindrances, in the presence of joy, happiness, tranquillity, and concentration, there is a feeling of great relief. The feeling of relief characterizing access to jhana increases to a sense of safety with the arising of jhana: safe from distraction, safe from hindrances, or, as the ancient scriptures describe, removed from the forces of Mara.

The jhanic factors of connecting, sustaining, delight, and joy will continue to strengthen. If your energy drops, you may find sounds or sensations intruding on the meditation. Gentle, joyful persistence is essential. If the mind becomes distracted, simply let the distracting perception be, and reconnect with the nimitta. Nurture equanimity; be happy to connect with the whole breath, or the light nimitta; direct your attention to whichever object is apparent there. Reconnect repeatedly, clearly aware of gladness infusing the connection. Keep lifting the mind up to its object. Use this power of vitakka to refresh the connection whenever the energy sinks or the attention scatters.

When the prerequisites to jhana are stable and sustained, focus the attention for just a moment on the distinctive absence of hindrances. Consider if true happiness can ever be found through sensory experiences. Once you achieve the certainty that happiness will not be found by getting more sensory pleasures or thinking more interesting thoughts, your commitment to inner exploration will deepen. Recognize that this variety of seclusion is a source of joy and relief. After reflecting in this way, continue to develop the basic practice of connecting and sustaining attention on the light that infuses the breath point.

Let go with relief and allow the withdrawal from thoughts, personal concerns, and sensations to continue, unforced and unbroken. Mental brightness will continue to increase. A sense of cohesion and mental unification will grow. Since at this stage concentration is still fragile, this deep release is often interrupted by distraction. Quickly but gently bring energetic interest to the connecting and sustaining activity.

With this practice, the mind is preparing itself for the altered state of jhana—a deeply absorbed state of mind that can retain its unity without effortful striving. When vitakka and vicara are strong and infused with delight, you won't need to continually refresh the connection or fuss with the energy. It is natural for the mind to stay attentive to that which is delightful. So harness this power of happiness and let it totally permeate the nimitta, allowing the mind to become increasingly stable, cohesive, and bright.

These references to delight, gladness, happiness, and rapture could cause you to expect dramatic ecstatic pleasures. The process is more subtle, however. A unified mind experiences such refined pleasures that, although the quiet presence of sublime happiness permeates consciousness and accompanies each stage of jhana, the jhanic factors will barely be noticed while in jhana. This is discerned primarily in the moments prior to absorption and upon emerging from jhana.

Are there thoughts and hindrances that you can set aside, or is there an absence of hindrances in the mind? When you perceive the genuine absence of hindrances, you will feel happy, the happiness I've described as "a great relief." Become sensitive to the subtle pleasant quality of rapture when connecting with the nimitta. When attention is quiet and steady, piti does not have to be gloriously exciting. Enjoy the ease of a mind that is growing in purity.

CHAPTER 11

Fearless Abidings—The First Jhana

Secluded from sensual pleasures, secluded from unwholesome states, I entered and dwelt in the first jhana, which is accompanied by thought and examination, with rapture and happiness born of seclusion.

—The Buddha[1]

I N NORMAL WORLDLY ACTIVITIES, we naturally orient our perceptions toward sensory impressions. We don't need to intentionally listen to hear someone approaching us. We don't need to make an effort to see the dog sitting on the lawn. We don't consciously resolve to feel the touch of a tool in our hand. Jhana, by contrast, represents a radical reorientation: perception recedes from its conventional relationship to sensory objects and attends to a narrow domain of mental factors distinctive to each stage of jhana.

Perception still functions, brightly and with alert mindfulness, but during absorption you are not aware of sounds and sensory impressions. Your attention is unified with the breath and supported by the energy of piti, the gentle contentment of sukha, and the various mental factors of alertness still active in this restricted field of jhana. Hindrances of desire, craving, and aversion do not arise. Energy is balanced and effort feels effortless. There is no need to vigorously refresh the connection with the nimitta, because the attention is already stable. Relaxation and stability are noticeably deeper than they are in conventional experience.

As you approach and enter the first jhana, thoughts are few and far between. Those that do arise are light and quickly dissolve. Without effort, the mind automatically resettles after each thought passes. If thoughts proliferate, triggered by associations or sensations, it indicates that jhana has not been established. If it feels as though your mind goes out to meet the objects of senses, even if you mindfully let go before a proliferating reaction is set in motion, seclusion is not firmly established.

THE FIRST JHANA

Aloofness from the hindrances gives rise to the characteristic happiness of the first jhana: *happiness born of seclusion* or *happiness born of detachment*. Detached from the hindering forces, consciousness is elated. By consciously experiencing the absence of the hindrances during access concentration, you have at your disposal a wholesome cause for generating greater happiness. Traditional descriptions of jhana include such observations:

> Having reached the first jhana, [...] whatever sensations of lust that he previously had disappear. At that time there is present a true but subtle perception of delight and happiness, born of detachment, and he becomes one who is conscious of this delight and happiness. In this way some perceptions arise through training, and some pass away through training.[2]

Observing the perceptions that arise and cease during absorption clarifies the conditions that support sustained spiritual pleasure. For example, you might have noticed that during the access stage the habitually restless wandering mind settles down. There was a presence of calm and an absence of restlessness. Noticing what is present and absent is a simple function of discernment that supports the integration of concentration *(samatha)* and insight *(vipassana)*.

The first jhana, like the state of access concentration, contains the subtle activity of initial and sustained attention (*vitakka* and *vicara*) and is infused with rapture and happiness (*piti* and *sukha*). The purification of mind becomes palpable. Brightness increases. The connecting and sustaining of attention are experienced with a gentle ease likened to the satisfaction of tidying up your house, or working in the comfort of your own home. Far from the threat of hindering disruptions, the one-pointed focus (*ekaggata*) intensifies and consciousness smoothly relaxes into absorption.

Comingling of the happiness factors of piti and sukha also mark the first jhana. Often *piti-sukha* is first experienced as a simple lightness in the mind; it need not be ecstatic bliss. If piti-sukha arises, even slightly, let it infuse the breath with pleasantness and suffuse the heart, mind, and body with this rapture and pleasure born of seclusion. Let this happiness cleanse, protect, and purify the mind.

Notice how you discern piti and sukha. Are the pleasurable vibrations located in the body or mind? Is coolness or warmth associated with this pleasure? Is the vibration wavelike? Rippled? Tingly? Showering? Pervasive? Brief or enduring? Nurture this characteristic pleasure through gentle interest and trusting attention. Intentionally saturate your body and mind with this pervasive happiness. Allow happiness and rapture to infuse the breath. Let the pleasantness brighten your connection with the breath. Although you may still perceive a general sense of physical pleasure, the mental component of pleasantness comes to the foreground. It is a joy based in relinquishment.

A sense of cohesion, confidence, focus, and unification harmonizes the energies. The traditional simile used to describe this unification is the skilled bath man or his assistant who kneads a mass of soap powder. He blends, kneads, and sprinkles it with water, until it is unified, congealed, and bound with oil, such that nothing oozes or escapes.[3] Allow that gentle activity of connecting and sustaining the attention to continue amassing mental energies, drawing in the energy of thought that might otherwise leak out. Like the bath man kneading the mass of soap powder, trust the capacity of directed and sustained attention to collect the mind so that no thoughts ooze out. Concentration condenses the diffused tendencies of feeling, thought, and perception into a cohesive, unified, and cooperative force.

The first jhana is deeply restorative to the mind and body. It is a wholesome and healing state of consciousness. Dwell within its domain for some time, saturating your being with the healing vibrations.

HARNESS THE POWER OF RESOLVE

The critical skill for encouraging the development of the jhanic factors and negotiating the shifts between jhanas is invoking the power of intention, determination, and resolution. The effect of intention is dramatically amplified in the sublime refinement of an undistracted mind. Resolution is directed through wholehearted dedication; it is an orientation of collected mental energies more than an attempt to accomplish a task. To gain access "at will without trouble or difficulty" to jhanic levels of concentration, you shift your reliance on the gross activity of energetically connecting and sustaining to a subtler power of mind that inclines toward the direction of your resolve. This subtle shift of effort releases consciousness into an absorption with the nimitta and resolutely lets go of any competing distraction. Once you form the resolve in mind (about which I say more below), you don't need to do anything more. In the limber mind near jhana, what we resolve upon appears to happen instantly, without additional striving. Yet setting a resolve does not itself create the new experience; rather trusting the wholesome power of your intention, all possible diversions are abandoned, and the energy of mind orients toward the resolve.

Although specific resolutions may appear to be verbal requests or instructions, you may not need to use words to express your resolve; you may find your own way to focus your determination and crystallize your intention with images, feelings, or mental gestures. Determination is not a verbal instruction that we give ourselves and then set out to accomplish, and the essential feature of resolution is not contained in specific verbal expressions, but in the focused power of energetic intention. A verbal expression, image, or feeling may help to coalesce the energetic resolve, opening your heart to your aim and supporting a disposition that eliminates all competing distractions.

The resolve may be inserted after access to jhana is firmly established—that is, when the jhanic factors are strong and clearly discernible, the hindrances are at bay, thinking is minimal and not distracting, and the attention rests steadily and happily on the nimitta. At that point, you strengthen the earnestness of your commitment by making a strong determination to attain the first jhana. You might silently aspire with the thought "May I experience full absorption," "May I attain the first jhana," "May the first jhana arise," or "May my mind be absorbed in the happiness born of seclusion." You could also reflect with energetic resolve on the traditional description of the first jhana: "Being thus secluded from sense pleasures, secluded from unwholesome states, may I enter and abide in the first jhana, which is with applied and sustained thought, and has happiness and pleasure born of seclusion."[4]

Although jhana can certainly arise without the impetus of a resolution, a little skillful nudging can escort the mind into the first jhana. A clear resolution can also crystallize the delineation between access and the first jhana. When you can move the mind through the light touch of intention, coarse applications of effort fall away. An intention gracefully planted when conditions are conducive is like a well-sown seed in a fertile field; it will grow on its own. Nurture the unfolding of jhana and enjoy its sprouting.

Be observant as this altered state of consciousness called the first jhana arises—and at the same time do not consider it a problem if it does not arise immediately. Happily continue to connect and sustain the attention on the breath infused with rapture and happiness. This is the fundamental practice that brings clarity and calm. Give your attention to the breath with or without absorption. You might periodically resolve for the strengthening of each of the jhanic factors, nonverbally or with: "May each jhanic factor grow strong."

A useful precaution is to set the resolve for a balance of factors: "May piti and sukha be balanced and firm." Piti can easily get revved up, whirling you right out of a calm balance and into intensely agitated bliss. Even if you don't consciously know which factors need to increase or decrease, setting the intention encourages intuitive wisdom to operate. Trust your nervous system to restore its equilibrium, allowing the jhanic factors to thrive in the background as your attention is consistently established upon the breath nimitta. Consciously directing the mind through resolve is not cheating, forcing, or contriving the experience.

One of the mysterious powers of intention is that it can accomplish things you don't consciously know how to do.

DISTINGUISHING ABSORPTION FROM ACCESS

The transition between access to, and absorption in, the first jhana is one
of the most difficult to discern. Most meditators will experience the
absorption several times, moving back and forth between access and first
jhana, before clearly distinguishing the two stages of concentration. The
difficulty resides in the fact that the mental factors present in access and
first jhana are identical. Both are marked by applied and sustained attention, rapture and happiness, and a coherent and unified focus. And yet a
distinctive shift in consciousness occurs in the first jhana: the focus is settled deeply inside the mind, utterly unconcerned with outer phenomena. Some people recognize the first jhana only after emerging from it,
by noticing its effect on consciousness. A distinctive swell of energy
accompanies jhana. Calm and largely unnoticed during the period of the
absorption, the mind-body system is recharged in a way that is quite different from what sleep, caffeine, entertainment, good news, or any
worldly spike of energy can accomplish. Please appreciate this inspiring
restoration; it stands in stark contrast to the exhausting pursuits of a distracted mind.

Although it may be difficult for beginners to identify the transition
between access to jhana and first jhana itself with certainty, discerning
the qualities of genuine absorption will clarify the path of concentration
enabling you to attain jhana in the future. The effort to discern these
states and factors also facilitates the direct perception of impermanence,
which I will address in more detail in Chapters 17 and 18. Although
shifting back and forth between first jhana and access to jhana might initially appear to stall the progression, it is my conviction that the clarity
that arises through a patient engagement with the essential features of
absorption is a valuable support for transformative insight.

WHEN DOES THE MIND BECOME ONE-POINTED?

The boundary between access to jhana and full absorption in the first
jhana is a subject of historical debate among Buddhist scholars and
practitioners. The controversy centers around a discrepancy between
the standard description of the first jhana found in early discourses,
which does not specifically list the presence of ekaggata (one-pointed

attention), and later discourses[5] and commentaries[6] that define the first jhana as possessing all five jhanic factors, including ekaggata. This discrepancy has led to a range of opinions regarding the question of whether one-pointed attention must be present for absorption. And if so, to what degree?

As scholars debate where the line between access, first jhana, and second jhana will be drawn, distinct schools of practice have evolved. Some teachers define the first jhana as a relatively light stage of concentration; they will confirm attainment of the first jhana when hindrances subside and the first four jhanic factors are developed, even if thoughts, sensations, and sounds still impinge on consciousness. Other teachers require a deeper absorption and do not declare the first jhana attained until one-pointedness has strengthened to such a degree that engagement with thoughts, sounds, and sensations is suspended. Do these approaches describe two valid but different jhanic systems within the Buddhist tradition? Different teachers have drawn the line in significantly different ways, leading to a controversial range of experiences that have been attributed to the first jhana. Some teachers move students through the stage of first jhana quickly, giving greater emphasis to the more intense factor of piti in the second jhana. Other teachers require prolonged absorption in deep states of the first jhana, milking that attainment to develop mastery over the entrance and exit from absorption, to clarify subtle mental factors, to wear away potential enchantment with pleasure associated with seclusion or personal success, and to permit the first jhana—as the basis of each further attainment—to mature.

My personal practice explored a number of approaches, however, I have come to value the sustained experience of the first jhana and now teach students to remain with the first jhana until it is very well established, attainable with ease, and that the transition between access to jhana and absorption in jhana has been experienced many dozens of times. However, I do not want to assert a definitive interpretation of exactly where the line must be drawn. Instead, I suggest that noticing what constitutes *an absorption* enables the student to enter the systematic progression jhana whenever they wish, given suitable conditions. Exploring the distinction between a mind that is absent of hindrances and possessed of strong jhanic factors but stimulated by perceptions from the sensory field, and a mind that is equally absent of hindrances and possessed of strong jhanic factors but is removed from sensory perceptions clarifies the unique experience of absorption.

We cannot know for certain what the Buddha actually taught; however, it seems clear that he did not specifically define the unfathomable depths of absorption. There are various depths of concentration, each having its own use and meaning. But for the cultivation of jhana, I believe that we can set this academic debate aside.

The different definitions do not need to interrupt our practical attainment of jhana. In my practice, I often experience the lighter state of consciousness quite quickly on retreats. Some teachers consider this a mark of the first jhana and recommend shifting to the second jhana to swiftly continue through the sequence of attainments. However, I have consistently found that when I simply continue to focus attention on the nimitta of light-breath, all five jhanic factors develop until the mind experiences a spontaneous, total, and unquestioned absorption characterized by a powerful but effortless single-pointed focus and accompanied by the subtle influence of the other four jhanic factors. Sometimes it takes several days of sustained attention for this shift to what I call *full absorption* to occur; however, when the shift happens, there is a sense of inner clarity and complete confidence regarding the absorption.

Ekaggata is subtle and difficult to discern in the early stages of practice. The coarser activities of vitakka and vicara tend to obscure it, but this does not imply that it isn't present. Ekaggata's function becomes more apparent after these first two active jhanic factors subside through the progressive development of concentration. It is my conviction that one-pointed attention is present in all the jhanas and is a defining feature of absorption. Therefore, I shall continue to describe the first jhana as possessing all five jhanic factors: vitakka, vicara, piti, sukha, and ekaggata.

SAFE AT LAST

Access to jhana can be likened to a radio whose volume is turned very low: the impact of sensory stimulation is minimal and obstructive states have dramatically diminished. With the arising of jhana, the volume is turned down even more—below the threshold of hearing. The delineation of absorptions can be imagined as a fence around the mind that prevents the hindrances from entering awareness. When access is established, the hindrances don't arise, but they are not far away. The mind is brightened by their absence, but you would not dare let down your guard. The seclusion of jhana separates the mind much further from obstructive states. In that depth of aloofness, you rest: safe at last. The heart is glad and happy. This is the happiness born of seclusion: a fearless abiding.

Traditional teachings consider absorption achieved when the jhanic factors of vitakka, vicara, piti, sukha, and ekaggata are so powerfully present that one can stay secluded from sensory experience and undistracted by thoughts for a long time without the need to refresh the attention by diligently returning to the breath. The *Visuddhimagga* describes this period as being the length of a night and a day. Whether one chooses to take that time frame literally or not, jhana is stable, undistracted, and undisturbed.

More contemporary teachers suggest resolving to remain in absorption for increasing durations. Start with twenty minutes of absorption uninterrupted by thought. Once that is easy to establish and repeat, make a determination for thirty minutes, then forty-five minutes, then one hour, two hours, and three hours. For a beginner to jhana practice, the nimitta may remain stable for only five or ten minutes before a thought or perception interrupts the absorption; often it is a thought about the meditation itself. But as practice deepens, consciousness will remain absorbed for a long time without difficulty. One Burmese master I studied with requested sustained absorption, without the intrusion of a single thought, for more than one hour of each sitting, during all meditation sessions in the day, for at least three consecutive days before he would give the instruction for the next jhana. Although I have not found any particular amount of time to be critical, jhanas are stable states of deep absorption, not brief encounters with bliss. In jhana there is no restlessness; nothing is present that would disturb the tranquillity. A meditator should be able to sit without internal disturbance for very, very long periods of time.

THE FIRST JHANA AS A BASIS FOR INSIGHT

Insight, for our purposes, does not refer to an intellectual understanding. In the context of meditation practice, insight refers to an undistorted clear perception that has the potential of liberating the mind from ignorance. Chapters 17 and 18 are devoted to the exploration of insight after emerging from jhana. This section briefly presents the practical shift between the concentration practices and insight practices so that each jhana can be used sequentially as a basis for insight as you progress through these levels.

Strengthened by absorption, concentration becomes the basis for insight: you allow the jhana to dissolve and shift to perceiving sensory phenomena. If you achieved deep absorption, you may not need to anchor the attention on a primary object during the vipassana aspect of the meditation session. Simply direct the energy of your accumulated samadhi to realize the true nature of all phenomena. Immediately upon emerging from absorption, observe the impermanent, changing nature of the jhanic factors as they fade. Once the jhanic factors diminish, continue to bring mindfulness to whatever mental and physical phenomena enter your awareness. If a sound arises, it is known as a moment of hearing: impermanent, undependable, and impersonal. As physical sensations occur, they are known according to their specific qualities: hardness, heat, coolness, or movement. They are also known by their general characteristics: inconstant, unsatisfactory, and empty. Whatever occurs—thoughts, emotions, hindrances or harmless thoughts—is met with stable mindfulness and the wisdom that apprehends them without attachment.

Commonly the meditator establishes jhana during the earlier portion of a sitting meditation session and then shifts to a vipassana mode for the later portion. You may find it useful to divide your meditation session in half. Or, you may weave back and forth between samadhi and vipassana practices as you feel inclined. Sometimes you might let the concentration grow by anchoring the attention with the breath for a few moments but not necessarily reentering absorption. At other times you might enter and exit jhana several times, tasting the deliciousness of a still mind and emerging again to experience the true nature of the dynamic world. In this exploration of perception you learn to sensitively escort the mind between the seclusion of jhana and the clarity of engaged contact.

This application of the purity of absorption to the complexities of living is the purpose of this training. The shift from unified absorption to the diverse explorations of insight will be explored in greater depth later in this book, but it is important to incorporate insight practice throughout the development of the jhanic states. Don't wait until you experience all four absorptions before you see clearly. Use whatever degree of samadhi you have accumulated and direct that stability of mind toward investigating how suffering comes about and how it can end. This clarity is the function of insight. Insight that arises out of the steadiness of first jhana concentration can be enough to end all suffering.[7] Play in the terrain that is safe and secluded from Mara. Frolic with a joyful heart, courageously exploring this undependable fleeting world.

If, after moving in and out of absorption many times, learning to enter and exit without trouble or difficulty, and using the first jhana as the basis for insight, the mind is not totally liberated, you have another option. You may grow disenchanted with the relative coarseness of applied and sustained thought. Interest may arise to further deepen samadhi. Rather than shifting out of jhana to vipassana, aspire to attain a more sublime degree of samadhi. With dispassion toward the first jhana, relinquish that quality of pleasure and aspire to attain the second jhana.

☞ FOR REFLECTION

Consider your relationship to the sensory field, now informed by a period of time secluded from sensory pleasures.

What is this body? What are feelings? What is your relationship to pleasure? Can happiness be found through the body?

After the meditation session, reflect upon the experience: In your experience, what is the significance of jhana, both in relationship to the state itself and to its effect on the mind?

CHAPTER 12
Drenched in Delight—The Second Jhana

Whatever wholesome states there are, they are all rooted in diligence, converge upon diligence, and diligence is reckoned the best of them all.

—The Buddha[1]

WITH THE FIRST JHANA well established, you may progress to develop more refined and sublime states of concentration. To facilitate entrance to the second jhana, direct the attention to the rapture and delight that is already perceivable in the first jhana. Allow the attention to stay with this manifestation of pleasure while relinquishing the movement of directing and sustaining. In the second jhana, rapture, contentment, and one-pointedness are the dominant forces. The factor of piti intensifies; however, without the agitation of directed and sustained energies, this pleasure stabilizes into a powerful experience of inner tranquillity. *Happiness and pleasure born of concentration* can now accompany attention into absorption.

From the second jhana onward, connection with the meditation object is sustained by trusting one-pointed unification with the object—a state in which the mind "locks" on to its object to settle there with rapt interest as consciousness consolidates. This absorption into the second jhana is characterized by a very refined quality of pleasure as the mind is submerged in this field of happiness. The traditional description of entering the second jhana says:

> With the subsiding of thinking and pondering, by gaining inner
> tranquillity and oneness (unity) of mind, he enters and remains in
> the second jhana, which is without thinking and pondering, born
> of concentration, filled with delight and joy. And with this delight
> and joy born of concentration he so suffuses his body that no spot
> remains untouched.[2]

Piti is an effervescent quality of pleasure that pours like a refreshing
fountain through the body at this point:

> Just as a lake fed by a spring, with no inflow from east, west, north
> or south, where the rain-god sends moderate showers from time
> to time, the water welling up from below, mingling with cool
> water, would suffuse, fill and irradiate that cool water, so that no
> part of the pool was untouched by it—so, with this delight and
> joy born of concentration he so suffuses his body that no spot
> remains untouched.[3]

The vibrational feeling of delight can be thrilling: intense ripples,
waves, and excitement pervade the body. Tremendous energy is
unleashed. The mind is keenly alert and focused, not drawn into the
diverse range of sensory perceptions. Staying unified within a field of
pure delight, this energy generates more focused energy, which further
intensifies the distilling process of mind. Posture is spontaneously
uplifted; spine, neck, and back align upward, buoyant against gravity. The
internal energy feels like a huge bright smile, although there is no physical movement of facial muscles. The rapture so thoroughly pervades
consciousness that no ripples, waves, jerks, or intense fluctuations are
apparent. Whether intense or mild, the rapture is steadily pervasive.

RESOLVING FOR THE SECOND JHANA

When you wish to shift to the second jhana, reflect on two disadvantages
to the first jhana, and one advantage to the second jhana. In the first
jhana, one is (1) dangerously close to the hindrances, especially restlessness and distraction; and (2) relying strongly on vitakka and vicara, which
are relatively coarse factors.

The second jhana is quieter; rapture, happiness, and one-pointedness are more peaceful. Make the clear and firm resolve, "May the second jhana arise," "May I attain the second jhana," or "May my mind be absorbed in the happiness born of concentration." Or use the phrasing of the sutta descriptions: "With the subsiding of thought and examination, I enter and dwell in the second jhana, which has internal confidence and unification of mind, is without thought and examination, and has rapture and happiness born of concentration."[4] This resolve may be the boost the mind needs to allow its reliance on vitakka and vicara to fade. Make the resolve, then let go. Let it do the work without interfering further.

Clear resolve can strengthen each state and its associated jhana factors. If absorption is *almost* happening—the factors are present and stable—but the attention is pulled to the fringes of absorption, employ the simple resolve: "May the second jhana strengthen and deepen," or "May the factors of the second jhana grow in clarity and balance." This can support unified attention with the nimitta, highlighting the quality of piti, without interfering in the settling that is occurring.

The second jhana is characterized by this particular blend of piti and sukha called the *happiness born of concentration*. Practice moving back and forth between the first and second jhana to sharpen your ability to distinguish *happiness born of seclusion* in the first jhana from *happiness born of concentration* in the second jhana. Look deeply into the experience of these states. You don't need to analyze every minute distinction; in fact, such detailed analysis could unravel into a discursive thinking process. A joyful mindful interest in what is and is not present is enough to highlight the

---

⌒ **FOR REFLECTION**

Observe how you experience these characteristic blends of happiness. How do they differ? What aspects are clearer or more intense in each? Is your experience physical or mental? What is the quality of the vibration—rippling, tingly, wavelike, pulsing, pervasive, smooth? What is the texture of mind in the second jhana as distinct from the first jhana? Is there any change in body posture? What is present and what is absent in each state of consciousness?

processes that unify the mind with the object of attention. By developing these first two jhanas, you will acquire the skills needed to progressively refine the mind.

MOVING TOWARD THE SUBTLE

The thrill of piti—drenched by delight, suffused with happiness—might at first be tantalizing, enthralling, even fun, but its intensity can give rise to annoyance. In comparison to the distractions of worldly life, any jhana appears smooth. From the perspective of higher absorptions, however,

---

☞ A FRESH ENCOUNTER WITH THE WORLD

When you emerge from the jhana, allow yourself to experience the impact of the flood of bodily sensations and environmental contacts on consciousness.

Feel the touch of your clothes; notice the sound of the refrigerator; experience the effect of light; sense the movement of air and the different temperatures at different points on your body.

Let life flow in.

There is nothing you need to do with sensations and sounds; let them be as they are: fleeting impersonal phenomena that continuously flow by.

During the hours that follow the meditation session, notice how you experience daily encounters with sight, sound, social encounters, sensations, and activities.

Did the previous experience of jhana have an impact on your everyday perceptions?

In my own experience, I found each jhana left a residue that inclined my experience in distinct ways. How do you experience the moments after the second jhana as distinct from the moments that followed absorption in the first jhana?

---

the first and second jhanas are relatively agitated weak states by virtue of their proximity to vitakka and vicara. This does not diminish their importance; they are incredibly useful states for rejuvenation, inspiration, and as a foundation for insight. After exploring the second jhana and shifting repeatedly between the first and the second jhanas, intentionally use the experience of the second jhana as a basis for a new perception of reality. Open the jhana and allow the jhanic factors to change. Observe how the experiences of mind, perception, and environment change. Dedicate time in your meditation for this insight (vipassana) component. The second jhana is a powerful foundation for direct insight for the very same reasons it is considered less stable: because of its proximity to thought. Vitakka and vicara are close by, readily available for your wise use. Engage them with the strength of a buoyant, energized, undistracted mind to perceive more directly the true nature of all things.

☞ FOR REFLECTION

Reflection after each jhana strengthens insight. Discover what can be learned from these altered states and how they may inform and affect daily perceptions.

How can the seclusion of jhana inform your present engagement with diverse things?

Are sense impressions graspable or controllable?

Is there any fixed place to stand in relation to the senses?

How does one affect or condition the next moment's experience?

If, however, you are not completely liberated from all forms of clinging when using the second jhana as a basis for insight, incline toward a more sublime state, even if you don't know what comes next. When piti fades, the mind prepares for a greater depth of samadhi. Because the concentrated mind is inclined to release whatever it perceives as coarse, development of higher consciousness continues through progressive stages of letting go.

CHAPTER 13
Absorbed in Joy—The Third Jhana

[W]ith the fading away of delight [the meditator] remains imperturbable, mindful and clearly aware, and experiences in himself that joy of which the Noble Ones say: "Happy is he who dwells with equanimity and mindfulness," and he enters and remains in the third jhana. And with this joy devoid of delight he so suffuses his body that no spot remains untouched.

—The Buddha[1]

SUKHA WAS ALREADY PRESENT during access concentration and the first and second jhanas, but only after the grosser factor of piti is stilled can the subtler factor of sukha attain center stage. Since piti no longer thrills, intrigues, or impresses, dispassion toward the coarseness of rapture grows. Perception simplifies, attention remains single-pointedly focused on the nimitta, and sukha comes to the fore. At this point, consciousness is unified with quiet joy, contentment, and peace devoid of delight.

The traditional description of the third jhana points to a specific subtle pleasure that comes from a mind at rest in equanimity: the happiness of unreactive mindful awareness. As you prepare to enter the third jhana, sukha shines brightly, filling consciousness with a smooth sense of contentment. Sukha has a deeply balanced quality of peace that is thoroughly but subtly happy. Distinctly different from the dazzling grandeur of piti, sukha feels creamy, like the texture of a perfectly prepared dessert pudding or sweet butter. Translators seeking English words to describe this ambiguous blend of happiness and equanimity, pleasure and equality, turn to such terms as "contentment," "happiness," "pleasure," "joy," or dissatisfied with such renderings, many contemporary teachers prefer to use the Pali term "sukha." I have found that as we repeatedly experience this absorption, practitioners sense for ourselves the unique quality of third-jhana happiness. You will come to know sukha through your experience of it.

A gentle lingering delicacy to sukha melts consciousness into its object, affecting the quality of attention even beyond the duration of the absorptions. When sukha is strong, conceptual divisions seem inconsequential and indistinct. Sukha tends to temporarily dissolve them, eliminating even subtle feelings of fragmentation or alienation. Experience feels seamless without the usual arbitrary divisions between consciousness and perceptions. There is virtually no content in the mind: no personal thoughts, no personal stories, no distracting or fragmenting perceptions. Social conventions, such as the use of calendars and clock time, will hold little relevance to the practitioner whose mind is saturated with sukha.

When consciousness is altered by the pervasive presence of sukha, nothing disturbs you. There is no sleepiness, no dullness, no energetic imbalances to shake the stability of this state; environmental sounds do not disturb the attention, nor does cold or heat. If physical discomforts such as chronic back pain should arise, the mind remains undisturbed. Although the meditator may recognize sensations of pain, pain may not be perceived as unpleasant, due to the saturation of consciousness in contentment. Muscle spasms can be recognized and wisely responded to, but the mind will be free of any unpleasant associations.

After deep experience of the third jhana, sukha will begin to permeate perception between meditation sessions—in any posture and any activity. During this phase of my jhana retreat, happiness saturated every aspect of the day. Deep contentment pervaded the experience of folding laundry, walking in the snow, standing in line, touching a doorknob, exercising. When the meditator is saturated with the feeling tone of happiness, there is no opportunity for unpleasant experience to occur.

One can sustain jhana for very long periods when consciousness is absorbed in sukha. You will not want to end the meditation session. This pleasant abiding is soothing, healing, and completely wholesome. It brings consciousness into a complete and deep absorption. Such a profound resonance of joy can deeply transform the shape of consciousness, restructuring the tendencies of perception toward happy states. Students often discover that, after a jhana retreat, a lingering residue of joy, patience, and equanimity naturally replaces the depression and irritation that would once arise in response to so many situations they encounter. Prolonged contact with sukha, periodically intensified by the potent field of jhana, can diminish conditioned tendencies toward depression, irritation, and crankiness. You can let sukha suffuse your entire being.

As the Buddha says:

> Just as if, in a pond of blue, red or white lotuses in which the flowers, born in the water, grown in the water, not growing out of the water, are fed from the water's depths, those blue, red or white lotuses would be suffused, filled, and irradiated with that cool water—so with this joy devoid of delight the monk so suffuses his body that no spot remains untouched.[2]

Allow the coolness of sukha to saturate every aspect of your being, like lotuses completely suffused day and night, inside and out, by cool pond water. Melt into it, welcome it, and let it purify your heart and mind. Drink deeply of this joy. Grow familiar with this unperturbed mind. Notice how settled and stable the mind is with this absorption. Absolutely nothing about the third jhana is unpleasant.

RESOLVING FOR THE THIRD JHANA

The third jhana may arise naturally with the fading of piti in the second jhana. You can easily accelerate the process, however, by intentionally relinquishing the coarsest jhanic factors. In the transition from second to third jhana, that would require letting go of piti. Make a definite resolve to allow the factor of piti to fade. Withdraw attention from it. Reflect on the coarseness of piti, and the proximity that the second jhana has to the gross qualities of the first jhana. Consider the greater refinement that sukha and ekaggata offer.

Then reconnect with the nimitta to enter into the third jhana. You can choose what you give your attention to and what you sustain interest in. Direct attention toward the nimitta with disinterest toward piti, and interest in sukha, resolving: "May I attain the third jhana," "May the third jhana arise," "May my mind be absorbed in sukha." Or use the traditional language: "Mindful, clearly aware, and equanimous, may I enter and abide in the third jhana, experiencing happiness devoid of delight."

USING THE THIRD JHANA AS A BASIS FOR INSIGHT

There is no need to hurry through the third jhana. Few people will want to rush once they taste this expansive and spacious joy. Although the third-jhana happiness is deeply calm, there is still a density to it, a relatively coarse quality. The feelings are entirely pleasant, so one does not experience the common coarseness of unpleasant feeling. In fact, third-jhana happiness is so wondrously calming and joyful to the heart and mind that I have never experienced anything distinctly unpleasant arising in this state—no aversive feelings of boredom, no agitation like the slight irritation of the incessant delightfulness of piti, no involvement with thought fragmenting the attention, no striving effort draining the energy, no craving to be anywhere else.

Nevertheless, sukha does begin to feel relatively coarse after some time. The fragile, conditioned nature of the jhana becomes obvious, and with that recognition dissatisfaction with the conditioned state arises, even though it is a thoroughly pleasant conditioned state. Satiated, the mind will naturally turn away from pleasure and incline toward something much stiller.

Many students find it difficult to fathom the possibility of growing tired of deep and pervasive contentment. Thus many of them linger in this stage, unaware of their subtle attachment to pleasure. At some point in this distilling process you must honestly reflect: "Am I willing to relinquish pleasant feeling?" Until you confidently embrace relinquishment, the happiness of the third jhana will remain seductive.

Jhana is a pleasant abiding. The purpose of developing samadhi, however, is to create the conditions most conducive for *liberating wisdom*. Be wary of the seductive danger of third-jhana happiness. Many meditators discover it as the most sublime happiness ever known, and you may too—but please do not stop there. As wonderful as contentment feels, it is not a reliable foundation for abiding happiness.

Since it is conditioned and volitionally produced, this sublime joy is ultimately undependable. Realization of this frees the mind from the seductive enchantment of pleasant states and prepares it to look elsewhere for freedom. The mind wants to be free, not simply experience temporary pleasures. Develop conviction in the potential of release and you will be able to allow this sublime joy to fade. Although there is no aversion to the third jhana, no craving for a different state, the mind naturally inclines toward a quieter stillness, to free itself from even pleasant feeling.

When you feel ready, allow the jhana to end and observe the changes that occur. Watch closely as the factors of the jhana (in this case, primarily contentment and unified singularity of mind) shift in the transition from altered to normal consciousness, from seclusion to sensory contact, from samadhi to vipassana practice. This is your opportunity to carefully observe the impermanence of subtle mental factors. Notice how you can distinguish a jhanic state from regular consciousness. Observe whatever is happening. And then, with a mind energized, clear, and freshened by concentration, dedicate the remainder of the meditation session to recognize the true nature of mental and physical phenomena.

If your mind becomes excessively distracted while you are observing changing objects, or if you feel it would enhance clarity to return to jhana, permit yourself to enter and exit jhana states at will. You can move among the first three jhanas, clarifying and strengthening each attainment. You can interweave the samadhi and vipassana practices in various ways, or structure the meditation sessions to methodically begin with samadhi and end with vipassana. Individual meditators will become sensitive to their energetic rhythms and can determine for themselves when to enter or exit the secluded states of jhana.

After developing the third jhana and using it as a basis for insight, you might grow curious about more refined levels of concentration. What state is beyond the happiness of a mind imbued with mindfulness and equanimity?

☞ FOR REFLECTION

After exploring the third jhana during meditation, notice if there are any effects on your disposition during daily activities.

For example, has your patience during political discussions increased? Has appreciation of spouse, partner, or intimate friends grown? Has your tolerance of an infirm relative changed? Notice the implications of being saturated with sukha and how this experience informs your life.

Reflect on the following questions:

Is happiness dependent on particular conditions, relationships, events, possessions, or attainments?

What, really, do I need to be happy?

CHAPTER 14
Radiant Calm—The Fourth Jhana

With the abandoning of pleasure and pain, and with the previous passing away of joy and displeasure, I entered and dwelt in the fourth jhana, which is neither painful nor pleasant and includes the purification of mindfulness by equanimity.

—The Buddha[1]

B Y THE TIME you have reached the threshold of the fourth jhana, the quality of your mind will be smooth, quiet, and exceedingly refined. After the third jhana, pleasure is relinquished and the heart is washed with the coolness of equanimity, *upekkha*. A very gentle inclination of interest is sufficient to realize the fourth jhana. You need do nothing except look beyond the happiness of pleasurable states.

The mind that is near the fourth jhana is extremely responsive to intentional thought. Consciousness instantly molds to the suggestion, whether your intention is to enter, expand, focus, release, deepen, or relax. You are not creating equanimity, since there is no need for striving. The energetic penetrating function of directed thought that supported the attainment of the first jhana is far too coarse to use now. Such vigorous endeavoring would feel abusive at this refined level of consciousness. The fourth jhana is an opportunity to surrender to your deepest spiritual aspirations.

Quietly reflect on the two disadvantages of the third jhana: (1) it is perilously close to the agitation of the second jhana, and (2) sukha is relatively coarse. Consider the advantages of the fourth jhana, namely that equanimity and one-pointedness are more peaceful. Gently give rise to a resolution: "May I attain the fourth jhana," or "May the fourth jhana arise," "May my mind be absorbed in equanimity," or "Beyond pleasure and pain, beyond happiness and sadness, may I enter and abide in the fourth jhana with mindfulness purified by equanimity."

These resolutions support the withdrawal of interest in sukha and incline the mind toward the feeling of equanimity. As sukha diminishes, it is replaced by a neutral feeling of equanimity. Give single-pointed attention to the breath nimitta infused with this quality of equanimity. Allow the mind to become absorbed in this stable yet vibrant state of equality.

RECOGNIZING THE FOURTH JHANA

The fourth jhana is characterized by a single-pointed focus with a neutral and equanimous feeling, a deep unification in this state, and the strange sense of not much else going on. Consciousness is pervaded by a subtle vibrational field that is neither pleasant nor unpleasant, yet it is perceivable as a feeling. Mind remains composed within itself in quiet still awareness, very remote from sensory contact. There is no excitement.

It is not a particularly happy state, but there is nothing to find here that is unpleasant or harmful. The bliss of the third jhana pales in comparison to the deep rest, sublime peacefulness, and profound sense of OK-ness at this stage. In the sublime stability of the fourth jhana, sounds, sensations, and other occurrences will mostly pass unrecognized. If intrusive external phenomena are perceived, breaching jhana and pulling consciousness briefly into contact with sensory stimuli, the experiences will be known from the perspective of equanimity.

For instance, if a loud sound is perceived it will not trigger conditioned responses of desire or aversion. On structured group retreats, the lunch bell is usually the most exciting moment of the day. Although it might ring nearby, it won't trigger the conditioned impulse to get up to go to the meal. The sound may be loud enough to intrude into consciousness, and with that contact there is awareness of hearing and the intelligent comprehension that it is the bell signaling the day's meal, but no habitual reaction is attached to the awareness. No urge is present to move from the meditation.

Unaffected by conditioned reactions of desire or aversion, the meditator's attention emerges only momentarily from absorption and easily resettles back into jhana. Although in retreat conditions few environmental objects are intrusive enough to penetrate the detachment of the fourth jhana, those that do arise and pass without disrupting this deeply balanced equipoise.

In the fourth jhana, you will feel as though you could sit indefinitely, like the yogis of old who sat unmoving for weeks at a stretch. There is no cause for disturbance while absorbed in this neutral feeling and steadiness of mind. Conventional body sensations are not registered. The breath becomes very, very shallow. Mindfulness continues with precision, and there is no reduction in attentiveness, but the physical field is beyond the boundaries of interest to the mind absorbed in the fourth jhana.

Experience this complete physical relaxation; however, out of compassion for the health of your spine, you might explore entering the fourth jhana with the resolve to relax with an uplifted spine. Let this profound equipoise saturate your consciousness, permeating every cell of your being with the unified experience of equanimity. As the Buddha's illustration states, "Just as if a man were to sit wrapped from head to foot in a white garment, so that no part of him was untouched by that garment—so his body is suffused, filled and irradiated . . . so that no part remains untouched by it."[2]

The mind can become so far removed from bodily experience that sensations may seem distant even after you emerge from the jhana. Equanimity can become so pervasive through deep absorptions that feelings normally associated with pain or pleasure simply carry a neutral quality. Even after emerging from absorption, the meditator may experience very strong sensations as primarily neutral.

Take the time to mindfully reconnect with the body and the world, gently stretch your limbs, feel the touch of clothes and the contact with water as you wash your hands. After emerging from jhana *do not sustain a state of disconnection* with the world: bring active energy to mindfulness on contact and invigorate your connection with the senses. Systematic withdrawal from worldly expressions is an important feature of jhana, but it would be a disadvantage for insight if sensory seclusion were sustained beyond the range of absorption. Insight frequently arises when mindfulness infuses sensory contact.

After emerging, give attention to embodied awareness, sensitively guarding the senses with the clarity of mindful presence.

EXPERIENCING EQUANIMITY

If your experience of the fourth jhana is deep and sustained, a strong sense of equanimity will continue between meditation sessions in relation to all contacts. Explore how equanimity feels in relation to climate, temperature, food tastes, other people's peculiar habits, broken equipment, daily choices of what to drink or wear. Equanimity supports a deep comprehension that things in the world are just following the way of the world. Things are the way that they are. As the Buddha said, "Such it is."[3]

Equanimity is not the static feeling most people imagine it to be. At this stage you can explore equanimity through its contrast to pleasure by shifting between the third and fourth jhanas, and jumping between all the previous levels. By comparing the qualities associated with each state, you can discern each factor and the feelings as they change. Recognize exactly what changes in each transition. Specifically notice what happens when the feeling-tone of sukha is exchanged for the feeling of equanimity. There is a vibrational tone to equanimity that is not bland or mediocre, but it is not the upbeat quality of sukha, and certainly not the intensity of piti. With the first four jhanas as a basis, you have four distinctively different states to explore. By moving through the jhanas in reverse order, you may learn about equanimity, contentment, and delight from a new perspective.

Equanimity is an extraordinary quality of the heart, necessary in life and vital in practice. It cools the heart, and lets the mind rest completely—steady and undisturbed. Following a deep absorption in the fourth jhana, the mind can feel so imperturbable that it is difficult to imagine ever reacting with desire or aversion. Many ardent meditators, saturated with the profound encounter with equanimity, briefly ponder if they have attained enlightenment. The problem with equanimity is, that, like all the previous states experienced in the development of concentration, it is merely conditioned. Like all mental states, it will change.

One of the profound teachings of the Buddha is that all conditioned things are undependable, unreliable, or unsatisfactory. This truth becomes vividly clear with the support of the stability of fourth-jhana samadhi. The mind is not busy fabricating stories, making excuses, weaving commentaries, developing strategies, or manipulating its relationship to all things in the futile quest to minimize the unpleasant. There simply is an absence of those ingrained reactions that fruitlessly attempt to adjust worldly conditions to support personal preferences and views. When the mind is profoundly balanced with equanimity, there is no averse reaction to the basic fact that nothing in the material world can bring satisfaction. The mind does not require further elaboration. The struggle ceases.

For example, in jhana you might sit unmoved for many hours at a stretch. In the course of time your mouth might dry; when the absorption ends you will feel thirsty. The sensations of thirst may or may not carry an unpleasant feeling tone. Influenced by equanimity, these sensations would not be coupled with craving, desperation, fear, or aversion. There may be no desire to quench them. The sensations will simply be known as they are, and a wise course of action will arise in response. You will simply drink some water, without the extra drama that an unsettled mind might interject into the moment.

A spasm or cramp is merely tension or pulsating heat. It is not terrible. It may not even be unpleasant. It can be known simply as a series of changing sensations. You might clearly feel sharp stinging sensations but not consider them painful. For the untrained mind, an added experience of aversion strengthens the motivation to change, seek help, or protect the body. However, with equanimity as your resource you won't need pain or aversion to protect yourself. Rather, intelligence determines a skillful course of action—to move, massage, or stretch a straining muscle. Wisdom is a sufficient guide.

When still saturated by equanimity after the fourth jhana, you might hear a spring bird song with magnificent detail—discerning fluctuations of melody and interactions with the wind. When mindfulness has been purified by equanimity, you will know it in its bare simplicity, without the extra involvement of liking or not liking, without the distortions of personal preferences, comparisons, and judgments. Equanimity is a deeply sublime happiness, not the happiness of a pleasant feeling, but a happiness experienced through the absence of unpredictable swings of pleasure and pain and reactions of desire and aversion.

Experience the positive and lingering effect of equanimity on consciousness. Go about your daily routine without the desire to control experiences, without demanding that things be your way. Confidence is based on the direct experiential knowledge that you don't need the biases of aversion, judgmental criticism, and personal greed to function peacefully in this world.

PURIFICATION OF MIND BY EQUANIMITY

In the quietude of the fourth jhana, the primary event is the progressive purification of awareness by equanimity. As the jhana is sustained, the power of mindfulness is clarified through the nonreactive qualities of this state. A mind influenced by equanimity is not buffeted and dulled by desire and aversion; it achieves a stillness that sharpens attention and clarifies awareness.

As the mind quiets, observe how equanimity affects your experience of things. How does equanimity affect the precision of mindfulness? How does the absence of desire and aversion affect your energy, focus, and concentration?

Consciousness influenced by the fourth jhana feels extraordinarily spacious. Look into the mind and recognize what is there and what is not there. Confidence develops when there is no craving, no aversion, no judging, no agitation, no preoccupations with self-interest, no unwholesome forces of any kind. Complete confidence is essential for the further development of samadhi. It cannot be assumed, however. It can only be found by looking into the mind and clearly discerning that there is actually nothing to fear. Notice what is present. Notice what is absent.

There is a path to peace and the mind will naturally incline toward whatever is deeper and purer. This inclination has been guiding you away from the gross aspects of worldly pleasures through the initial four jhanas. You won't need to coerce your mind down the path, cajole it, or bargain with it. By this point in the process there is a momentum in the practice. It may feel as though the mind is finding its own way home, and you are just along for the ride. Watch the natural settling of the mind as it follows its innate inclination toward peace.

A mind purified by jhana is beautiful!

USING THE PLIABLE, MALLEABLE, WIELDY MIND

From the stability of the fourth jhana, several options are available for further development. The ancient discourses present the possibility of using the fourth jhana as the springboard for "wielding the various kinds of spiritual power,"[4] such as mind-reading, seeing into the future, or recollecting past lives—even duplicating the body, or flying through the air. Although these possibilities are interesting, this book limits itself to a discussion of the two other traditional options. By continuing in the scheme of absorptions, you can experience a further sequence of *four formless attainments*. More importantly, you can use the fourth jhana as the basis for insight to purify the mind of all forms of attachment, defilement, and delusion.

The mind in the fourth jhana is extraordinarily agile, malleable, unified, clear, and stable—very fit for the work of insight meditation. It has become an effective tool to direct toward the resolution of suffering. After sufficiently permeating the mind and heart with the calm clarity of the fourth jhana, turn your now limber attention to the dissolving of the jhana. Observe the jhanic factors as they change. Observe all phenomena. Again you may enter or exit the jhana, or return to lower jhanas as you feel so inclined. Sense for yourself what supports the clarity of insight into the nature of things.

Samadhi sharpens the mind. Use it to develop an undistorted comprehension of life.

☞ EQUANIMITY AND ENGAGEMENT

When you emerge from the fourth jhana, direct mindfulness to the basic components of experience: pleasantness, unpleasantness, and neutrality of feeling.

Observe the feelings carefully.

Notice what reactions they trigger.

Practice fully experiencing the clarity of feeling without the extra formations of desire, aversion, and delusion.

Allow feeling to be simply a feeling, without adding attachment.

Continue your discernment of experience and development of insight as you go about your daily activities.

What does the experience of deep equanimity reveal about your engagement with life?

CHAPTER 15
How Deep Is Deep Enough?

Try to be mindful, and let things take their natural course.
Then your mind will become still in any surroundings, like a
clear forest pool. All kinds of wonderful, rare animals will come
to drink at the pool, and you will see the nature of all things.
You will see many strange and wonderful things come and go,
but you will be still. This is the happiness of the Buddha.

—Ajahn Chah[1]

CONTROVERSY HAS HISTORICALLY SURROUNDED the practice of jhana. The primary point of contention is the depth
required to designate a state as jhana: How deep is deep? How
stable is stable? How secluded does the mind need to be before the experience can reasonably be considered a jhana?

Some teachers in Asia and the West recognize fairly light levels of
natural samadhi (unified concentration) where bright joy steadily infuses
perception. They liberally apply the term jhana to any arising of the designated configuration of jhanic factors. Other teachers reserve the term
jhana for a depth of seclusion that permits no sensory impressions whatsoever. Most teachers fall somewhere between the two extremes.

Although the jhana states are succinctly described in the discourses
of the Buddha, the question remains: "What exactly entails a jhanic
experience?" One teacher[2] illustrates this controversial issue with a
simile of eight pools of water. One may skim the surface of the water,
wade in, swim on the surface, or dive in deep. However one enters, to

whatever depth, the pools of water are still the same pools. The eight jhanas remain the same even though the depth of experience differs depending upon how one engages with them.

The controversy over what constitutes the jhanic experience raises several questions. Should *no* thoughts arise—or only wispy thoughts that don't move the mind off its chosen point of focus? Must practitioners hear *no sounds* in jhana, or do they simply find that the mind is unmoved by the sounds that are perceived? Is there any perception of body and posture in jhana? Is physical perception suspended in the higher jhanas but not the lower, or is bodily perception abandoned as a basic precondition of the first jhana?

Teachers offer various views based on their distinct experiences. I am not sure that strict objective criteria can be applied to absorption. I prefer to let the individual practitioner determine this for her- or himself. With practice, you can gauge for yourself how liberally or conservatively you wish to apply the term "jhana" to your experience.

It is my hope that the question of "How deep is deep enough?" will become inconsequential when one comes to understand jhana practice as a progression of relinquishment. By stabilizing the mind and growing familiar with the jhanic factors, you'll soon come to a functional determination yourself. A personal sensitivity coupled with experientially developed criteria for absorption will be more useful for deepening concentration than deeply exploring the contrasting viewpoints of the traditional debates. You will learn to steer your own process. You will know when to rest the attention deeper in absorption, when to intensify the factors of concentration, and when to shift between jhanas or dissolve the seclusion entirely and see things as they are.

If we get trapped into arguing over the definition of a jhana's depth, we miss the opportunity to abandon at least some level of unwholesome forces and cultivate some degree of wholesome states. It is simply wiser to dwell with a mind suffused by joy or equanimity at any depth and to any degree than to indulge the comparing tendencies of mind or cower under the weight of historic controversies.

The depth that is possible for a concentrated mind is unfathomable. The Buddha listed depth of concentration as one of the four conditions that were incomprehensible and unfathomable: if obsessively considered it can never result in an answer, only in insanity.[3] However, should you choose to apply the term jhana liberally to states lightly saturated by jhanic factors, please don't presume such states represent the full potential of jhana. The early discourses of the Buddha describe very deeply secluded states.

For example, a student of Alara Kalama was once bragging that his teacher had sat unmoved by the roadside while five hundred carts passed by. Upon questioning, Alara Kalama stated that he was fully conscious and awake, and yet did not hear or see the five hundred carts passing nearby, even though his robe was splattered with mud. The Buddha then shared his experience of sitting through a violent rainstorm with thunder and lightning that killed two men and four oxen. He also described being fully conscious and awake, yet did not hear or see the storm.[4] Deep absorption describes a state removed from conventional sensory perceptions; however, it is not a dull or mindless state. Attention is keenly aware of the subtle mental phenomena that characterize each jhana. During jhana, the Buddha was steady, unmoved, and apparently unaware of external commotion—with mindful attention focused internally, he remained happily absorbed in jhana.

The early discourses contain a description of the chief disciple, Sariputta, sitting deeply absorbed when a passing mischievous spirit clobbered him on the head. He remained entirely undisturbed by it— only later commenting that he had a slight headache.[5] Physical assault describes a rather extreme test; however, it is quite reasonable to experience sustained states of consciousness that are flooded with exquisite purity, delight, happiness, and equanimity. For prolonged periods there can be exceedingly refined states of alertness during which bodily and postural sensations are completely excluded from awareness. There is no feeling of pain, no sense of touch, no perception of temperature, no sounds, no awareness of birds, of doors opening and closing, bells ringing, people walking in and out, or heaters turning on and off. There is no consciousness of day shifting into night or night into day, although the events occur.

Such depth of seclusion is certainly possible. When absorption is terminated and consciousness emerges from this controlled withdrawal, a dramatic moment of heightened awareness occurs—everything is sensitively and vividly known. One recognizes light, sounds, sensations, and the flow of dynamic life as they actually are. Consciousness, purified by the temporary seclusion of absorption, opens to meet this precious and fleeting existence in supreme clarity.

While developing this methodology, you may often observe periods in which the jhanic factors are strongly established but you don't feel an altered state of absorption. The jhanic factors are vibrant and dominant and yet the mind seems slightly removed. It may feel like you are watching them from a slight distance or through a glass window. Sometimes the only mental factors in your field of view will correspond to standard descriptions of jhana. If asked to describe what was present and absent in your mind, you might offer a textbook description of jhana, but you don't feel genuinely confident.

In a phase such as this, hindrances won't arise, due to the vibrancy of the jhanic factors. Everything looks right on the surface. However, the meditator's relationship with jhana is still tenuous—thought, effort, and sensations periodically intrude. The mind has not completely released into the cradle of jhana; it is not full absorption. To understand the quality of this phase, imagine yourself standing on the threshold of your house. You are looking inside through the open front door, but you have not yet stepped inside. You are looking inward, but you can still feel the outside temperature. This phase marks a natural transition; I would not call it jhana until a deeper immersion has occurred. When conditions for absorption do occur, the experience is like entering the house and closing the door behind: you feel more relaxed, safe, confident, and at ease in the welcome seclusion.

Even after absorption is established, you may experience your detachment periodically weakening as a result of an influx of a minor thought or environmental intrusion, and then effortlessly reestablish itself. Like an ebb and flow the mind momentarily surfaces from the depths, or returns to the thinner fringes of a concentrated field, then effortlessly sinks back, deep and centered. A good analogy for this experience is a minor breach that quickly closes by itself, or a tiny leak in concentration that is immediately plugged. Although imprecise, these images convey a general sense of the way altered states can fluctuate without disturbing the evolution of concentration.

Each level of attainment presents a new opportunity to consolidate the energies of mind. Working each jhana, you strengthen the absorptions while simultaneously developing a mind that is malleable and wieldy. There is no need to abbreviate this process for the sake of efficiency. Each attainment should be thoroughly developed and examined before resolving for the next jhana.

During a daily practice at home, meditators may find that although they can attain stable states of unification supported by strong jhanic factors, these states lack the sensory withdrawal characteristic of deep jhana. Seclusion can be supported by choosing a quiet and solitary location for meditation, closing and locking the door, meditating in the early morning before family members wake up, unplugging the telephone, and turning off computers, cell phones, faxes, and any other equipment that produces sound. For many practitioners, retreat conditions are necessary for deeper detachment. And even in retreat conditions, some practitioners will find that their minds simply do not enter absorption, even though they practice diligently. Nevertheless, the mental composure cultivated through concentration practice, energized by jhanic factors, will add an exponential degree of clarity to vipassana practices regardless of whether or not deep absorption is attained.

Spend whatever time you need to fully explore each state; don't rush through this system. The Buddha compared a meditator who hurries on to higher jhanas to a foolish mountain cow who wanders seeking greener pastures.[6] This mountain cow does not know the terrain and is not skilled in moving about the mountain. She leaves one pasture but gets lost and is unable to find that greener pasture or return to her home.

It is essential to lay a strong foundation of skill through practice in these first four jhanas before advancing to the more subtle formless states. Learn precisely how each nimitta changes and what shifts in each transition. As you make each discovery, move back and forth many times to learn if your observations describe consistent characteristics. Confirm your understandings through repeated reflections. Diligent practice will enable you to "obtain at will, without trouble or difficulty, the four jhanas that constitute the higher mind and provide a pleasant abiding here and now"[7]—the classic description of an adept.

After attaining stability in the jhana and clarity regarding its components, scrutinize the jhana even more closely until you genuinely recognize the conditioned aspect of concentrated states. Reflect that the state has been volitionally produced, is impermanent, and subject to change. Once you recognize the undependable quality of all conditioned states, you cease to adhere to things that are changing and conditioned—which you have probably figured out by now includes just about everything! Even if conditioned states are exquisitely delightful and pleasant, a mind intent on peace and freedom will look beyond their fleeting pleasures.

Undertake this investigation with an infusion of a gentle but potent interest. When you are interested in something, you naturally look very closely to understand the true nature of what is perceived. Observe jhanic experience with the innocent interest of a child fascinated with the movement of a beetle walking over pebbles. Or take your inspiration from the astronomer who repeatedly gazes through a telescope and patiently considers the movements of stars. Adjust the quality of investigation so that your observation does not impede the functioning of the subtle states. Overly vigorous investigation can agitate the distilled mind.

LOOK CLOSELY

When removed from sounds, thoughts, and varied sensations, the mind settles into its essential features. When the mind is thus concentrated, conditions are superb for clear seeing. If, however, you remain too long in deeply still absorptions, the factors of mindfulness and investigation can grow sluggish, inert, or dulled through disuse. Perception might feel rusty rather than agile if it remains sunk for too long in deep seclusion. The mind sometimes can feel stretched thin by excessively sustained absorptions, perhaps too thin to want to encounter chaotic confrontations with sensory phenomena.

Attentive to the dynamic balance of calm unification and mindful interest, a wise meditator moderates the duration and depth of absorption and adjusts the practice to obtain a useful blend of energy, tranquillity, and clarity. This may require moving between the jhanas more frequently, entering and exiting the jhanas in shorter intervals, intertwining the practices of samadhi and vipassana.

Develop the ability to move flexibly, like an accordion, flexing and extending awareness. Once this system is learned, meditators will find it remarkably easy to slide into deep states. There is no value, however, to falling into jhana like soiled linen tossed down a laundry chute. No skill is involved in going straight down. At all times each state should remain responsive to the meditator's intention and afford a flexible basis for insight. Although jhana produces a beautiful, still peacefulness, if attention emerges disoriented, or with the critical faculty of mindfulness dulled or impaired, it is not the right concentration taught by the Buddha.

⌒ CULTIVATING MASTERY

The following exercises drawn from the traditional teachings can strengthen the absorptions and cultivate mastery in jhana. I recommend that meditators engage with these exercises from the time that the first jhana is well established, exploring and enhancing their concentration regarding each jhana before advancing to the next level.

EXERCISE ONE Expand the experience of each jhana by suffusing, drenching, filling, and pervading consciousness with the dominant jhanic factors. Experience the broad, full, and spacious quality of mind utterly absorbed in the pertinent flavor of happiness (gladness, rapture, contentment, or equanimity).

Then intentionally narrow the focus to a one-pointed clarity with the nimitta. Let the attention pulsate from broad recognition to a more narrowly focused one; alternate between these two modes while maintaining unification with the pertinent jhanic factors. Let piti, sukha, or upekkha intensify with the narrow focus and permeate the mind and body in the expanded mode.

EXERCISE TWO Work with a very soft whisper of intention to move between the jhanas. The jhanic mind is so malleable that even a subtle intention will have a dramatic impact; the bare arousal of a simple resolution will be quite enough. Learn what is enough, and what effort is too coarse for the refinement of each state. Incline toward doing less; trust the gentler options. Let these shifts happen without force and without difficulty.

EXERCISE THREE Skill in determining the duration of an absorption is essential for attainment of formless perceptions. This skill is developed by diligent practice. Prior to entering a jhana, resolve to emerge at a predetermined time. Start with five, ten, or fifteen minutes; if that goes well, try thirty, forty, sixty, or one hundred and twenty minutes.

EXERCISE FOUR Know clearly what is present and what is absent in each jhana. Observe carefully. After emerging from absorption, consciously reflect upon your observations. Notice the texture of mind: is it malleable, flexible, limber? How does attention respond to intention? In addition to the primary five jhanic factors, take note of all the mental factors that arise in jhana. Become aware of how these mental factors function in the altered state of jhana. How does energetic effort affect the quality of the absorption?

Recognize mindfulness functioning when no sensory object is present. Let interest discern which faculties are active or dormant. Through these explorations you will know from your own experience, without the slightest hesitation, without referring to ideas or texts, what characterizes each jhana and how to distinguish each state.

After establishing at least the first three jhanas, incorporate the next two exercises.

EXERCISE FIVE Clarify the entrance into and defining features of each jhana by moving back and forth through the sequence of jhanas. Develop skill and greater awareness by moving in forward order, reverse order, by systematically skipping first through the odd numbers (jumping from the first to the third jhana and then back to the first jhana), then through the even numbers (jumping from the second jhana to the fourth jhana and back to the second jhana), and then jumping between jhanas in a random order.

EXERCISE SIX Attain each jhana directly from access: access to first jhana, exit and return to access; access to second jhana, exit and then return to access; repeat this process through all levels of jhana. You can achieve this most easily by connecting with the whole breath before and after each absorption.

CHAPTER 16
Summary of Meditation Instructions

A T THIS STAGE it would be valuable for us to review in summary form the meditation instructions we have covered in this book. This chapter provides a checklist for jhana practice that you may refer to as you establish the sequence of absorptions and review before moving into the final stages of our exploration of the jhanas as a means to liberation.

INITIAL ATTITUDES AND CONDITIONS

1. Guard the mind with mindfulness.
2. Establish a stability of mindful attention in the present moment.
3. Have a clear intention to focus on your meditation object: the breath.
4. Incline the attitude of the meditation toward stability and composure.
5. Understand the practice as a refinement of relinquishment rather than an accumulation of attainments.
6. Enjoy each opportunity to abandon an unwholesome state or repetitive thought.
7. Cultivate attitudes of mind that are bright, spacious, and relaxed.
8. Temporarily set aside other meditation systems while you are establishing this singularity of focus. Permit your meditation practice to be utterly simple.

9. Cultivate confidence that this practice works—jhana is attainable. For over 2,600 years meditators have used these techniques to discover profound peace. Trust that the practice will work for you too—your mind is no exception.

BEGINNING THE FOCUSED MEDITATION TECHNIQUE

1. Connect and sustain the attention at the point of occurrence of the breath with diligent penetrating interest.
2. Count 1–10–1, 1–10–1 for a few minutes to strengthen the focus on the breath.
3. If distracting thoughts persist, count 1, 1, 1, 1, 1, 2, 2, 2, 2, 2, 2, 3, 3, 3, 3, 3, 3, . . . reconnecting repeatedly as you attend to the whole breath.
4. Learn to abandon all unwholesome states.
5. Notice mind as it brightens and coheres. Notice the arising of the jhanic factors.
6. Infuse the awareness of breath with delight and happiness while steadfastly focusing on the breath.
7. Examine the experience of the absence of hindrances to become familiar with the quality of an undefiled awareness.

ESTABLISHING ACCESS TO ABSORPTION

1. Notice when the physicality of the sensations diminish and a dominant luminosity arises in the mind: the appearance of the counterpart sign (nimitta).
2. Shift the attention from the physicality of sensory experience to this radiant light or to the bare mental functions of directing and sustaining attention.
3. Resolve for the growth and increase of the jhanic factors.
4. Gladden the mind with the perception of the absence of hindrances; learn to trust your mind by abiding without hindrances.

SEQUENTIAL PROGRESSION

1. When the mind is very bright, cohesive, undisturbed by thoughts, and unhindered by desire, aversion, or doubt, insert the resolve: "May I enter and abide in the first jhana."
2. Let the mind rest in the purity of this state.
3. Observe the inward quality of mental cohesion in the first jhana.
4. Allow vitakka and vicara to settle, then focus with rapt interest on the nimitta to attain the second jhana.
5. Become dispassionate toward piti as it fades in order to shift to the third jhana. Let the mind unify with the subtle happiness of sukha.
6. Relinquish any attachment to sukha to attain the fourth jhana.
7. Follow the single-pointed stillness into a stable absorption characterized by a neutral expression of equanimity.

STRENGTHENING ABSORPTION

1. Alternate between a narrow focus on the nimitta and the expansive energy of diffusing, pervading, and suffusing consciousness with the rapture, pleasure, or happiness distinctive of the jhana.
2. Let the happiness saturate the entire body and mind.
3. Sustain the jhana gently, with joy, interest, and ease.
4. If the seclusion begins to weaken with the influx of a few thoughts, infuse attention with interest to maintain the unification.
5. Avoid trying to adjust the jhana; a detached equanimous observation that values the separation from unwholesome states is often enough to release back into absorption.
6. Give attention to the stability, quality, and clarity of each jhanic factor.
7. Develop the agility to enter and exit without difficulty.
8. Jump between the levels of jhana.
9. Rest deeply in each of these pleasant abidings.
10. Relax, doing nothing, observing quietly.
11. Trust the concentration to deepen on its own.

USING JHANA AS A BASIS FOR INSIGHT

1. Examine what is present and what is absent in the mind in all stages.
2. Relinquish the seclusion after each absorption. Let the jhana dissolve and observe the dissipation of the jhanic factors and the secluded state.
3. Become aware of all things as they naturally occur.
4. Use each stage as a basis for insight before aspiring to the next level.
5. Take a moment to consciously bring the session to a close with a dedication, a reflection on the session, recommitment to your aim, gentle movement, or contemplation of the relevance of the meditative experience for your life.
6. Allow the experience of jhana to consciously inform your life.

PART IV
Doing the Work of Insight

CHAPTER 17
Three Doorways to Insight

When extraordinarily blissful, clear states arise from insight meditation practice, do not cling to them. Although this tranquillity has a sweet taste, it too must be seen as impermanent, unsatisfactory, and empty. Absorption is not what the Buddha found essential in meditation. Practice without thought of attaining absorption or any special state. Just know whether the mind is calm or not and, if so, whether a little or a lot. In this way it will develop on its own. . . Nevertheless, concentration must be firmly established for wisdom to arise. To concentrate the mind is like turning on the switch, and wisdom is the resulting light. Without the switch, there is no light, but we should not waste our time playing with the switch.

— Ajahn Chah[1]

I T IS UNLIKELY that insight will occur as a spectacular event marked by celestial music and fireworks. It will be much simpler: seeing things without attachment, as they are, rather than as we wish they were.

There is a story about a wisely foolish Sufi saint, Mullah Nasrudin:

Mullah was walking down the village street when some street kids began to throw stones at him.

"Don't do that, and I will tell you something that will interest you," Nasrudin said.

"All right, what is it? But no philosophy," the street kids replied.

"The Emir is giving a free banquet to all comers."

The children ran off toward the Emir's house as Nasrudin warmed to his theme, " . . . the delicacies and the delights of the entertainment . . ."

He looked up and saw them disappearing in the distance. Suddenly he tucked up his robes and started to sprint after them. "I'd better go and see. It might be true after all."[2]

Too often we ascribe reality to our desires and lose touch with what is true in the present moment. Is your experience of seeing, smelling, hearing, thinking, and sensing clear, or is it distorted by misperception?

Imagine you are walking along a forest path at dusk and see something partially coiled and partially stretched across the path just a step or two ahead. Startled as the thought of a snake occupies the mind, you stand frozen with fear. As you are caught in the grip of this misperception, your heart races, fear overtakes your mind, and then—afflicted with a flurry of emotional responses—your mind jumps back and forth between strategies of escape and scenarios of danger. As you stand motionless, wondering which way to step to avoid the snake, you notice that the snake has not moved. Looking more carefully you discover that it is not a snake; it is only a rope.

The story of the snake and the rope is a familiar rendering of the problem of seeing clearly. This ancient teaching story has been retold for thousands of years reminding us that problems are solved by clear seeing. We don't turn a snake into a rope. We don't need to make things different than they are. We simply bring our attention to the reality of things. When encountering conditioned phenomena, we observe their fundamental characteristics as *impermanent, unreliable,* and *not self.* Armed with the striking clarity of this knowledge, the mind can find nothing to cling to, crave for, or identify with.

IMPERMANENCE, UNSATISFACTORINESS, AND NOT-SELF

The Pali term *vipassana,* generally translated as "insight," literally means "clear seeing." Vipassana is not simply a meditation technique. Vipassana is fundamentally about clear perception. Liberating insight may manifest when a meditator clearly recognizes three specific characteristics—*anicca* (impermanence), *dukkha* (unsatisfactoriness), and *anatta* (not-self)— because they diminish the tendency to cling.

Everyone has experienced phenomena changing. Weather changes. Bodies alter with age. All material and mental conditions are impermanent and inconstant. Things increase and decrease, expand and contract, begin and end. Awareness of change is not shocking to most people. Few, however, penetrate this fundamental perception sufficiently to arrive at a state of liberation through not-clinging.

Undoubtedly you have experienced the unsatisfactory, undependable, and stressful quality of things as they decay, break, or are lost. Pain is an obvious expression of suffering. Dukkha, more subtle than mere physical or mental pain, reveals the underlying undependable aspect of things. A deeper understanding of dukkha arises when we recognize that impermanent experiences cannot be a reliable basis for happiness. You might experience this quality of dukkha not only through explicit suffering, but also in the subtler discontent of, perhaps, wanting just a little more.

Whether you realize it or not, you have probably experienced the absence of an inherently existing essence we call *self.* You are not who you were yesterday. Your cells change. Experience changes. Ideas, opinions, and feelings change. Which one, if any, of these provides a stable definition of you? Examine your perceptions to discover if you can find someone behind your experience. Is there a fixed essence called *self* to whom your life happens? We all taste, but who or what knows the taste? We see, but who or what sees? Look deeply into your experience of perception. Does this sense of self that we conventionally call "I" have color, shape, location, or attributes? Is there an intrinsic being lurking behind the face, inside the rib cage, or in the elbow who would claim experiences as *I, me,* or *mine?* Usually the sense of a continuous self arises when we identify with thoughts, affiliations, or possessions. Yet when we examine our experience closely, nothing can be found that allows us to say, "This is really self."

Confusion arises when the term *anatta* is misunderstood as *no-self,* rather than *not-self.* The language of *no-self* sometimes creates a false impression that Buddhist teachings negate existence, whereas the teachings of *not-self* invite a precise investigation into what exactly the concept of self relies upon. What does the term *self* refer to?

Insight into anatta does not require a blanket negation of self-constructs. Through investigation we discover that every experience of body, mind, perception, or feeling is in fact not self. Self does not exist as a thing; self does not exist in anything. When we have clearly perceived this, identification with experience fades and the mind rests in profound detachment and ease. The insight into anatta manifests in the moment you are not taking life personally.

Vipassana offers systematic approaches—such as mindfulness with breathing practices, techniques that develop mindfulness of body, emotions, and mental states, and skills to investigate present-moment perception—that heighten awareness of the three primary insights. When directly perceiving anicca, you do not cling. When deeply perceiving dukkha, you do not cling. When clearly perceiving anatta, you do not cling. Shine the spotlight of attention onto these three characteristics until it results in liberating insight.

Recognizing these three characteristics is called *seeing with wisdom*. When you see with wisdom, you replace your former infatuation with sensory experience with an attention that is markedly disenchanted. This is an important distinction for the meditation practitioner to perceive. You do not *practice* disenchantment. You practice clear seeing; disenchantment naturally ensues. When you see with wisdom, the deluded view that seeks gratification through the senses ends. The connection with the senses continues, but it is altered by this perspective of disenchantment. Observing the fragile qualities of existence, you become disenchanted with conditioned things as a foundation for happiness. When you recognize that fleeting phenomena are not under your control, your enchantment with self-grasping ceases. When you perceive clearly, you discover a liberating disenchantment.

This transformation constitutes insight.[4]

FETTERED BY DESIRE

To experience liberating wisdom, you do not need to abandon particular *objects*. Objects and experiences are not the problem. The trouble lies

---

✎ HIGHLIGHTING DISENCHANTMENT

Observe the quality of disenchantment as it occurs in simple ways: perhaps as you turn away from attractive perceptions, or change tasks throughout the day.

What does the mind feel like when it is enthralled with a sensory experience?

What occurs when that seduction ends?

As you walk around the block and see a beautiful sunset, or as you savor a delicious meal, notice the moment when you are seduced into the experience.

Then observe the moment when the mind releases that enchantment and moves on to the next thing. No one exists transfixed the entire day by a single sensory pleasure.

Observe disenchantment occurring as you move from one activity to the next; as you are attracted to and then fail to notice various sensory stimuli; as you make this food choice, then that; and as you alter your recreational preferences.

Highlight and study mundane experiences of disenchantment in your daily routine.

Then, during formal meditation, observe this same dynamic. Disenchantment plays an essential role: it makes the seclusion of the first jhana possible. Notice the function of disenchantment in the transitions between jhanas, as each factor is released. Observe closely as it arises in a moment of clearly perceiving the impermanent, undependable, and empty nature of things.

---

in the indulgence, attachment, infatuation, and confusion that presumes "things" can be the basis of lasting happiness. Don't let go of objects; *release the grip of clinging and attachment* instead.

A simile the Buddha repeatedly used describes a black ox and a white ox yoked together.[5] One would not say that the black ox is the fetter of the white ox, or that the white ox is the fetter of the black ox. The yoke is the fetter. This simile can be applied to our experience.

Thoughts and experience are the black and the white oxen; desire, titillation, and clinging constitute the yoke that fetters. We abandon the yoke; thoughts and experiences remain.

Sometimes people don't recognize the fetter of desire because they are entranced by the hope that *this* sensation, *this* idea, *this* sight, *this* taste, *this* meditative experience will be the one that will "do it once and for all," that will bring ceaseless happiness. As you review your previous sensory experiences, consider how many sensory contacts you have already had in your lifetime. Were any capable of providing secure pleasure? If these didn't make you happy and peaceful, why would another one do it? Have you learned from your experience that conditioned phenomena are not a cause of lasting joy?

Jhana may be considered a bend in the metaphorical road to awakening, the place where the vista opens onto a breathtaking insight. Eventually, however, the selective attention that jhana depends upon must also be relinquished as the mind opens in a full response of living insight. Ultimately the path leads beyond the force of grasping, beyond the duality of this and that, things and nothings, confinement and spaciousness, form and formlessness, and beyond any subset of concentrated states. The freedom of release reveals something beyond the equipoise of equanimity and concentration.

Insight can arise at any time—in the midst of mundane daily interactions or during profound spiritual quests. A flash of insight may bring new perspectives to personal psychological patterns or inspire creative ideas for a project at work. A surprising vision might arise and inspire a painting. Or, you may find yourself mysteriously oriented toward something utterly sublime. As your awareness expands beyond self-interest, you might awaken to a realization of what the Buddhist tradition refers to as the unconditioned, the ultimate, the inexpressible, the immeasurable, the deathless—the end of all distress.

IN THIS FATHOM-LONG BODY

The Buddha taught that everything you need for liberating insight can be found by looking into your own experience. "It is in this fathom-long

---

⌒ SENSING PRESENT AWARENESS

Right now, as you are reading these words, sense present awareness, that natural open knowing of things as they are.

Feel the contact with your chair, feel the temperature of the body, feel the sensations of the breath moving, notice the sounds in the environment, sense the texture of the pages on your fingertips.

As you experience the simplicity of present-moment contacts, without dwelling on or preferring any particular perception, feel the factual flow of experience.

Notice what you are experiencing in this moment.

Experience now, without past or future, and see if there is any problem with the present.

Let this experience of simple and clear presence register within.

Look into the present moment and see what it is.

What is your relationship to present-moment experience?

---

body with its perceptions and thoughts that there is the world, the origin of the world, the cessation of the world, and the path leading to the cessation of the world."[6] Don't look for fancy insights or expect huge openings of heart. Rather, just see what happens when you allow your basic relationship to sensory experience to be relaxed and free of grasping.

If we expect freedom to be a far out and spectacular experience, we may miss the intimacy of the timeless expression of an unbound mind. Repeatedly the Buddha referred to liberation not as an isolated, reified state, but as something more accessible: a wise and peaceful encounter with everyday sensory contact. He taught that "the supreme state of sublime peace" manifests as wisdom regarding all sensory contacts, and summarized it as "liberation through not clinging."[7] Whatever understanding we have must be brought to bear on our sensory experience. Since it is in our sensory contact where grasping may erupt, there is where we will come to know a profound absence of clinging.

BENEFITS OF CONCENTRATING THE MIND

Many benefits come with practicing jhana: making space in the otherwise hectic bustle of your days; learning to disentangle yourself from chronic distraction; and enjoying the pleasures of a unified mind. These are alluring and valuable aspects of concentration practice. From a Buddhist perspective, however, they are merely the fringe benefits, not the reason for concentrating the mind.

The only reason for developing samadhi genuinely worth your time is that it supports liberating insight, insight that will ultimately allow you to become free from all distress. Concentration is the ground out of which liberating wisdom arises. The Buddha advised us to develop concentration, because, "one who is concentrated understands things as they really are."[8] Understanding the interdependence of wisdom and concentration is fundamental to creating an effective and balanced spiritual life.

Wisdom goes beyond insight into the ways you are habitually distracted. With the steadiness of samadhi, your awareness can penetrate subtler aspects of experience: the pervasiveness of change and the undependable quality of conditioned things. In particular, it will discover the subtle forms of clinging, where the illusion of "I" arises and clings to perceptions. Samadhi supports this sustained inquiry so that deep truths can be realized.

The traditional instructions describe jhana as the process that makes the mind "fit to be worked" or "fit for work."[9] The Buddha used the analogy of purifying gold to describe the purification of mind. Gold is worked until the metal becomes pliant, strong, malleable, pure, and ready to be shaped into any ornament or object the goldsmith desires to produce.[10]

> There are these five corruptions of gold, corrupted by which gold is neither malleable nor wieldy nor radiant but brittle and not properly fit for work. What five? Iron is a corruption of gold, corrupted by which gold is neither malleable nor wieldy nor radiant, but brittle and not properly fit for work. Copper . . . Tin . . . Lead . . . Silver . . . These are the five corruptions of gold, corrupted by which gold is neither malleable nor wieldy nor radiant but brittle and not properly fit for work. . . .

So too, there are these five corruptions of the mind, corrupted by which the mind is neither malleable nor wieldy nor
radiant but brittle and not rightly concentrated for the destruction of the taints. What five? Sensual desire is a corruption of the
mind . . . ill will . . . sloth and torpor . . . restlessness . . . doubt is a
corruption of the mind. These are the five corruptions of the
mind, corrupted by which the mind is neither malleable nor
wieldy nor radiant but brittle and not rightly concentrated for
the destruction of the taints.[11]

The meditative process enables you to overcome these classic five
hindrances, to purify the mind, and make it pliant and responsive to your
deepest intentions, until nothing remains to corrupt attention. The traditional texts describe the quality of mind that is ready to work as: "concentrated, purified and cleansed, unblemished, free from impurities,
malleable, workable, established, and having gained imperturbability."[12]
The seclusion of jhana preserves mental energies and the mind grows
remarkably bright, malleable, and fit for work. Thus, jhana prepares the
mind to solve the problem of suffering.

As a child I enjoyed sharpening my pencils—cranking the handle of
the sharpener that was mounted on the classroom wall and watching the
shavings fill the container below. I'd sharpen a bit and then inspect the
point, sharpening more and more until I was satisfied with the point.
Sometimes I would sharpen away the better part of the pencil seeking a
refined point. Now I have a small battery-powered pencil sharpener on
my desk. It reminds me of the purpose of concentration. Concentration
sharpens the mind; it serves no purpose, however, to seek a perfectly
refined state. Once the mind is sufficiently clear and sharp, use it. Just as
it is childish to enjoy sharpening pencils so much that we shave until the
pencil finally disappears, we should not fritter away our time just playing
with jhana. We can apply whatever degree of mental refinement we
develop to a purpose: attaining liberating insight.

Time goes by, retreats end, health fades, and inevitably death comes.
Life progresses quickly. How much concentration is needed for insight
will depend upon the practice conditions, inclinations, interests, and disposition of each individual. There is no objective measurement for how

sharp a pencil needs to be to write, or how deep an absorption needs to be for insight. A pointy pencil that sits in a desk drawer is of little value. A concentrated mind that merely abides in pleasant states is equally friv- olous. Whatever degree of concentration you are able to establish will be your resource for awakening. Use it to free the mind!

WHAT IS THE WORK THAT NEEDS TO BE DONE?

Even though astonishing, almost miraculous powers can be generated through jhanic levels of concentration, the Buddha forbade his monas- tics from displaying such attainments. We don't develop the mind to feel concentrated or impress friends.

The Buddha's teachings guide our attention toward those particular insights that have the potential to liberate. A mindfulness practitioner is trained to observe both the specific and general characteristics of phe- nomena. For example, anger is specifically characterized by heat, agita- tion, tension, pressure in the head, coarseness of thought, and rudeness of speech. Pain is specifically characterized by sharpness, burning, searing, pulsing, and stabbing. The characteristics associated with lustful fantasies are longing, infatuation, clinging, and greed. When we are truly mindful of these experiences, we know anger, pain, and lust; we understand how these emotions function.

And as I've said, vipassana meditation also encourages the recogni- tion of general characteristics: impermanence, unsatisfactoriness, and emptiness. For example, when your attention becomes entangled in a planning scenario, investigate your thinking by noticing the particular qualities attributed to that thought—it might be excited, joyful, resent- ful, pleasant, or peaceful. Then observe how thought is subject to change. Perceive the beginning and ending of thoughts. Recognize the universal fact that thought is an unreliable foundation for happiness: because it changes, thought cannot be a lasting source of security. Investigate the lack of intrinsic essence to thought; see that there is no permanent entity to whom this thought refers. Mindfulness allows you to discriminate specific and general characteristics in any perception. A willingness to investigate makes it possible to open to the universal qualities that all things share.

And yet, it is important to resist the urge to grasp insight. Observe all perceptions with detachment. If you become fixated on a vipassana technique, jhanic attainment, or perception of impermanence, you are just as trapped as if you were attached to a tuna-fish sandwich. Fascinated with observing change, otherwise diligent students sometimes falter. Stagnation can occur if repeated observations of impermanence are hailed as the markers of success. Any form of attachment, to jhanic pleasures or to the brightness of insight, can halt progress. The self will try to take a stand upon these attainments, creating an illusion it exists through association with meditative accomplishment. Then the entrapping concept of "being a meditator" is born. Recognize this construction; it presents the dangerous first step toward attachment to the concept of "a realized self."

Sometimes you may have great insights—and indeed insight can feel so pleasing, vast, and luminous that one confuses it with the satisfaction of completeness. Vigilance is necessary to see if the liberation is truly lasting, or if it rigidifies around a view of enlightenment. Observe if the ease truly ends clinging or is merely the recollection of a peaceful moment that passed. Continued alertness in the midst of profound "Ah-ha" experiences keeps the examination alive until you are certain that there is no more work left to do and your deepest intention is fulfilled.

Let go of every fixation. Ultimately this is a path of release. The mind may attempt to construct itself on any foundation: through attachment to blissful jhanic states; by becoming "the one who lets go"; by being "the meditator who understands change." Observe and laugh at the antics of the mind. Coax it to release its hold, even its attachment to good things. Uproot any place you find yourself stuck in, whether it be with the pleasures of the tranquil mind of jhana or in the clarity of insight. Resist the urge to keep score of your insights. Assessing your meditation practice only fuels grasping.

Willingness to let go is indispensable. Every stage of this path requires a complete relinquishment of both the struggles and the delights, pleasant experiences and painful ones. Even the states of samadhi that you diligently cultivate must, in the end, be relinquished.

The refined sublimity of the final formless state is considered "the best object of clinging,"[13] but the Buddha encourages disciples to not cling even to the base of neither-perception-nor-non-perception, because only "[one] who is without clinging attains Nibbana."[14] Any form of clinging, even to concentration, is undesirable. As you see the limitations of each conditioned state, the state will dissipate. Every refinement you cultivate will dissolve. Regarding all the wholesome and wonderful developments of concentration, including all the levels of jhana, the Buddha said, "That, I say, is not enough. Abandon it, I say; surmount it, I say."[15]

This discipline is not a practice of preferring one thing over another, of taking the subtle and leaving the gross, or of trading petty sensual desires for jhanic bliss. In mastering the jhanas, you will have sequenced through an extremely refined system of relinquishment to develop the capacity to let go. One of the greatest insights regarding things is also obvious: "Whatever is subject to origination is subject to cessation."[16] Whatever perceptions arise cannot be clung to. The Buddha's instruction was "to abandon desire for whatever is impermanent, suffering, and not-self."[17]

You don't really need to let go of much—only the delusion of misperception. In doing so, you will quickly discover the ultimate peacefulness of the Buddha's instruction, "Abandon what is not yours; this will lead to your happiness for a long time."[18]

Insight is immediate recognition that moves consciousness beyond the fragmentation of the conceptual mind. It is an order of knowing not bound by the intellect nor limited to ideas and concepts; very often it cannot be reduced to language. Yet insight has the power to release the tension of attachment and end the strain of clinging.

Seeing things as they are will open you to the truth of being. You will rest at peace in the fluidity of sensory contacts while in the midst of active living. Insight does not depend on retreat conditions, silence, or secluded absorption states.

Insight that matters transforms our lives!

CHAPTER 18
A New Way of Seeing

When the eyes and the ears are open, even the leaves on the trees teach like pages from the scriptures.

—Kabir

J HANA CREATES A UNIQUE FRAME OF MIND to observe the changing nature of things. Quietly emerging from absorption, the mind is stable, strong, and energetic as it meets the dynamic flow of things. The concentration you accumulate through samadhi can be your vantage point for insight.

This chapter explores the transition from seclusion to contact, from samadhi to vipassana—how to utilize jhana to flexibly shift from concentrated states into the clarity of sensory contact.

Sustained absorption in happy states changes the shape of the mind, affecting its tendencies and patterns, inclining it toward joy and ease. Concentration alone, however, does not have the power to make us free. We must join concentration, mindfulness, investigation, and wisdom to generate an unshakable deliverance from suffering. Concentration temporarily suspends preoccupation with desires and aversions and provides relief through a state of desirelessness. However, this peace is born of seclusion, not wisdom. It depends on specific conditions and hence is vulnerable to change.

The effort it takes to sustain jhana reveals the defect of jhanic states. Notice what you must do to sustain absorption in jhana. That subtle intentional effort reveals the limitations of the conditioned state: jhana is produced through volition and effort and hence vulnerable to change.

The moment jhana dissolves—the shift from the seclusion of absorption to the perception of the senses—provides a strategic opportunity for insight. Thoughts, sensations, and images arise. How this flood of impressions is perceived will have a deep impact on the mind. This is due to the purity that accrued during jhana. When a mind is concentrated, it feels less "sticky," less prone to grasp at things it likes or react against things it does not like. This dispassion provides a bridge between the peaceful secluded state and direct, wise contact with worldly life. Insight backed by the potency of jhana has tremendous strength to free the mind from suffering.

EXAMINING THE DISSOLUTION OF JHANA

When the mind is absorbed, there is little complexity and few causes of distraction. In other words, there is not much going on! Mindfulness is still functioning within jhana, although one is not mindful of ordinary sensory contacts. The mind is vividly alert, but sensory stimulation is not perceived. Hindrances may arise after jhana; however, while the jhanic factors are dominant, the mind remains at ease.

The Pali Canon likens applying reflection to the emergence from jhana to an archer practicing with a straw target before going into battle.[1] A meditator who observes the characteristics of impermanence, unsatisfactoriness, and not-self revealed within the less complex conditions of a concentrated mind later applies that understanding to the potentially confusing encounters of worldly life. The limited range of factors present in a concentrated mind make for safe and easy practice. In particular, subtle insights that arise during jhana practice are often related to this narrow range of pleasant states. We can see, for example, the impermanence of rapture, the undependability of sustained attention, and the impersonal quality of consciousness. In this safe practice ground, the meditator can explore the unreliability of pleasure as a basis for real happiness, then boldly shift beyond this protected arena of absorption to realize insight without boundaries.

Observe how jhana dissolves and perception engages with the sensory world. Many changes occur as the factors of concentration diminish. Notice how qualities of happiness, pleasure, cohesion, concentration, one-pointedness, and equanimity change during the transition from deep jhana to sensory experience. They may increase or decrease. They may disappear altogether. The energies of piti, sukha, and upekkha may take on a more physical quality, with energy pulsing through the body. Observe the impermanence and conditionality of the dominant jhanic factor during this transition.

The meditator has invested a great deal of time and energy in cultivating these jhanic attainments by developing the qualities of a refined, concentrated, and beautiful mind. She can now watch these very factors, so lovingly nurtured, as they dissipate. This is the pivotal moment for investigation: *Is there any clinging or attachment?*

Attachment to the pleasant experience of absorption is an inherent risk in jhana practice. Look carefully for any attachment to happiness, rapture, and concentration. The very investment made in achieving absorption creates the opportunity for attachment to slip in.

Practicing jhana as the basis for insight is a little like the practice of the Tibetan sand mandala. These extraordinary ornate paintings are made of colored sand. Their construction demands years of training and diligent attention. No matter how perfectly formed, the painting is ritually destroyed and literally brushed away once completed. Similarly we carefully construct samadhi, but lurking beneath our efforts may be an unseen desire for permanent satisfaction. As you move out of jhana, experience how the conditioned impermanent quality shines gloriously.

The cultivation of wholesome states within jhana occurs within the broader context of practicing non-attachment. Even slight attachment will be seen truly as suffering to such a clarified mind. We create these strong jhanic states in order to watch them dissolve, and thus train the mind in nonattachment. We strive for the best possible experience meditative effort can bring and then, by design, must witness its demise. Jhanic factors are our straw target. Jhana, as the basis for insight, fuses development of what is wholesome with complete relinquishment of any perception that consciousness might fix on.

The residue of absorption can bring a spacious clarity to vipassana practice. It is worthwhile to explore how the mind unified through samadhi meets sensory contact. In the transition period immediately following absorption, observe the factors change. After they have diminished, gently allow mindfulness to meet whatever else may be occurring in the body and mind. The breath may become apparent. Attention may be drawn toward sounds. The flood of sensory data sometimes feels intrusive, overwhelming, and confusing; don't worry—quietly watch it all unfold. Simply recognize sensations and thoughts as they arise and change. With a calm and stable mind, examine the nature of sense impressions and do not be swept away by conceptual proliferation or reactivity.

Be curious as you meet the sensory world. What happens when you hear a sound? During absorption, you perceive no sounds, but when jhana dissolves, you hear all sorts of things: a person moving, a bird outside, the drips of a water faucet, your own breath. How does consciousness know it is hearing, or what it is hearing? Inquire: *Is this a simple experience of hearing, or does my mind move toward the sound, constructing a relationship that postulates self, preference, desire, or aversion?*

In jhana there were no bodily experiences. In a post-jhana state, there may well be pain, pleasure, or sensations of warmth and coldness. You will become aware of your posture. How are these physical experiences known? Are they felt with a balanced mind, or is there a critical commentary attached? In absorption, there are no hindrances of desire or aversion. But without the protection of seclusion, these mental states may arise again. Notice if judgment, comparison, or confusion arises. Do perceptions stimulate desire, craving, fear, aversion, or agitation? Work with whatever hindrances you find. Having practiced letting go of attachment to tranquillity, happiness, and rapture as your "straw target," now you can use these skills to abandon coarser painful hindrances. Understand them as nothing more than changing mental states.

Explore how perception occurs. Notice if the mind wraps itself around objects by conceiving of things as *I, me,* or *mine.* Observe very carefully what happens when you shift from a secluded state into the non-secluded state of sensory perception; the first moment is critical.

Open to that instant between the seclusion of jhana, before perception constructs fixed concepts. Notice especially the quality of mind that is unfixed, and how fixation occurs. As you perceive this transition, reflect: *What is the activity of fixation?* Examine whatever occurs as if this were your first encounter with life.

The "higher" jhanas do not necessarily yield better insights than the "lower" ones. For liberating insight, the first jhana has all the conditions you need. The first four jhanas plus three formless perceptions are traditionally used as a direct basis for insight, and insight from the perspective of the last formless attainment is gained through reflection. Whatever concentration is established as you move through the jhanas can be applied progressively to seeing the nature of things. It is always possible to create another vantage point for insight by deepening the concentration to the next level of absorption. On the other hand, you may be liberated in the early stages—after all, why not? It is a simple matter of not-clinging!

EXITING JHANA

Within the field of absorption, perception is restrained. After absorption ends, sensations and thoughts arise uninvited—the beautiful ones as well as the forbidden. Absorption states are like a fenced-in ring, an arena where only certain factors are allowed inside. In order to establish jhana, you guarded and restrained the mind. After you emerge, the quality of practice shifts remarkably as restraints are lifted. Without emphasizing tranquil and happy feelings, without rejecting challenging emotions, you can experience the present moment with an awareness as vast as a huge bowl that holds all things. Accept the flow of everything, balanced in the midst of it all.

The powerful energy accumulated through jhana can meet any experience without bias. Be careful not to squander this concentrated energy. The momentum of attention as you emerge from absorption can be very strong. Channel this energy toward insight. Don't let it scatter. These initial post-jhana moments may be disconcerting or invigorating. It matters little whether the perceptions are calming or agitating. As you encounter the world of sensory experience, examine that contact. The jhanic mind might be revitalized and fresh, or cautious and delicate. Respect the depth of absorption; take the transition slowly and gently. Feel your way into a mindful encounter with the dynamic world without force.

To exit jhana, there is no need to actively abolish the jhanic state. Ceasing to hold the factors in one-pointed awareness is usually sufficient. If you need a stronger demarcation, try exiting with a resolve such as: "May I abide in full awareness," "May jhana dissolve and I see all things clearly," "May I rest in open clear awareness of what actually occurs." Or, make a mental gesture of opening the mind as you would open your fist. However, if you have been practicing with determining the time of absorption before entering each jhana, you may well find that the jhana automatically crumbles when the time period is reached.

Let go of expectations that something marvelous will happen when jhana dissolves. Don't be too disappointed if the world is just as wacky, painful, and imperfect as when you entered absorption. Of course it is! An explosive destruction of all defilements the moment you exit jhana is unlikely to happen. More typically the quiet mind simply knows ordinary experience as it is. Nothing fancy. Awareness meets whatever is arising without craving for more or less. Experiences remain ordinary. It is the absence of discontent that is extraordinary.

Examine how the mind emerges and meets the phenomenal world. Notice how the mind naturally apprehends perceptions. Do experiences of seeing, hearing, smelling, thinking, and feeling construct a sense of becoming someone through sensory encounters? Are experiences possessed as *mine*?

Whatever you notice is OK; you needn't manipulate the tendencies. Bring enough interest to notice what this mind is doing and how it functions. Relax in full wakefulness; observe without trying to control phenomena. Trust the strength of samadhi and have faith in your aspiration to awaken. There are no preconceptions to impose upon the experience of the present moment.

Everything is known as it really is: empty ephemeral phenomena arising out of nothing and passing away into nothing, leaving no litter, no trail, no trace. What an amazing world! And it is continuously revealed to anyone ready to behold it. If mind attends to the various changing objects in the sensory field such as sounds and sights—fine. If mind attends to perceptual functions such as how things are known—fine. If it attends to jhanic factors such as the diminishing or intensification of sukha or upekkha—fine. If it recognizes habitual dynamics, such as self-grasping or what the Buddha calls "mine-making" and "I-making"—fine. If it rests in a deeply profound release of all suffering—fine.

MORE ON THE INSIGHT PHASE OF PRACTICE

During the insight phase of practice, you may employ a variety of vipassana methods:

You can practice vipassana by observing the rise and fall of the breath at the abdomen, or by systematically moving the attention through the body, from the top of the head to the tip of the toes.

You can shift the attention between various touch points in the body.

You may rest with an open awareness of the present.

You may incline toward reflection.

You may contemplate death, observe the fluctuations of pleasant and unpleasant experiences, contemplate how the mind is affected by moods, states, and dispositions.

You may focus on the apparent construction of self.

You may develop any of the many vipassana techniques preserved by Buddhist tradition.

Or, you may abide, simply noticing when there is clinging and when there is no clinging.

There is no single right way to experience the truth of the present. Some practitioners will be inspired to employ traditional systematic exercises, others may be inclined toward less structured or intuitive explorations. Trust the process to unfold according to the wholesome force of your intention. When the mind is not running away with thoughts and sense impressions, it is open to insight. Allow this potential for insight to manifest, supported by curiosity and direct observation of reality, with or without the superstructure of formal vipassana techniques.

Simply observe the moment. Reflect: *Did you "organize" the present moment like this; did you somehow cause it to be this way?* When coming out of jhana, you may be flooded with sudden bursts of sensations. Piti and sukha may flood the body with pulsing sensations. In sharp relief to the seclusion of jhana, there may be a multitude of haphazard phenomena occurring at every sense door—birds twittering, dogs barking, heat, the tingling contact of hands, thoughts arising. Bare contact with sensory life can spark the simple but profound knowledge that all this is happening without your control. It is not constructed according to your personal design. Reflect: *Since you did not organize this, maybe you don't need to resurrect habits of worry, manipulation, and judgmental comparisons that dominate most human perceptions.*

The basic perception is simply that "I" did not organize it. "I" can't control it. It is not "my" personal story, not the defining feature of "my" life. You may then wonder, what is this "I" and "mine" anyway?

Observe: *Is experience simply being known?* Or is there a secondary process of "I-making" and "mine-making" intertwined with perception? "Not-self" is not merely a Buddhist concept to understand intellectually. It must be experienced. With the stability of a concentrated mind, you will know for yourself when, how, and if self-grasping arises in a moment of contact. You will also know when perception is crisply free from the distortions of what we can playfully call "*selfing.*"

It is helpful to bring this understanding into the meditation practice. Wisdom and equanimity encourage acceptance through a present relationship with whatever is happening. Can you be present with dullness as well as with clarity? Are you interested in irritation as well as appreciation? Are both the experience of the unconcentrated mind and the concentrated mind worthy of being recognized? Mindfulness is without bias, prejudice, and preference. It readily recognizes whatever occurs. Through that total acceptance, insight into all things unfolds. Insight can quench a craving heart, like a tall glass of lemonade on a sultry summer's day quenches the thirst. It is distinctly refreshing, tantalizing, exciting—tart and sweet at the same time.

Tremendous happiness can follow insight. Experiencing change without the entanglement of attachment provides a joy greater than anything tasted in jhana. Contemplate the fading away of attachment with a big relaxed grin. Allow direct insights to resonate deep within the heart.

In the quest for liberation, the transitory states of jhanic delights have a practical function, but no intrinsic value. Enlightenment is not a special secluded state. Enlightenment is defined as the eradication of lust, hate, and delusion. When you are in the midst of sensory contact, let insight dissolve any residue of lust, anger, and confusion, and radically transform your relationship to life. This is the greatest seclusion; this is the end of all suffering.

Sit in the midst of things, occupying the vantage point traditionally likened to a great throne that overlooks the city from a palace high up on the hill. Here, perched above the kingdom, a king observes all the daily functions that keep the city prosperous and safe. Assume your royal seat, observe all that occurs from this perfect vantage point. Awareness is naturally unsoiled, unruffled, unattached. You need do nothing, and there is nothing you need to undo. Empty experience, unpossessed and uncontrolled, appears and disappears, forms and dissolves.

Throughout this book I have referred to two practices: samadhi and vipassana. As facets of experience, they can be distinguished but not divided.

Conventional distinctions seem to divide calm abidings from the mindful investigation of perception; however, we simultaneously develop samadhi and vipassana. Since each jhana is conditioned and volitionally produced,[2] insight is integrated into the jhanic attainment. "Right concentration" is described as that concentration which has "release as its object."[3] The wisdom of release is a defining feature of concentration. The stability of concentration and the wisdom of release are inseparably intertwined.

Realization occurs as an undivided and limitless expression of not clinging—including not grasping views that separate samadhi and vipassana.

PART V

Experiencing the Formless Dimensions

CHAPTER 19
Without Boundaries:
Exploring the Infinite

We live in illusion and the appearance of things. There is a reality. We are that reality. When you understand this, you see that you are nothing. And being nothing, you are everything. That is all.

—Kalu Rinpoche[1]

THE FIRST MILESTONE in the development of jhana occurred when you achieved the transition between the stage of access to jhana and genuine absorption in the first jhana, radically reorienting your consciousness from the dispersal of sensory perceptions to an internal unification. To explore beyond the fourth jhana, you will need to take another quantum leap.

The shift from the fine material base of the fourth jhana to the formless perceptions begins with the clear recognition of feeling as feeling. A subtle but almost material density is intrinsic to the functioning of feeling. The fourth jhana brought feeling to its culmination: the neutrality of equanimity. What lies beyond perception and feeling? This inquiry guides awareness into the immaterial spheres.

The four formless spheres of perception share two factors with the fourth jhana: equanimity and unity of mind. The perception that characterizes each successive immaterial state, however, is more peaceful than preceding perceptions. The higher attainments are aptly described by their names: the sphere of infinite space (the fifth); the sphere of infinite consciousness (the sixth); the sphere of no-thingness (the seventh); and the sphere of neither-perception-nor-non-perception (the eighth).

Before moving to explore these higher states in your meditation, ask yourself: *Am I willing to abide without any reference to form or senses, without orientation to thoughts or mental structures?* If you are not sure, then stay with the fourth jhana. It is not prudent to force the formless spheres to occur. They are delicate states that some people find unnerving or dissociating. If you have a history of mental instability, drug use, depression, anxiety disorders, hallucinations, or if the four material jhanas are difficult for you to attain, it would be wiser to concentrate on attaining a stable grounding in the four jhanas, which provide an excellent and entirely sufficient basis for insight.

The formless spheres are not needed for liberating insight. In fact, many practitioners find that the lower states are a *more* effective basis for insight. The tranquillity of sustained absorption in formless spheres can inhibit investigation, a factor vital to the dynamic examinations needed in insight practice. Most of the teachings on jhana in the early discourses culminated with insight after the fourth jhana. Only on selective occasions did the Buddha teach disciples to explore these more altered states of consciousness.

Since some practitioners enter into these formless states uninformed, such states merit inclusion in this book. Some practitioners will find that after the saturation of happiness and peace of the four jhanas, the mind naturally inclines toward contemplating consciousness unsupported by form. This contemplation is a pure examination of mind without the obstruction of sensory objects, and without consciousness fractured by a material object to be aware of.

THE SPHERE OF INFINITE SPACE

> By passing entirely beyond bodily sensation, by the disappearance
> of all sense of resistance, and by non-attraction to the perception
> of diversity, seeing that space is infinite, he reaches and remains in
> the sphere of infinite space.[2]

This passage is the ancient instruction for attaining the base of the perception of infinite space. This occurs as an extension of the fourth jhana. Absorption in the fourth jhana leads to release of interest in diverse perceptions and allows attention to incline toward the element of boundless space. If the concentration is ripe for this experience, the attainment will occur that simply.

The *Visuddhimagga* recommends resolutely directing attention to the space left by the removal of the previous nimitta, as though one is "striking at" the sign of space with the thought of "space, space" until absorption occurs.[3] Some teachers recommend imagining the edges of your bodily field expanding out to facilitate this shift—filling the room, the area, the solar system, until finally you imagine expanding to encompass the entire universe.

I recommend a less elaborate approach: bare relinquishment. This simple and relatively uncontrived approach will work when the mind is prepared. From the fourth jhana simply relinquish all engagement with the four aspects of perception listed in the Buddha's instruction: bodily sensations, resistance, attraction to diverse perceptions, and any defining boundaries. Give your attention to whatever aspect of space you may intuit as you sense space as infinite. Relax and observe the basic aspect of space. Like a waterfall filling a pond, mind rushes in to rest in the spacious expanse.

Space has no direction—it is neither up nor down, neither in nor out. In space, there is no relationship to body or breath, no physical vibrations intrude, and conventional references are inadequate to describe a spatial field. It is a perception that is unconfined and without borders. Space is not big like a sky filled with stars; it is not small like a speck of dust. It is literally a perception without reference, formations, structures, distinctions, or particulars. It is without bounds. Infinite space cannot be described by its proportions, measurements, or dimensions. It is neither infinitely large nor infinitely small. Referential distinctions don't apply. Since material forms are absent, nothing exists to create diversity.

This is a direct perception of the fundamental aspect of infinite space. It is not a concept, idea, or notion of what space looks like, nor an experience associated with ideas. It is, rather, the simple and direct experience of infinitely extensive space known in consciousness, one glimpse into the nature of mind.

☞ EXPLORING THE SPACE BETWEEN

As you go about your daily activities:
   Notice the space between things.
   Notice the pause between breaths.
   Notice the space between thoughts.
   Rest at ease with a spacious attention.
   Notice the aspect of space whenever and wherever you can.

BOUNDARIES ARE MIND-MADE

Boundaries are arbitrary mind-made distinctions. In the perception of infinite space, the mind rests in the experience of non-locatability and non-confinability: the boundaryless nature of reality.

Contemplate this dimension: What is the separation between your hand and this book? What is the distinction between your body and the chair you sit on? Where does one end and the other begin? The perception of space invites the contemplation of how things are interrelated.

Relative stability or instability of the formless spheres is determined by the texture of mind in the fourth jhana. If your glimpse of infinite space is short-lived, if thoughts interrupt the seclusion, or the attention gets drawn out by sensations (even cooperative thoughts such as a thought about the meditation experience or mundane sensations such as a perception of breath), then you have not completely turned away from the sensory sphere. You have not set aside fully your attraction to diverse worldly perceptions. Since there is nothing to "do" in the formless realms, if you aspire to greater stability, the work must be done from the lower jhanas. Stabilize the equanimity and single-pointed focus in the fourth jhana, or strengthen mindfulness and equanimity on contact as you go about your days.

Attainment of these formless perceptions unleashes incredible energy. When the perception of form is released, tiredness vanishes; sleep might feel impossible. There is no agitation in either body or mind, yet one feels plugged into an unfathomable source of energy. Even though you may not feel the physical need to sleep, don't be fooled! The intensity of this energy demands that you care wisely for yourself. Mental balance and sanity still require a little sleep. You may need to moderate the amount of time spent in formless perceptions so that sleepless periods are not excessively prolonged beyond a few days at a time.

Undertaking an exploration of the formless dimensions of consciousness is a delicate investigation, best done with wisdom, a qualified teacher as guide, and in the protected conditions of retreat. If you are accessing formless perceptions, your consciousness is pretty far outside the ordinary framework of conventional mental functioning. Although this extreme saturation in peaceful and happy abidings may produce a sense of being invincible, you may not be as balanced as you think.

☞ FOR REFLECTION

In quiet moments after the concentrated meditation has ended, ask yourself:

What is the mind?

What are its boundaries, color, shape, location?

If you cannot find a location for mind, does this affect how you might conventionally refer to mind as a thing that you own?

EXPLORATIONS OF EMERGENCE

Explore options for emergence from the stability of the base of infinite space. For example, you might want to return to the fourth jhana for a while and practice insight from there. Shifting back and forth between the perception of space and the equanimity of the fourth jhana will clarify the experience of feeling and equanimity, highlighting what actually changes between these two levels. You might feel the vibrational field of equanimity in a new way. You might intuit the experiences of form, sense contact, and the body from a new perspective.

As you integrate the attainment of the jhana and reflect on its effect after emergence, you can let the formless perceptions inform your experience of all things. Sometimes you will notice more by moving through the jhanas in reverse order rather than in ascending order. When you move in reverse order, the lower jhanas' sense of density enhances your dispassion. The pleasant qualities that previously seemed so divine can appear almost repulsive when viewed from the perspective of formless perceptions. This viewpoint can dislodge residual enchantment with pleasure and unbind the heart from attachment to conditioned forms. You will come to know that things are fundamentally unsatisfactory, even the pleasures of equanimity.

The significance of this practice is the myriad ways in which it trains the mind to let go. When even the exquisite states of jhana feel coarse and unsatisfying, why would one cling to anything in this world? Again and again you will see there is no lasting happiness to be found through things, objects, ideas, and perceptions.

If you still haven't attained this insight, take the system to the next level. Perhaps that perspective will convince you that nothing is worth clinging to. Although practice systems can become exceedingly reified, the lesson to be learned is always the same: don't attach to anything!

☞ FOR REFLECTION

From the perspective of infinite space what can be relinquished?

In what ways do you remain identified with form?

Is there attachment to your body, appearance, health, or particular thoughts?

Consider: Are you really those thoughts? Are you really this body? Can you be limited to those frameworks of conceiving?

THE SPHERE OF INFINITE CONSCIOUSNESS

The next stage does not add anything to experience; it would be absurd to even attempt to "add something" to space. What does occur is shedding the perception of infinite space. Then, what is left to perceive?— the consciousness that was aware of infinite space. You turn attention around to perceive that which knows space. Now infinite consciousness becomes the base through which the mind unifies. This consciousness is a brilliant expanse of unbroken knowing.

The transition from the perception of infinite space to the perception of infinite consciousness entails a miniscule shift. No strain is involved, no effort to push space away, no attempt to grasp hold of consciousness. You simply become aware of the basic lucid cognizant quality of mind. The traditional phrasing is: "By passing entirely beyond the sphere of infinite space, seeing that consciousness is infinite, [one] reaches and remains in the sphere of infinite consciousness."[4]

This shift reveals an awareness that is utterly radiant and without bounds. Unrestricted lucidity has no fixed dimensions. Luminous clarity abides undefined by space and time, unrestrained by particular objects. In this state, the mind is exceptionally buoyant, light, and bright. Energy continues to seem unlimited when the mind is not heedlessly consumed by binding consciousness to diverse objects of perception. There is enormous comfort in this undistracted wakefulness. Mind is quiet and content within itself, feeling no pull into relationship through perceptions. There is no agitation, nothing to resist, nothing to gain in this extraordinarily energized and potent state of complete relaxation. With nothing to disturb your ease of concentration, you can remain absorbed for many hours at a time.

Formless dimensions are too subtle to permit active investigation. Consequently, intentional movement between these states is necessary to provide conditions for contrast and moments of reflection that can reveal the characteristics of the states themselves, and potentially liberating insights into the nature of mind.

Sequence through the lower states in reverse order, and jump between jhanas. Your mind may bounce up again into formless spheres, buoyant like a helium balloon, but coax it to return periodically to the first four jhanas. Let the experience mature by integrating your awareness of both form and the absence of form. Know consciousness in its infinite, unbounded, and unlimited aspect, and recognize how consciousness functions when engaging with mundane sensory perceptions and feelings.

Consciousness is recognized in its infinite dimension. Consciousness does not need to be bound by any object that is known. Like the perception of infinite space, infinite consciousness is neither big, large, and expanded nor infinitesimally small. It is not measurable or definable. Without boundaries, it cannot be condensed or disturbed. It is not limited by association with things. Affected by this bare perception of infinite consciousness, the texture of awareness grows very soft, open, allowing, and transparent.

After emerging from this absorption, you may find that sights, sounds, thoughts, and sensations come and go of their own accord with little or no interference from your mind. You might taste a prolonged experience of clarity without a fixed standpoint for perception; knowing is activated without grasping particular things that are known.

After some time, however, the impact of multiple sensations may stimulate familiar attachments, personal views, and comparisons. This is an opportune time for contemplating perception. The perspective gained in experiencing the infinity of consciousness is a wonderful platform for calling into question the habitual association of consciousness with its objects. Everyday innocuous experiences may become fixed perceptions.

When grasped by the mind, perceptions can become the basis for constructing a sense of being me. Not only is the external experience grasped, but an internal attachment to the one who experiences is formed. Habits of self-grasping construct a personal standpoint. This is the habit of the mind. Remembering the infinitude of consciousness, you will recognize that this formation of self-grasping is unnecessary, and then relax. Clinging is not inherent to perception. Self-grasping is merely a superfluous function, utterly trivial from the perspective of the infinite evenness of consciousness.

There is much to learn through these rare perceptions. Touching an infinite capacity of awareness casts age-old habits of identification in a new light. Let yourself laugh at the amazing absurdity of a mind that tries in vain to cling. From the perspective of infinite consciousness, grasping things is ludicrous. Why would a mind without bounds, vast beyond any concept of vastness, ever reduce itself to identification?

Why would consciousness restrict itself to the knowledge of some particular thing?

Infinite consciousness is a profound experience. Although it is softer and more subtle than the knowing of space, it is not entirely peaceful. When this conditioned aspect of the base of infinite consciousness is understood, you will realize how to move beyond its limitations. The way into the next state will be spontaneously apparent.

When the subtle veil of infinite consciousness lifts, no-thingness is instantly exposed.

☞ FOR REFLECTION

Is knowing defined by what is known?

Can you know only objects or is there a knowing beyond objects?

What is the nature of knowing?

THE SPHERE OF NO-THINGNESS

To examine the next stage of concentration, drop the perception of infinite consciousness and notice what is left. No-thing remains! Directly perceive the absence of things. You will notice that perception is still functioning; however, it is not meeting any particular object. To describe the base of no-thingness, the *Visuddhimagga* uses the illustration of entering a hall where everyone has left. Upon entering the hall, you perceive that there is nothing there. You do not think about the people who have left. Rather, you experience a clear steady perception of the absence of things. The concept of absence will become the subtle object for attention.

As the Buddha says,

> By passing entirely beyond the sphere of infinite consciousness,
> seeing that there is no thing, [one] reaches and remains in the
> sphere of no-thingness, and [one] becomes one who is conscious
> of this true but subtle perception of the sphere of no-thingness.[5]

Mind does not need to be defined by things. In the seventh jhana there is no thing to grasp, no thing to be, no place for consciousness to form, collect, and land. From this perspective of voidness, the coarse desire for sensory pleasure is incomprehensible. The perception of emptiness can shatter a lifetime of preoccupation with protecting our roles, reputations, successes, and possessions. What really matters in life? Exploring the empty essence of mind puts one face to face with the barest of facts. In the face of no-thing, what matters?

Contemplate this question, letting it mature your heart in unlimited love and compassion. Align your life with the knowledge of what is of deepest significance. Discover what can hold its value in the face of the unfathomable mystery of emptiness. When you are motivated by wisdom, compassion, profound love, or a commitment to awakening, steadfast courage will be unstoppable. Supported by the unshakable quality of emptiness, you will be undeterred by the transient hardships that compassionate service often requires. Graced with knowledge of the true nature of things and no-things, we find our relationship to everything is clarified. The fundamental misperception of things that creates the illusion of *I, me,* and *mine* is unearthed. Nothing exists with which to identify a self-concept. Nothing exists to claim as mine.

THE SPHERE OF
NEITHER-PERCEPTION-NOR-NON-PERCEPTION

To explore samadhi further, turn the attention away from the absence of things and allow it to alight on that which took no-thingness as its object. From the knowing of no-thingness, turn mindfulness back on that which was aware of no-thing. This requires that you withdraw from the *movement of perceiving.*

Imagine this as the function of perception folding back into itself without turning itself into another object of perception. The *Visuddhimagga* suggests one use the thought "peaceful, peaceful" to strike at the "nonexistence of no-thingness." Unruffled awareness pervades the dimensionless knowledge of this attainment. The mind stills, imbued with trust, utterly relaxed and unmoved.

There is no clear characteristic here to describe, yet a stability of mind is known. In this attainment, the absence of things is not perceived. Nothing is perceived. Although awareness is clear and steady, you cannot say what the steadiness is fixed upon. It is a state of deep quiet, completely free of elaboration. The ability to move the attention, give rise to an intention, or make any effort at all is completely stilled. Here most mental functions rest in abeyance. The mind is calmed beyond the range of sounds, sensations, thoughts, intentions, and aspirations.

This sphere of neither-perception-nor-non-perception is referred to as *not non-perception,* because you *can* recognize it. It is referred to as not-perception because you *can't* recognize anything about it. Hence a state that is a perfection of simplicity has gained a rather long and awkward name.

This state of neither-perception-nor-non-perception is, for obvious reasons, difficult to describe. Although there is little that can be "known" about it, it creates a profoundly smooth texture in the mind. The general experience is one of incredible softness of mind. The mind simply rests, soft and stable, simple and quiet. There is absolutely nothing to do in it. In fact any activation of intention, feeling, resolve, or mental activity abruptly ends the absorption. Nothing is there to relax into or let go of, so even the subtle intention of release has no merit. Only a residue of mental factors are present, and these are in a dormant state; they are not functioning or active. You know the attainment and its effects upon consciousness by means of reflection after emerging from the sustained perception.

Two traditional images try to describe the subtlety of this state. The first image is of a bowl with a residue of oil in it:[6]

An attendant wants to serve his master some rice gruel. He tells the Master, "I have brought rice gruel, but your bowl has oil in it."

The Master replies, "Go get that other bowl and pour the oil into it, so this bowl can be used to serve the gruel."

The attendant responds, "There is no oil to pour out."

This is the analogy for the base of neither-perception-nor-non-perception. Just as there is neither oil nor non-oil, but a residue of oil remains, so it is with the base of neither-perception-nor-non-perception:

perception is not engaged by taking up objects, and yet perception is not absent. There is a residue of the functions of feeling, perception, mental formations, and consciousness; however, all are temporarily dormant.

The *Visuddhimagga's* second example uses water as the metaphor:[7]

A novice and an elder monk who is nearly blind are traveling between villages. The novice sees water on the road ahead and says to the elder, "There is water ahead sir, get out your sandals."

The elder responds, "Good, let us take a bath. Where is the towel?"

The novice responds, "There is no water for bathing."

The illustration of the presence of water that is not usable tries to describe the residue of formations that are suspended and inactive. Perception is arrested in a state in which it cannot perform its function.

If you cannot accomplish anything, nor direct the attention, you might wonder: of what use is attaining the sphere of neither-perception-nor-non-perception? The base of nothingness is actually considered the supreme base for insight. The base of neither-perception-nor-non-perception is too subtle to use as a ground for direct insight. One must emerge from this absorption, then turn the attention back in a reflective process to comprehend that it, too, is conditioned and volitionally produced. So why bother to develop it?

By virtue of its greater degree of peacefulness, absorption in the base of neither-perception-nor-non-perception will provide a dispassionate view toward the perception of no-thingness. The exquisitely pervasive peacefulness of the sphere of neither-perception-nor-non-perception naturally ends any residual attachment for the previous attainment of the sphere of no-thingness. There is no direct defect in the base of neither-perception-nor-non perception to contemplate, except that you can't stay there, because it is conditioned and volitionally produced.

Otherwise it might be utter perfection.

THE CESSATION OF PERCEPTION AND FEELING

Most references in the early discourses to deep concentration include only the four jhanas. In some, however, all eight attainments are elaborated: the four material jhanas and the four formless perceptions. In a few discourses, a ninth state is presented: the cessation of perception and feeling. It is the final attainment in the sequential distilling of mind, and might be read as the crowning achievement and the culminating conclusion to the practice. There is, however, significant dispute regarding what this attainment might be, and what relationship this attainment might have to liberation.

Venerable Sariputta's experience describes the process of entering this attainment as follows:

> Again, bhikkhus, by completely surmounting the base of neither-perception-nor-non-perception, Sariputta entered upon and abided in the cessation of perception and feeling. And his taints were destroyed by his seeing with wisdom.
>
> He emerged mindful from that attainment. Having done so, he recalled the past states, which had ceased and changed, thus: "So indeed, these states, not having been, come into being, having been, they vanish." Regarding those states, he abided unattracted, unrepelled, independent, detached, free, dissociated, with a mind rid of barriers. He understood: "There is no escape beyond." And with the cultivation of that attainment, he confirmed that there is not.[8]

This description treats the cessation of perception and feeling like the absorptions, as a temporary state that is attained through the relinquishment of previous states, and suggests that it can be used as a basis for insight through reflection. However, the state of cessation—like the formless abidings—is not classically considered to be an absorption, since there is nothing for the mind to absorb. Yet the state of cessation of perception and feeling can be attained and has a distinctive effect on consciousness, although that effect is so refined that nothing whatsoever can be apprehended about it.

For the adventurous, the *Visuddhimagga* presents a simple method for entering this attainment: one resolves to attain cessation while still at the level of the base of no-thingness since no intention can arise beyond that. In response to the resolve, consciousness will momentarily pass through the sphere of neither-perception-nor-non-perception and then cease. It is traditionally recommended that one take precautions to protect one's body and property from fire, robbers, and weather, invoke protection from deities, and make a clear determination regarding the time of emergence from the attainment. What value this attainment may have is highly speculative. However, it does seem that its greater degree of refinement dislodges any residual attachment to the base of neither-perception-nor-non-perception; it may serve as a cleansing, the final purification of perception.

I do not recommend striving for this attainment. No clear consensus has emerged regarding the exact nature and significance of the attainment of cessation of perception and feeling. An impressive degree of insight, as well as concentration, may be a prerequisite for this attainment. The Theravada tradition suggests that only a person who has reached the third stage of enlightenment by eradicating the defilements of personality view, doubt, greed, and hate, is capable of attaining the cessation of perception and feeling. Some scholars argue that this attainment describes the state of an enlightened mind after death.[9] Some practitioners report experiencing this subtle state even though they make no claims to enlightenment. Others believe it may be attainable by someone with strong concentration, but only someone with deep insight can stabilize the attainment. Other practitioners describe side affects such as an odd disorientation, almost a destabilization of consciousness. Who can say for certain what it actually is and who has genuinely experienced it? Due to the extreme subtly of this state, I recommend the basic cultivation of concentration and insight. If you should wish to explore the attainment of cessation of perception and feeling, however, I strongly urge you to find a qualified teacher.

The cessation of perception and feeling is so refined that nothing can be perceived while in it, or about it, and yet the texts tell us that Sariputta reflected upon it. How can "seeing with wisdom" occur, as Sariputta described, in a state that has no mental functions and no perception? Presented as the conclusion of the refinement of perception, cessation would hold little significance for liberation. Some teachers resolve this dilemma by describing cessation not as the temporary peaceful abiding that concludes the jhanic system, but equates the cessation of perception and feeling with the ultimate cessation of suffering. Cessation becomes a synonym for Nibbana. There is support for this view from many discourses, such as: "This is the most peaceful, this is the goal superior to all, that is to say, the stilling of all formations, the relinquishing of all essentials of existence, the exhaustion of craving, cessation, Nibbana."[10]

In this context, cessation is referring to a continuous state of liberation—the cessation of suffering.

The Buddha was renowned for word-play, using conventional terms in unconventional ways to dislodge assumptions that prevent immediate realization. The term may draw attention to what really needs to cease: craving, clinging, attachment, and suffering.

NOT A MARK OF SKILL

Meditators engaged in long-term practice may enter these boundless dimensions fairly easily, sometimes suddenly and deeply, like sliding down a laundry chute. The mere experience of these rarified states is not the mark of skill. They occur as a natural result of a momentum of concentration. When they arise, it is essential to work skillfully with them so that they mature as an attainment, not as another passing altered perception to amuse the self and add status to the spiritual persona.

Some personalities latch on to the dramatic occurrence of formless perceptions with pride, attributing significance to their practice simply because these perceptions arise. Other personalities withdraw in fear, overwhelmed by the altered state of consciousness. Some people ride into this energy in the spirit of full abandon. Some are curious, comparing the experience with what the book says on the subject. Others resist the powerful vortex of this extraordinarily empty power. Some wander, bewildered and confused by the intensity of the occurrence, intermittently drawn in by its power and uncertain if it is a good thing to do. These differences in temperament are insignificant because all these reactions are mere superficial personality traits. Some children love to ride roller coasters; others cry. So what?

Once the perception of form has been released in the transition from the fourth jhana to the immaterial bases, the draw can feel like a powerful vacuum pulling you into its realm. There is no particular value to being sucked in. Gravity naturally pulls all children down the playground slide; the energy of formless spheres naturally pulls the concentrated mind into its field. Skill develops through the ability to enter and exit without trouble or difficulty. The skilled practitioner should be able to emerge from jhana at any time. These states are described as "controlled perceptions" in the Buddha's discourses. They are not seductive episodes to glorify the concentrated practitioner.

Do not limit your practice to *surrendering* to these states: *examine them!* Withdraw from the stability of the attainment and then establish it again, absorb and emerge, move in and move out many times, according to your resolve. Let your resolve grow strong and guide your exploration of these transitions, at your choosing. Contemplate and reflect upon the attainments. This is the work to be done regarding the formless spheres. The depth is inherent.

You can do nothing to strengthen or deepen them, but your skill can still grow in proximity to this dynamic empty expanse.

DIFFICULTIES AND DANGERS OF FORMLESS DIMENSIONS

What you experience in these attainments influences your ordinary perceptions. It is important to be connected with the senses and the body during the times consciousness is not absorbed. Sometimes following a period of extended exploration of these formless perceptions, normal daily tasks will seem confusing. Decision-making might become difficult. If these states are sustained for long periods, the meditator might feel vulnerable, disoriented, easily startled, even nauseated when emerging from concentration.

Be gentle with the transition from deep meditation to the complexity of daily tasks. Immaterial jhanas are not something to dive into right before a staff meeting at the office or before piloting an airplane or scuba diving. They are certainly not to be undertaken for frivolous recreation. If you feel vulnerable or if there is any difficulty reestablishing embodied awareness, give careful attention to how you emerge.

Come out slowly, gradually shifting sequentially through the lower jhanas, adding each mental factor one by one, until your consciousness regains its orientation to physical life. Limit the time you spend in any of the higher attainments. Develop mastery by predetermining the duration and emerging according to your timed intention. Enjoy conscious movement practices during the day, like walking, yoga, or *qi gong,* to maintain a parallel embodied practice.

If they are balanced with mindfulness and investigation, the formless attainments can provide a fascinating and powerful view into emptiness. But, if recklessly sustained for too long, they backfire, temporarily diminishing the meditator's capacity for investigation. For the skillful meditator, formless perceptions can provide experiential knowledge of consciousness without boundaries: an intimate realization of emptiness. Despite their conditioned and fabricated nature, these states lead to an experience of an unwavering clarity, pure like space—timeless and dimensionless.

The transformation of perception in these formless states is quite marked. Altered perception usually lingers, informing later sensory contacts. You may feel quite light, as though you are gracefully floating through your routine, rather than walking. The entire visual world may appear transparent and insubstantial. Trees, buildings, traffic, people—all might appear substance-less, coexisting like exquisitely choreographed flags, dancing together, interacting, but lacking the density that creates conventional demarcations.

☞ FOR REFLECTION

With these higher states (and indeed with any meditational attainments) you gain another perspective on reality and access a potential platform for liberating insight. After emerging from each level of concentration, activate the mind by asking yourself:

What does this teach me?

What does this reveal about how I live?

Is this experience conditioned and subject to change?

What is the significance of this experience?

What does it show me about the end of suffering or the nature of mind?

What is there to cling to?

This is not a state of confusion; one clearly knows the distinction between a tree and a fire hydrant. The mind functions, intelligence operates, but consciousness is filled with an infinitely extensive radiance that pervades all perceptions. It is not helpful to try to sustain these lingering effects of formless attainments, nor replace conventional perceptions with these "spiritually advanced" perceptions. Their value is simpler. They provide an opportunity to cease to cling to conventional perception. They are not intended to encourage attachment to an altered perspective.

JUST LET GO, AGAIN

By progressively releasing, consciousness inclines toward the subtlest states. To gain access to jhana, your consciousness had to recede from obstructive states of mind, such as desire, aversion, and restless thinking. To establish the successive jhanas you abandoned the grosser factors, revealing more refined factors. The agitated movements of vitakka and vicara were released, the rippling vibrational excitement of rapture fell away, and the gentle warm wash of sukha diminished until you rested in the utterly still unification of the neither-pleasant-nor-unpleasant feeling.

The shift from fine material jhanas to formless states required the release of binding fascination with diverse perceptions. When the perception of infinite space was dismissed, infinite consciousness shone brightly. Once dispassion toward infinite consciousness developed, nothingness came to the fore. With the release of the perception of absence, the function of perception itself tranquilized.

You can read and comprehend descriptions of each level. But you cannot know successive levels for yourself until the previous coarser faculties fade. Although it may seem that these are things that you do, enforce, or make manifest, you do not make these states occur. Like love, they are dimensions of unwavering trust that are unresponsive to command.

You can't do much in any of these formless spheres of perception. You might try to "let go" but even the attempt to release is effortless. There simply is nothing to push against, nothing to resist, nothing for the effort to rub up against. Finally humbled, you allow every concept of effort to fall away. Awareness shines with spontaneous radiance.

Relax, let the practice mature; allow it to guide you through the experience of emptiness.

This is the inevitable inclination of awareness.

CHAPTER 20
Realizing Emptiness

There is an island (in the river of being)
An island which you cannot go beyond.
It is a place of nothingness,
A place of non-possession and of non-attachment.
It is the total end of death and decay,
and this is why I call it Nibbana.

— The Buddha[1]

WHEN MAGNIFIED to metaphysical proportions, the concept of emptiness, sometimes called "voidness," can seem bewildering—yet the *realization* of emptiness is profound in its simplicity. The realization of emptiness is a perception of pristine purity; it is neither complex nor abstract. It is a profound encounter with the nature of things. Emptiness is not reserved for the privileged elite. Emptiness is not a state that will be gained in the future, in a particular place or time, or by means of a particular technique. Emptiness is already the basic fact of existence.

Nothing actually exists the way we conceive of it, as the Buddha said: "In whatever way we conceive, the fact is ever other than that."[2] The failure to understand emptiness keeps people enthralled by the stories the mind fabricates as it wanders in a trance of hallucinated narratives. Reality cannot be perceived with such distortion. A concentrated mind has the strength to penetrate the layers of conceptual proliferation and allow a direct experience of reality to occur.

⌒ **FOR REFLECTION**

What do you assume the realization of emptiness describes?

Is it a place? A thing? An experience?

Is it a fascinating attainment that will elevate your self-esteem, fix your personality quirks, and resolve personal problems?

Is this an experience that you fear or desire?

How would you recognize the experience of emptiness?

Why is the realization of emptiness considered a spiritual attainment?

THE THOUGHT "I AM"

Thoughts determine our personal experience of the world. Our concepts affect the way we perceive our lives. When you are mindful and bring attention directly to meet a thought, what do you find?

Meditative investigation explores, among other things, these questions: What is a thought? Does a thought have color or shape? Is it housed in a location? Does it travel a certain distance?

The greatest illusion created by the thinking mind is the concept of itself. If I asked you, "Who is thinking?" you might reply "I am thinking." What is this "*I*" to whom you attribute your activities? The thought "*I am*" is the fundamental concept obscuring the void nature of things.

Buddhist tradition considers the thought "*I am*" to be the great catastrophe of birth: a birth that leads inevitably to death. Every time "*I*" arises in a moment of sensory contact and claims experience for itself, this birth of self recurs, caught in the cycle of dualistic formations. Without the deluding dualistic concepts of self and other, what would conceal the exquisite purity of the empty space of all phenomena? Suffering arises as we try to sustain the illusory creation of self. When that project ceases, the depth of ease is unimaginable. Endless energy becomes available. The mind awakens to a knowing beyond knower and known; it opens to a timeless lucid awareness.

One of the fundamental instructions my teacher H.W. L. Poonja gave was to "follow the *I-thought* back to its source and stay there." Catch the *I-thought* and trace it to its root. Where did it arise? Where does it cease? What is its basis and support? Follow the "I-thought" back and you will rest at ease—at home. Worldly attractions may arise and pass like a magic show. The mind, without the tether of identification, however, is not allured by diverse concepts.

Mindfully observe where, when, and how a thought arises and disappears. Ponder: what is a thought? This inquiry need not produce specific answers. Inquiry into thought unveils the very illusions that have been giving credence to the formation that is conventionally assumed to be *self.* You'll discover that each distinct thought of *I, me, mine,* and *myself* is impermanent—thoughts change and end.

The Buddha declared, "No other thing do I know, O monks, that changes so quickly as the mind. It is not easy to give a simile for how quickly the mind changes."[3] Any belief constructed on such rapidly changing expressions will inevitably be an unreliable foundation for consciousness. Anxiety proliferates when consciousness relies on the unstable support of concepts. Thinking about ourselves, we are preoccupied until death. This cycle of unrest continues, agitating the mind and keeping concentration far away.

MINDFUL OF NON-CLINGING

Wisdom replaces foolish responses with considered, skillful actions. But you can go further than reconditioning your mind to respond with wisdom. It is also possible to realize a quality of wisdom more profound than skillful manipulation of old patterns: a direct encounter with life, beyond concepts, beyond thought, beyond the personal, and beyond mind. So, how do you cross over from skillful and wise reflections on the conditioned to a realization of what is unconditioned?

When you let go of a desire or reaction and feel the peace of release, at that moment examine the quality of mind. Are you still focused on the release of an object, on the letting go, on the wise action you took? Or can you simply rest within the release of the not-clinging? Informed by wisdom, you took the appropriate action: you considered cause and effect, repeatedly reflecting on the wholesome and unwholesome roots of your endeavors. But did you stop there to marvel at how well you handled the situation? Or, in that moment of deep peace, did you look deeper? What is the nature of the experience of non-clinging itself? Look into the direct experience of liberation through non-clinging without being fascinated by methods, meditation objects, progress, or feelings. Get to know those moments free of clinging as the release that is the manifestation of wisdom.

Often the mind comes in at critical junctures and either doubts your path or claims the experience for itself. Even after a profound insight, you may find a little thought arising that clings to the skillfulness of your action or attributes significance to your experiences, turning an otherwise profound encounter with reality into just another conceptual story with a spiritual subplot. Reveling in the spiritual experience, you might think about how that profound event arose, or how lucky "I" am to have had this awakening.

At this juncture, having discovered a meditative tool to use and apply, people often want to test their new tool by advising others about how to fix their problems. Sharing your wisdom may seem generous, but it can also stop the exploration before it is complete. Subtle identification with spiritual experience keeps us grasping the methods and techniques. Meditators can become attached to the path and stop short of the triumphant goal.

The Buddha described the dangers of self-grasping infiltrating the profound experiences of peace. He warned, "And when this venerable one regards himself thus: 'I am at peace, I have attained Nibbana, I am without clinging,' that too is declared to be clinging."[4] Experiences of profound peace will occur in the course of a meditation practice. But the Buddha pointed the way to a liberation beyond any definable state, beyond any formation where the concept of I might arise to distort experiences through self-grasping.

BEYOND THE PRACTICE

When letting go is understood as a practice that is done over time, it is seen as conditioned. The decision to let go is informed by wisdom. This act of letting go, however, is not the ultimate expression of release. *Go beyond letting go.* Let go of this approach too. Don't turn release into another method to cling to.

The Buddha's famous simile of the raft is one of the great illustrations of wisdom and letting go. The Buddha described the building of a raft to use to cross the river of suffering. Arriving at the other shore, one does not carry the raft on his shoulders but leaves it on the bank and travels unburdened, liberated from all attachments, even the attachment to what helped him arrive at his destination. You must untangle any clinging to method, technique, rights and rituals, views, concepts, knowledge, and experience—once they have done their job.

Spiritual experiences may occur, jhana can be attained, insights may be won, but you needn't be proud of yourself on that account. In one discourse, Sariputta is described in discussion with the Venerable Samiddhi, whose clarity and able manner while engaging in Dhamma discussion elicited great praise from the chief disciple. The sutta ends with a wonderful reminder: Sariputta remarks to Samiddhi, "Well spoken, Samiddhi, well spoken! You have answered well the various questions put to you. But do not be proud of yourself on that account!"[5]

Attainments can easily become a basis for self-grasping with the thought, "I attained" or "I did not attain," distorting the experience and entrapping the mind yet again in the age-old pattern of self-interest. Sariputta describes his emergence from each jhana without any sense of *I, me,* or *mine* in relation to those attainments. He describes each jhana and remarks, "Yet friend, it did not occur to me, 'I am attaining the first [second, third, etc.] jhana,' or 'I have attained the first jhana,' or 'I have emerged from the first jhana.'"[6] And Ananda speculates, "It must be because I-making, mine-making, and the underlying tendency to conceit have been thoroughly uprooted in the Venerable Sariputta for a long time that such thoughts did not occur to him." Sariputta had abandoned these notions of *I, me,* and *mine,* in relation to all things—even refined spiritual abidings. Whether you are immersed in the chaotic encounters of everyday living or in the refined absorptions of jhana, keep a watch out for any formations of *I, me,* and *mine,* where you may become ensnared. These formations of self-grasping are among Mara's many baited hooks.[7]

Although on many occasions we confront obstacles, we often abide free of clinging, identification, and misperception. Experience those moments of non-clinging; they point to something beyond the repetitious practice of alternately clinging and letting go. When the mind is naturally settled in a stable and open clarity, it is ripe for contemplation. What happens, then, when you ponder what is unconditioned, uncaused, beyond cause and effect, the end of the path?

Let your love of freedom carry you into an inquiry beyond the known. It will guide you safely from the conditioned to the unconditioned, from the relative aspects of wisdom and skillful living to realize something beyond mind, effort, and actions. The desire to be free is not the kind of desire to abandon midstream. The desire for liberation inspires the practice—and leads to the end of desire.

As H.W. L. Poonja said, "Have only one desire in your life, the desire for freedom. Only this desire will not allow any other desire to trouble you."[8]

ABIDING IN VOIDNESS

There are several dialogues recorded in the early Buddhist scriptures of an awed companion exclaiming that the Buddha or his chief disciple Sariputta exhibited a radiant glow that permeated their complexions.[9] In reply, the Buddha or Sariputta explain that they often "abide in voidness," and that it was this abiding that produced the radiant appearance. Perception beyond mundane fixation on objects will have an effect on consciousness, mind, and body. This may manifest as the radiance depicted by artists in paintings of saints with halos, surrounded by auras, rainbows, and lights beaming in luminous glory.

Ananda, who served as the Buddha's attendant for the last twenty-five years of the Buddha's ministry, once asked the Buddha to elaborate on the remark, "I often abide in voidness."[10] The Buddha described three general avenues into the perception of emptiness: (1) knowing things as void of what is absent; (2) knowing as present only what is there; and (3) knowing just that amount of disturbance that is actually occurring in the current conditions. This means a meditator will recognize what factors are present, what factors are absent, and accurately identify the gross factors that agitate the state.

In a progression that parallels the development of jhana, the Buddha described increasingly subtle experiences of emptiness, beginning with the simple departure from the complexities of urban life by retreating to the forest, progressing through the stilling of conceptual proliferation and experiencing the formless perceptions, until finally culminating in a direct experience of emptiness.

At each level the meditator is instructed to reflect upon perception: recognize what is present in each state; recognize what is absent in each state; know each state as conditioned, impermanent and subject to cessation. This is the same process used to reflect on the defects of each jhana. We examine every experience until we have stabilized the recognition of craving's absence.

With the undistorted knowledge that craving is absent, one is capable of realizing liberation. With this understanding comes the distinct and specific knowledge, "It is liberated." This instruction points to an interesting distinction between the absence of craving and the "positive knowledge of liberation." Direct and clear knowledge is a crucial step. Without it, our conditioned perception may think, "There is nothing here," rather than apprehending the freedom. Like a fish that does not know it is in the water, the conceptual mind may fail to recognize emptiness by attributing to it the characteristic of being empty. The freedom inherent in emptiness may go unrecognized if we are looking for an experience to attain. The subtle searching for something to happen in our meditations may cause us to miss the seminal realization of emptiness.

In this teaching on the gradual descent into voidness, the Buddha's guidance continues with indefatigable detail. The meditator is asked to recognize not only what is absent in the liberated mind (i.e., craving for sense pleasures, self-construction, and ignorance), but also what is present (i.e., "It is liberated"). The only disturbance to be found is "connected with the six sense bases, dependent on body and conditioned by life." Life continues; our senses, bodies, and minds function; only the causes of suffering have ended. This sequential reflection on what is absent and what is present, and what degree of agitation (coarse factors) remains, constitutes the structure of examination that we apply to every level along the approach to emptiness. The Buddha summarizes this progressive reflection with a simple instruction on how to realize emptiness: "Regard it as void of what is not present and understand that which is present as "this is present." These instructions are not mysterious, esoteric, or confusing. As you follow the approach to jhanas presented in this book, you will reflect in the same manner upon the presence and absence of formations at every stage of concentration. Knowing what is present and absent, the heart relaxes with the deep stillness of acceptance. Non-attachment, non-struggle, and non-contention pervade both the practice of jhana and the realization of emptiness.

The Tibetan master Dilgo Khyentse Rinpoche described all the events of life whether pleasant or unpleasant, kind or critical, as "just the echoes of emptiness."[11] Just as there is no reason to feel elated or depressed if you shout flattery or insults at a cliff and those words are echoed back, so it is with all of our experience. All the sounds, sights, and sensations of the entire universe "are without any real essence. They are just ungraspable empty echoes."[12]

Many classic illustrations of emptiness refer to the tricks of magicians. Things seem to appear and disappear, but the magician, knowing his tricks, is not fooled by his own performance. Like the magician, we live in the world but are not fooled by it or by our own contrivances. It is possible to experience the physical senses and think with the mind and not be deceived by the antics of grasping.

There is a traditional story of a parent standing with a child under a clear night sky and pointing to the moon. If the child fixes her attention on the pointing finger (that is, the concept or practice method), she will never perceive the moon for herself. She must turn her attention away from the pointer in order to recognize the moon. This shift from fixation on the finger to a direct perception of the moon requires an act imbued with faith and curiosity. It is a movement from the known to the unknown, from the familiar to the unfamiliar.

We have refined perception through our systematic exploration of the jhanas. Now we can turn the attention away from things that are defined by form or formless perceptions to discover what is beyond this dualistic spectrum. Freedom is not found in the constrained states of absorption. The Buddha described this movement from the known to the unknown in this way:

> Whatever states are included there comprised by form, feeling, perception, volitional formations or consciousness: he reviews those states as impermanent, as suffering, as a disease, boil, dart, misery, affliction, alien, disintegrating, as empty, non-self.
>
> Having reviewed them thus, his mind turns away from those states and focuses upon the deathless element: "This is peaceful, this is sublime: that is the stilling of all formations, the relinquishment of all acquisitions, the destruction of craving, dispassion, cessation, Nibbana."[13]

Here we meet the term *deathless element*. This is not a place or a thing, but rather an experience of the end of the solidifying formations of grasping. The term describes an insight in which life is vividly apparent, but not set in opposition to decay and death. The nature of things blazes forth in supreme non-dualistic clarity.

Dispassion toward conditioned perceptions arises through reflection on the facts of conditioned phenomena, in this case within the framework of deep concentration. The mind lets go of the attachment that has kept it bound to the cycles of birth, decay, and death. Once you know beyond all doubt that jhana, although sublime, is subject to conditioning, birth, decay, and death, the mind naturally will seek another route to freedom. The method is utterly simple: turn the attention from all that is conditioned; don't grasp a concept of the deathless. This is the meaning of the metaphorical instruction to turn one's attention from the finger to the moon. Following upon relinquishment, the entire mass of conditioned perceptions may fall away, revealing the potential for a liberating recognition of the deathless element—sometimes called an experience of emptiness.

THE LAND-FINDING CROW

As I have emphasized repeatedly, the discourses of the Buddha tell us very simply what we must do to have the experience of emptiness: Don't cling.

The *Visuddhimagga* offers additional instruction in the illustration of an ocean-faring ship that keeps a land-finding crow on board.[14] Periodically the crow is released to fly free while the sailors observe the direction of its flight. If the crow does not return, the sailors assume it found land and steer the ship in the path of that crow. This analogy suggests that a meditator, in releasing consciousness from the cage of identification with mind-body processes, allows the mind to fly unburdened by desires, fears, personality formations, or concepts. This opening of the mind beyond fixation invites the realization of what is unbound—"the other shore" of the ocean of suffering.

If the mind is released from fixation but does not discover the deathless property, it returns to a state of deep equanimity, just as the land-finding crow returns to its nest until the next opportunity to fly free occurs. When your mind is very still and equanimous, release all holds. Abandon all fixation—to the subtle as well as to the gross. Then observe the flight of the mind. Let go of the pleasant absorption of jhana and send the mind out like a land-finding crow to discover a peace beyond contrived formations. This release has a fearless quality.

When you have seen the defects of conditioned reality deeply enough, your mind will let go. This release may have the gentle quality of a sparkling bubble popping, the simplicity of a clenched fist unwrapping, or the power of a home run swing in baseball. The feeling of release may vary, yet it will be release beyond anything that we can produce through effort.

BEYOND DEPENDENCE, WE MEDITATE

The Buddha taught meditation that was not fixated on objects, not entranced by form, and not dependent on the formless perceptions. He used sensory experiences, the four jhanas, mental states, and the four formless spheres as the means to cultivate the mind; however, he cautioned that meditation is not to be bound by these.

The Buddha described meditation as a negation of all possibilities where attention might become fixated:

> He does not meditate with a mind obsessed and oppressed by ill
> will, sloth and torpor, restlessness and worry, and doubt, and he

understands as it really is the escape from them. He does not meditate in dependence on earth, in dependence on water, in dependence on fire, in dependence on air, in dependence on the base of the
infinity of space, in dependence on the base of the infinity of consciousness, in dependence on the base of nothingness, in dependence on the base of neither-perception-nor-non-perception, in
dependence on this world, in dependence on the other world, in
dependence on what is seen, heard, sensed, cognized, reached,
sought after and examined by the mind, and yet he meditates.[15]

Yet, freed from attachment to both form and formless perceptions,
we still meditate. What is this meditation that is not dependent upon a
meditation object and that is not defined by a posture, a perception, or a
technique? What is meditation that is not limited by perception of physical or mental objects, not defined by the cultivation of spiritual factors,
and not bound by space and time?

To understand it, we must consider meditation beyond the confines
of disciplined practices that cultivate certain factors of mind. The
Buddha's teachings lead to an experience of emptiness and the realization of liberation from fixation, not bound to concepts and conventional
perceptions. It is unborn, unchanging, unfabricated, and dimensionless.
It cannot be characterized as a thing, a place, or a function. The experience of emptiness is revealed when grasping has ceased and when consciousness is not reaching toward perceptions to construct a sense of "I"
in relationship to mental, physical, or environmental contacts. The cessation of these formations awakens such an unwavering state of pure rest,
beyond all extremes and fabrications, that it may be referred to as abiding in voidness, resting in emptiness, or the realization of the deathless.

Contemplation of emptiness requires a mind open to the simplicity
of what is. Glimpses beyond conventional reality will occur during meditation. Let these glimpses inspire release.

Each day allow the release of non-clinging in little and big ways.
What can you know when you cease the habit of seeing the world
through familiar formations of *I, me,* and *mine?* When you observe the
insubstantial nature of things or experience the emptiness of thoughts,
you are simultaneously recognizing the meditator's lack of substance.

An emptiness attributed only to the phenomenal world wrongly posits an observer who is viewing the emptiness. Emptiness then becomes conceptualized and the meditator is trapped again by this reference to spiritual success. Don't get stuck holding a dualistic vision of a quiet mind that looks out on objects and sees their emptiness.

The stability of a concentrated mind can see the emptiness of thought without becoming sucked in by the habitual pull of grasping. This is one of the important advantages of samadhi: it supports the release of *all* positions of fixation—subtle or gross, internal or external.

CONCEIVING THINS OUT

When concentration is strong, perception commonly appears altered. You may emerge from formless spheres to meander about your day seeing things rather differently. These are extraordinary states of consciousness. By definition, they are altered states. After attainment of a formless state, you may see the world as brighter, clearer, more luminous, empty, and substance-less. The density of things may seem to have evaporated. Perceiving transparency is only a conditioned altered state when attributed to the corporeal objects of the world. Such perceptions come and go with meditation, and may or may not be of any significant benefit. This shift in perception, however, can point to another way of relating to things—a knowledge that thins the conceiving out of experience.

The activity of clinging generally creates a subtle feeling of density in the mind. Attachment is the real burden, not perception. A tree does not need to be lighter. A building does not need to sparkle in radiant clarity. There is no reason to reduce the corporeality of the world. The specific density of worldly things is not your concern. Leave that to nature.

Ceasing to insert self into phenomenal experiences is more useful than the altered perception of jhana. When asked "What is the deliverance of mind through voidness?"[16] the Venerable Sariputta taught, "Here a bhikkhu, gone to the forest or to the root of a tree or to an empty hut, reflects thus: 'This is void of a self or of what belongs to a self.' This is called the deliverance of mind through voidness." Experience is distorted by the delusion of self-interest whenever a concept of self creeps into perceptions. Rather than directly perceiving the nature of life, we conceive things in relation to "me." Conceiving of things as mine, or who I am, or relating through a position of me, is the primary problematic distortion of perception.

Most people find that much of the day they are not actually aware of their direct experience, but removed from it by a commentarial layer of concept. We conceive of our experience and view ourselves within the experience, but rarely meet experience free of this chronic distortion of conceiving of self through contacts. Quietly drop into the flow of your actual sensory experience. You can do this while you work, while you eat lunch, while you talk on the telephone, while you stretch your body, while you sweep the floor or chop vegetables. Become aware of the present moment. Notice what is actually happening rather than believe a concept about the experience. Drop out of the concepts in the mind, and intimately wake up to reality, here and now. You don't need altered states of consciousness to awaken!

☞ TRY THIS: TAKE A WAKEFUL WALK

The next time you take a walk notice if you are aware of present-moment experience.

Bring awareness to present-moment sounds, temperature, textures, and movement.

Anytime the mind gets lost in thoughts about things that are not here and now, let go of the seduction in thought, and reconnect to just walking.

See what you might notice about the sensations of movement.

Notice the contact with the earth.

Relax into a wakeful walk.

Feel the sensations where your skin contacts clothes.

Notice the sounds and activities in the environment.

Delight in seeing something you have never noticed before.

LIVING WITH UNWAVERING CLARITY

The spiritual journey may not come to final completion with a single glimpse into emptiness—or it may. Either way, the Buddha instructed his disciples to continue awareness practice. The Buddha instructs Sariputta, in the wake of sublime attainments, not to dwell on the sublime qualities of emptiness, but to diligently consider the state of his mind when he walks on the path to the village.

The Buddha brings the realization of voidness down to earth. He tells Sariputta to consider: Did any desire, lust, aversion, delusion, or hate arise with regard to things seen, heard, smelled, or cognized? He instructs him to review his mind to ascertain if there are any activities or conditions in which attachment to sensory encounters or defilements in the mind remain unabandoned. And he instructs him to review his mind for positive qualities—mindfulness, effort, investigation, rapture, tranquillity, concentration, equanimity, confidence, and wisdom—to determine if any wholesome factors are as yet uncultivated. Should he find an unwholesome factor present, he should make an effort to abandon it— but "if by reviewing he knows there was no desire . . . then he can abide happy and glad training day and night in wholesome states."[17]

Spiritual experience matures by reflecting on the presence or absence of states. If you were hoping that the experience of emptiness would bring you to a quick spiritual retirement, these teachings might disappoint you. The Buddha encouraged his disciples to continue cultivation of wholesome states long after hindering forces are abandoned.

This way the mind is emptied of all greed, hatred, and delusion. It is emptied of all suffering.

EPILOGUE
Fearless and Awake

Enjoying everything, simply leave it as it is and rest your weary mind.

—Longchenpa

THE PRIMARY PURPOSE of undertaking any spiritual discipline is to free the mind from suffering. Although concentration brings states of pervasive bliss, beyond concentration lies liberation. Concentration alone, regardless of the level of jhanic attainment, does not extinguish the roots of attachment. A practitioner with a range of meditative skills can discover the integrated awakening that includes relinquishment, effort, wisdom, virtue, mindfulness, concentration, and investigation.

This awakening manifests in a free engagement with complex daily responsibilities as pervasively as it does during the sublime tranquillity of formal sitting meditation. The mutually supportive twin practices of concentration and insight develop a profound capacity to let go—the essence of liberation. Freed from the burden of habitual attachments, consciousness encounters the ever-changing, sometimes challenging, and sometimes exhilarating experiences of life with a stable clarity that ultimately frees the heart of all resistance.

From a conventional perspective, experiencing the sequentially distinct levels of jhana might appear to be a significant personal attainment. However, the accomplishment that transforms consciousness is revealed through release of self-interest, rather than individual gain. Insights of genuine worth on the spiritual path generally amplify humility rather than attainments. The further we progress in the development of mind, the less we are inclined to claim success. Each attainment is an experience of release, and progress comes through deeper abandonment. As you explore the calm abidings available to the undistracted mind, consciousness is gloriously simplified—freed of its preoccupation with personal attainment.

Belief in the significance of personal progress depends upon the delusion of a self-centered orientation. Measuring our individual worth by the outcome of our actions, however, inevitably perpetuates struggle: victors suffer to protect their "success"; losers suffer in "defeat." Once caught in this trap of gain and loss, success and failure, we feel happy when we attain absorption, and disappointed when we are distracted.

In reality, however, there is no role for "self" in spiritual attainment. The paradox consists of this: a brief glimpse into the unfathomable depths of the concentrated mind shatters personal ambition and reveals the utter impossibility of self succeeding in the spiritual arena. Attainment in a spiritual practice is "no attainment"—a fundamentally not-personal experience of reality.

Whatever level of individual accomplishment you master in this progressive training, don't stop short of complete awakening—the release of all attachment, the ending of conceit. The primary endeavor is to free the mind—beyond perfect equanimity, beyond form and formless, beyond the conceivable and the doable, beyond all constructs of self—and beyond the blissful states of jhana.

Shortly after meeting H. W. L. Poonja in India, he told me: "You are just a half-step from liberation." That was exciting! I had traveled to India, I was committed to the spiritual path, and earnestly sought enlightenment. I assumed he meant I was on the right track and very close to awakening; I felt very inspired.

One day, as I was chopping cabbage in the kitchen, it suddenly became completely obvious—liberation was *always* only one half-step away. A full step would imply fixation—seeing a pretty scarf and growing attached it, touching a filthy rag and getting caught in a reaction of disgust, mulling over an opinion that solidifies a self-image, chopping onions or lighting a candle with a view that the task *should* be performed in one particular way. Fixation can form in the perception of sensory experiences, views and opinions, self-concepts, or ways of performing tasks.

Whether through the stylized form of ritual practices, the mundane routines we perform at work, or the mental patterns we reinforce, fixation—the attachment of the mind to its perception—can take root. This is the full step: a step involves lifting the foot, moving it forward, and placing it down.

A half-step would be just lifting, moving—not landing. The very activities that reinforce fixation can be simplified. When chopping carrots, just chop the carrots, without attachment to outcome. When seeing a beautiful sight, appreciate the pleasant sight without triggering possessiveness. When performing a function, whether lighting a candle, cleaning the toilet, articulating a perception, or answering the telephone, let the action be simple: just the action without the addition of attachment.

When I came to understand about the half-step, I understood that the mind does not need to land and fixate on objects, concepts, views, or perceptions. We do not need to perpetuate attachments in order to make daily-life decisions, to function at work, to socialize in our communities, and to live a full life.

Wisdom is a much more trustworthy guide than attachment. The metaphor of the half-step describes a wise and unattached movement through life. Liberation is not discovered by traversing a distance; it cannot be measured in terms of "near" or "far." Awakening is always available when the mind is not attached.

The practice of jhana requires a steady cultivation of relinquishment. From the initial endeavor to focus a distracted mind, to the clarity of insight, jhana as a basis for insight is a practice of release. Reflect upon the expressions of letting go you have developed through these concentration exercises. You have practiced letting go of distracting sounds, repetitious thoughts, habitual judgments, hindrances, and harmful impulses. You have developed skills to rest at ease when difficult emotions and physical pain occur. As the mind purifies, letting go becomes more subtle.

By cultivating and then relinquishing the jhanic factors, you fortify consciousness before liberating the mind from fascination with these sublime pleasures. The fading away of attachment to diverse perceptions permits an exploration of formless dimensions. Insight into boundless perceptions and vast emptiness transforms consciousness, freeing it from bondage to coarse temporal delights. This is the basic progression developed through deep concentration.

As you abandon each attachment, a profound event is simultaneously occurring. Each experience of letting go teaches the mind to discern and remove the fundamental patterns of clinging, craving, and identification—not merely how to resolve a particular challenge. We discover the problem of attachment. We learn to "take the problem out of life."[1] When you find yourself struggling at home or work, consider: Where does the problem lie? Where can peace be found?

Not every challenge requires an external solution. By looking into the mind, we may discover that the problem lies in attachment to a view that does not correspond to the truth of things. Attached to opinion, preference, or fantasy, we suffer. Through sequentially refined experiences, the practitioner of jhana as the basis for insight learns to identify states of subtle fixation, clinging, and attachment, and that clarity frees the mind from attachment.

More important than the step that takes you into jhana is the step that takes you out again. How do you emerge to live your life? Can you engage at home and at work without the tension of grasping?

Ideally, jhana practice will develop calmness, clarity, equanimity, joy, letting go, and wisdom that you can apply to the more chaotic activities of life: cooking, working, planning, cleaning the house, engaging in conversations, balancing your accounts, raising your children, living with pain or illness. The important skill to develop is not the capacity to attain deep absorption, but rather the ability to abide undistracted and unattached in the diverse field of life.

The qualities developed during jhana will enable you to encounter life with the confidence to open to the truth of things without attachment. You can let the world be as it is, active or still, quiet or noisy. A liberated mind is equally at rest in the dynamic interplay of perception, feeling, and thinking, in relationships, love, and work, as it is in the silent abiding of the jhanas. You will discover a quality of presence that is undisturbed by your daily responsibilities and social contributions.

My grandmother was eighty-six years old when she had a series of heart attacks. Admitted to the intensive care unit of a local hospital, she was resuscitated each time her heart stopped. She was dying; however, the attempts to keep her alive continued until we met in a family-doctor conference and made the decision to not resuscitate. With nothing left to do, nothing to accomplish, produce, or attain, others went home. I stayed by her bedside and sat with my Grammy for the remaining hour of her life. The struggle had ended. This was a time to be present, steady, and connected to the profundity of a life ending.

Concentration supports the capacity to remain present—a stability that is not blind to the painful moments of life. In fact, by remaining undistracted, we are connected with the difficult truth of things. Undistracted attention does not require the secluded states of absorption. We find peace in the fact of things, open to the difficult and beautiful moments of life. We are fearless and awake.

Although we may practice for some time in seclusion to develop our meditative skills, concentration brings forth a profoundly intimate connection with existence. Paradoxically, jhana is cultivated in seclusion, yet this practice reveals intimacy and undivided love. Feelings of separation and alienation are impossible to sustain in the purity of undistracted presence.

Steadied by jhana we have no attachment to anything, and we connect to the true nature that underlies everything.

NOTES

Introduction: From Focused Concentration to Fearless Awakening

1. M. 36:31–37

2. Alara Kalama instructed the Buddha through the seventh level of absorption, and Uddaka Ramaputta instructed him through the eighth level (M. 26). Upon completing his studies the Buddha realized that he had mastered all that his teachers could teach. Disappointed that these attainments did not bring his mind "to peace, to direct knowledge, to enlightenment, to Nibbana" (M. 26:15) but only to a temporary abiding, Siddhartha Gotama left the communities of these great teachers and undertook years of austerity practice.

3. A. v:176

4. S. 35:118

Chapter 1: Cultivating the Focused Mind

1. A. VI:55
2. A. III:100
3. M. 19
4. S. 48:10

Chapter 2: Joy of Seclusion

1. Rumi, *Birdsong,* translated by Coleman Barks.
2. This is a formulaic reference to the jhanas repeated in many discourses. See M. 66:19–21 as an example.
3. Dhp. verse 290
4. S. 1. note #525
5. M. 27:17; M. 39:12; M. 51:18; M. 107:8; M. 125:20
6. S. 22:88
7. S. 35:63
8. Poonja, H. W. L., *The Truth Is* (Lucknow, India, 1995).
9. S. 21:10
10. Ud. 1:10, from *The Island: An Anthology of the Buddha's Teachings on Nibbana,* by Ajahn Pasanno and Ajahn Amaro.
11. Ud. 8:1, Nanamoli, Bhikkhu, *Life of the Buddha According to the Pali Canon,* Kandy, 3rd ed., Sri Lanka: Buddhist Publications Society, 1992.

Chapter 3: Happiness

1. Ud. 2:2
2. A. VI:55
3. Vism. XII:60–66
4. Ud. 3:2
5. M. 89:12
6. S. 36:19
7. D. 21
8. S. 36:19
9. S. 36:19
10. Sn. verse 61
11. M. 10:32

12. Perception in the fifth, sixth, seventh, and eighth levels of attainment is released from all perception of form and feeling. These states are so refined that the Buddha sometimes distinguished them as "peaceful abidings" rather than "pleasant abidings." M. 8:2–9

13. M. 59:16

Chapter 4: Equanimity

1. S. 35:130

2. Adapted from the translation of the Commentary to the Dhammapada verses 227–230 by E. W. Burlingame in *Buddhist Legends,* first published 1921.

Chapter 5: The Wisdom of Letting Go

1. Sn. verse 1098

2. Ud. 2.1; Ud. 4.1

3. Joseph Goldstein

4. M. 37

5. M. 36:8

6. M. 66

7. M 66·17

8. M. 22:40

9. S. 36:12(2)

10. S. 36:6

11. S. 36:6

Chapter 6: Dynamics of Emotion

1. Maharaj, Sri Nisargadatta, and Surdhakar Dikshit ed., and Maurice Frydman trans., *I Am That* (Durham, NC: Acorn Press, 1997).

2. A. IV:117

3. A. IV:165

4. S. 35:95. The same progression is repeated regarding each of the six senses (eye, ear, nose, tongue, body, and mind).

5. S. 36:6

6. S. 36:6

7. M. 36:32

8. M. 36:30

9. D. 2

10. M. 36:35–37

11. S. 36:14(4):

> Bhikkhus, suppose there is a guest house. People come from the east, west, north, and south and lodge there; khattiyas, brahmins, vessas, and suddas come and lodge there. So too, bhikkhus, various feelings arise in this body: pleasant feeling arises, painful feeling arises, neither-painful-nor-pleasant feeling arises; carnal pleasant feeling arises; carnal painful feeling arises; carnal neither-painful-nor-pleasant feeling arises; spiritual pleasant feeling arises; spiritual painful feeling arises; spiritual neither-painful-nor-pleasant feeling arises.

Chapter 7: Effort, Ease, and Intention

1. Dilgo Khyentse Rinpoche, quoted from *Awakening The Buddha Within,* by Lama Surya Das, page 70.

2. S. 6:15(5); D. 16

3. M. 19

4. A. VI:55

5. S. 1:1

6. M. 78

7. The translation of karma is "action."

8. A. VI:63

9. M. 78

10. M. 53:19; M. 16:27; M. 51

11. M. 4:32

Chapter 8: Calming the Restless Mind

1. M. 78

2. A. x:60

3. Mackenzie, Vicki, *Cave In The Snow: Tenzin Palmo's Quest for Enlightenment* (New York: Bloomsbury Press, 1999), page 170.

4. It. 94; M. 138

5. M. 138

6. M. 138

7. A. III:99

Chapter 9: Happiness and the Five Factors of Absorption

1. Sn. verse 1103

2. Sn. note to sutta #2. Traditionally Mara is said to be accompanied by ten armies. His ten primary obstructive forces include (1) Sense Desire, (2) Discontent, (3) Hunger and thirst, (4) Craving, (5) Lethargy and drowsiness, (6) Cowardice, (7) Uncertainty, (8) Distraction and obstinacy, (9) Gain, praise, honor, and undeserved fame, and (10) The extolling of oneself whilst disparaging others.

3. S. 5:5, verses 532–535

4. S. 4:22, verse 489

5. M. 151

6. Vism. VIII:200

7. S. 4:20, verse 486–487:

> *If there were a mountain made of gold,*
> *Made entirely of solid gold,*
> *Not double this would suffice for one:*
> *Having known this, fare evenly.*
> *How could a person incline to sensual pleasures*
> *Who has seen the source whence suffering springs?*
> *Having known acquisitions as a tie in the world,*
> *A person should train for its removal.*

8. M. 111

Chapter 10: Access to Absorption: At the Threshold of Peace

1. It. 4:11; A. IV:11, 11

2. D. 2:75

Chapter 11: Fearless Abidings—The First Jhana

1. S. 28:1

2. D. 9:9–10

3. D. 2:76

4. D. 2:75

5. M. 111; M. 43
6. *Visuddhimagga*
7. M. 52

Chapter 12: Drenched in Delight—The Second Jhana
 1. A. x:15
 2. D. 2:77
 3. D. 2:78
 4. S. 28:2

Chapter 13: Absorbed in Joy—The Third Jhana
 1. D. 2:79
 2. D. 2:80

Chapter 14: Radiant Calm—The Fourth Jhana
 1. S. 28:4
 2. D. 2:82
 3. S. 35:130
 4. A. 3:100

Chapter 15: How Deep Is Deep Enough?
 1. Ajahn Chah, quoted from Jack Kornfield and Paul Breiter, *A Still Forest Pool: The Insight Meditation of Achaan Chah* (Wheaton, IL: Theosophical Publishing House, 1985).
 2. Leigh Braisington is an American Dharma teacher who has tirelessly brought jhana into the mainstream of vipassana practice. He has generously shared numerous stories and examples that helped to clarify these states and offered a thoughtful reading of this manuscript.
 3. A. IV:77, *Handful of Leaves,* volume 3, translated by Thanissaro Bhikkhu:

> There are these four inconceivable things that are not to be conjectured about, that would bring madness and vexation to anyone who conjectured about them. Which four?
>
> 1. The range of powers a Buddha develops as a result of becoming a Buddha.

2. The range of powers that one may obtain while absorbed in jhana.

3. The mechanism and precise working out of the results of karma.

4. Conjecture about the origin of the world.

4. D. 16:4.27–33
5. Ud. 4:4
6. A. ix:35
7. M. 53:18

Chapter 17: Three Doorways to Insight

1. Quoted from Jack Kornfield and Paul Breiter, *A Still Forest Pool: The Insight Meditation of Achaan Chah* (Wheaton, IL: Theosophical Publishing House, 1985), p. 89–90

2. Shah, Idries, *The Pleasantries of the Incredible Mulla Nasrudin* (New York: E.P. Dutton, 1971), page 22.

3. M. 106:5

4. For more on this topic see Buddhadasa Bhikkhu, *Handbook for Mankind,* Chapter v, on the Three Trainings.

5. S. 35:232; S. 35:233

6. A. iv:45

7. M. 102:25:

> This supreme state of sublime peace has been discovered by the Tathagata, that is, liberation through not clinging, by understanding as they actually are the origination, the disappearance, the gratification, the danger, and the escape in the case of the six bases of contact. Bhikkhus, that is the supreme state of sublime peace, discovered by the Tathagata, that is, liberation through not clinging.

8. S. 35:99–100; S. 35:160–161; S. 22:5–6; S. 56:1–2

9. Vism. xii:14

10. Three discourses that use the analogy of purification of gold—A. iii:100,1–10; A. iii:11–15; S. 46:33

11. S. 46:33

12. D. 2:97

13. M. 106:11

14. M. 106:12
15. M. 66:16; S. 35:74
16. S. 35:162–164
17. S. 35:101

Chapter 18: A New Way of Seeing

1. A. 11:36
2. This argument was made by Keren Arbel in her unpublished dissertation, *The Attainment of Cessation of Perception and Feeling: A Study Of
   Sannavedayitanirodha in The Pali Nikayas,* submitted to the University
   of Bristol October 2004.
3. S. 48:9; S. 48:10, note #194

Chapter 19: Without Boundaries: Exploring the Infinite

1. Quoted from Joseph Goldstein's *The Experience of Insight* (Boulder,
   CO: Shambhala Publications, 1983).
2. D. 9:14
3. Vism. x:9
4. D. 9:15
5. D. 9:16
6. Vism. x:51
7. Vism. x:54
8. M. 111:19–20
9. Keren Arbel, unpublished dissertation on *The Attainment of Cessation
   of Perception and Feeling: A Study of Sannavedayitanirodha in The Pali
   Nikayas,* submitted to the University of Bristol, October 2004.
10. A. x:60, also see M. 26:19

Chapter 20: Realizing Emptiness

1. Sn. verse 1094
2. M. 113
3. A. i:v8
4. M. 102:24
5. A. ix:14
6. S. 28

7. M. 106:2; Sn. 61; S. 35:230

8. From author's personal notes.

9. M. 151, M. 121

10. M. 121

11. Khyentse, Dilgo Rinpoche, *Heart Treasure of the Enlightened Ones* (Boston: Shambhala Publications, 1992, page 43).

12. Ibid.

13. A. ix:36; M. 64; A.ix:36

14. Vism. xxi:65

15. A. ix:10

16. M. 43:33

17. M. 121

Epilogue: Fearless and Awake

1. Oral teaching from my mentor and dharma teacher, Christopher Titmuss.

BIBLIOGRAPHY

PRIMARY SOURCES

Bhikkhu, Thanissaro. *Handful of Leaves,* volumes 1–4. San Diego: Metta Forest Monastery, 2002.

Bodhi, Bhikkhu, trans. *The Connected Discourses of the Buddha: A Translation of the Samyutta Nikaya.* Boston: Wisdom Publications, 2000.

Fronsdal, Gil. *The Dhammapada: A New Translation of the Buddhist Classic.* Boston: Shambhala Publications, 2005.

Ireland, John D., trans. *The Udana and the Itivuttaka: Inspired Utterances of the Buddha and The Buddha's Sayings.* Kandy, Sri Lanka: Buddhist Publication Society, 1997.

Nanamoli, Bhikkhu, trans. *The Middle Length Discourses of the Buddha: A Translation of the Majjhima Nikaya.* Edited and revised by Bhikkhu Bodhi. Boston: Wisdom Publications, 1995.

Nanamoli, Bhikkhu, trans. *Visuddhimagga: The Path of Purification: The Classic Manual of Buddhist Doctrine and Meditation.* Kandy: Buddhist Publications Society, 1991.

Nyanaponika Thera and Bhikkhu Bodhi, trans. and ed. *Numerical Discourses of the Buddha: An Anthology of Suttas from the Anguttara Nikaya.* Walnut Creek, CA: Alta Mira Press, 1999.

Saddhatissa, H., trans. *Sutta Nipata.* London: Curzon Press, 1994.

Walshe, Maurice, trans. *The Long Discourses of the Buddha: A translation of the Digha Nikaya.* Boston: Wisdom Publications, 1995. (Originally published under the title, *Thus Have I Heard,* 1987.)

OTHER WORKS

Bhikkhu, Buddhadasa. *Handbook for Mankind*. Bangplad, Thailand: Dhammasapa, 1998.

Das, Lama Surya. *Awakening the Buddha Within*. New York: Broadway Books, 1997.

Goldstein, Joseph. *The Experience of Insight*. Boulder, CO: Shambhala Publications, 1983.

Khyentse, Dilgo Rinpoche. *Heart Treasure of the Enlightened Ones*. Boston: Shambhala Publications, 1992.

Kornfield, Jack and Paul Breiter. *A Still Forest Pool: The Insight Meditation of Achaan Chah*. Wheaton, IL: Theosophical Publishing House, 1985.

Lauck, Joanne Elizabeth. *The Voice of the Infinite In the Small*. Mill Spring, NC: Swan Raven and Co., 1998.

Mackenzie, Vicki. *Cave in the Snow: Tenzin Palmo's Quest for Enlightenment*. New York: Bloomsbury Press, 1999.

Maharaj, Sri Nisargadatta, and Surdhakar Dikshit ed, and Maurice Frydman trans. *I Am That*. Durham, NC: Acorn Press, 1997.

Nanamoli, Bhikkhu. *Life of the Buddha According to the Pali Canon*. 3rd ed. Kandy, Sri Lanka: Buddhist Publications Society, 1992.

Pasanno, Ajahn and Ajahn Amaro. *The Island: An Anthology of the Buddha's Teachings on Nibbana*. Redwood Valley, CA: Abahyagiri Buddhist Monastery, 2008. (Forthcoming as this book goes to press.)

Poonja, H.W.L.. *The Truth Is*. Lucknow, India, 1995.

Rumi, Jelaluddin. *Birdsong*. Coleman Barks, trans. Athens, GA: Maypop Books, 1993.

Sayadaw, PaAuk Tawya. *Knowing and Seeing*. Revised ed. Kuala Lumpur: WAVE Publications, 2003.

Shah, Idries. *The Pleasantries of the Incredible Mulla Nasrudin*. New York: E.P. Dutton, 1971.

INDEX

Page locators in **bold** *indicate information that appears in boxes in the text.*

ABOUT THE AUTHOR

 SHAILA CATHERINE began her meditation practice in 1980, at the age of seventeen, and has accumulated over seven years of intensive silent retreat experience. She has taught since 1996 in the United States, India, Israel, England, and New Zealand. Shaila studied at the Sharpham College for Buddhist Studies in England, and dedicated several years to studying with masters in India, Nepal, and Thailand. Since 2003, Shaila has focused on developing concentration and jhana practice, completing over fourteen months in jhana-based retreats primarily at the Forest Refuge of the Insight Meditation Society in Barre, Massachusetts. She founded Insight Meditation South Bay in Mountain View, California, and leads retreats and courses on the cultivation of concentration, mindfulness-based insight meditation practices, and the contemplative study of the Discourses of the Buddha.

Insight Meditation South Bay
www.imsb.org

ABOUT WISDOM PUBLICATIONS

WISDOM PUBLICATIONS, a nonprofit publisher, is dedicated to making available authentic works relating to Buddhism for the benefit of all. We publish books by ancient and modern masters in all traditions of Buddhism, translations of important texts, and original scholarship. Additionally, we offer books that explore East-West themes unfolding as traditional Buddhism encounters our modern culture in all its aspects. Our titles are published with the appreciation of Buddhism as a living philosophy, and with the special commitment to preserve and transmit important works from Buddhism's many traditions.

To learn more about Wisdom, or to browse books online, visit our website at www.wisdompubs.org.

You may request a copy of our catalog online or by writing to this address:

Wisdom Publications
199 Elm Street
Somerville, Massachusetts 02144 USA
Telephone: 617-776-7416
Fax: 617-776-7841
Email: info@wisdompubs.org
www.wisdompubs.org

THE WISDOM TRUST

As a nonprofit publisher, Wisdom is dedicated to the publication of Dharma books for the benefit of all sentient beings and dependent upon the kindness and generosity of sponsors in order to do so. If you would like to make a donation to Wisdom, you may do so through our website or our Somerville office. If you would like to help sponsor the publication of a book, please write or email us at the address above.
Thank you.

Wisdom is a nonprofit, charitable 501(c)(3) organization affiliated with the Foundation for the Preservation of the Mahayana Tradition (FPMT).